DEATH AND CHILDREN: A Guide for Educators, Parents and Caregivers

EDITORS
Steven Viton Gullo
Paul R. Patterson
John E. Schowalter
Margot Tallmer
Austin H. Kutscher
Penelope Buschman
with the editorial assistance of
Lillian G. Kutscher

A Foundation of Thanatology Text

Tappan Press
Dobbs Ferry, New York • 1985

Copyright © 1985 by Tappan Press, Dobbs Ferry, N.Y.

ISSN 0-930-194-152

UWEC McIntyre Library

EAU CLAIRE, WI

CONTENTS

Preface
The Editors

PART I. PERSPECTIVES FOR EDUCATORS

1. Philosophy of Education an Teaching About Death   1
   Elvira A. Tarr

2. Guidelines for Death Education for Young Children   7
   Dixie R. Crase and Darrell Crase

3. Death Education: Some Issues and Suggested Practices   15
   Carolyn C. Maurer and James Muro

4. Death Education – From the Beginning   28
   Robert C. Slater

5. Education for Living (Including Death)   35
   Norma Gayle Schmidt

6. Death and the Classroom Teacher   38
   Louise Bates Ames

7. The Developmental Approach to Death Education for Children   41
   Ellen S. Marbach

8. Children and Death – A Biophilosophical Perspective in Death Education   47
   Arlene Seguine

9. "Sometimes I Think About Dying": Helping Children Write About Death   59
   William Wertheim

10. Factors to be Considered in Designing a Program of Death Education for Teachers   64
    Rudy Alec and Joseph Sayles

PART II. PERSPECTIVES FOR PARENTS

11. On Understanding and Coping With Death During Childhood   79
    Stephen Viton Gullo and Edward H. Plimpton

12. Juvenile Crime and Its Relationship to Concepts of Death   93
    Caren Elin

13. The Adolescent and Death *Lynne S. Schneider*	101
14. Memory and the Child's Ability to Mourn *Betty C. Buchsbaum*	109
15. Some Insights from Counseling Bereaved Parents *James Zimmerman*	120
16. Literature for Young People: Nonfiction Books About Death *Joanne E. Bernstein*	127
17. The Topic of Death in Children's Literature *Phyllis L. Schneider*	134

PART III. PERSPECTIVES FOR CAREGIVERS

18. The Impact of Death of a Psychotherapist on Emotionally Disturbed Children *Boris M. Levinson*	144
19. A Child's Delayed Reaction to Death of a Parent: A Case Study of a Thirteen Year Old Girl *Phyllis Cohen*	151
20. A Multidisciplinary Approach to the Care of the Terminally Ill Pediatric Patient in the Hospital *Joseph T. Bianco and Irene Trowell*	169
21. Chronic Illness and Death in Childhood: Recommendations for Improvement of Current Educational and Management Deficiencies *Antoine K. Fomufod*	172
22. The Child as a Hospital Patient *Anneliese Sitarz*	178
23. Psycho-Medical Inconsistency in Preadolescent and Adolescent Leukemia *William James Liccione*	181
24. Issues of Consent in the Treatment of the Child with a Deadly Disease *James L. Gibbons*	192
25. On the Side of Live: Living with a Life-Threatening Illness *Iris Cutler*	199

EDITORS

Stephen Viton Gullo, Ph.D., President, Institute for Health and Weight Sciences' Center for Healthful Living, Manhasset, New York; Assistant Clinical Professor, School of Dental and Oral Surgery, Columbia University.

Paul R. Patterson, M.D., Emeritus Professor of Pediatrics, Albany Medical School of Union University, Albany, New York

John E. Schowalter, M.D., Professor of Pediatrics and Psychiatry, Yale University School of Medicine; Chief of Child Psychiatry, Yale University Child Study Center, New Haven, Connecticut

Margot Tallmer, Ph.D., Professor of Psychology, Hunter College of the City University of New York, New York

Austin H. Kutscher, D.D.S., President, The Foundation of Thanatology; Professor of Dentistry (in Psychiatry), Department of Psychiatry, College of Physicians and Surgeons, Columbia University

Penelope Buschman, R.N., Babies Hospital, Columbia-Presbyterian Medical Center, New York, New York

CONTRIBUTORS

Rudy Alec, Division of Teacher Education, College of Education, Wayne State University, Detroit, Michigan

Louise Bates Ames, M.D., Gesell Institute of Child Development, Yale University, New Haven, Connecticut

Joanne E. Bernstein, Ph.D., Assistant Professor, School of Education, Brooklyn College of the City University of New York

Joseph T. Bianco, M.D., Misericordia Hospital and Medical Center, Bronx, New York

Betty C. Buchsbaum, Ph.D., Adjunct Attending Psychologist, New York Hospital-Cornell Medical Center; Assistant Clinical Professor of Psychology, Albert Einstein College of Medicine, Bronx, New York

Phyllis Cohen, Adjunct Faculty, College of Staten Island, New York, New York

Darrell Crase, Ph.D., Professor of Health Education, College of Education, Memphis State University, Memphis, Tennessee

Dixie R. Crase, Ph.D., Associate Professor of Child Development, College of Education, Memphis State University, Memphis, Tennessee

Iris Cutler, M.Ed., Instructor in Pediatrics, Cystic Fibrosis Center, Hahnemann Medical Center and Hospital, Philadelphia, Pennsylvania.

Caren Elin, Educational Research, Northridge, California

Antoine K. Fomofud, M.D., M.P.H., Howard University Hospital, Washington, D.C.

James L. Gibbons, Director, Department of Chaplaincy Services, University of Chicago Hospitals and Clinics, Chicago, Illinois

Lillian G. Kutscher, Publications Editor, The Foundation of Thanatology, New York, New York

Boris M. Levinson, Ph.D., Emeritus Professor of Psychology, Yeshiva University, New York, New York; Blueberry Treatment Centers, Inc., Brooklyn, New York

William James Liccione, M.S.W., Ph.D., Social Psychologist and Counselor, Division of Hematology, St. Louis Children's Hospital, St. Louis, Missouri

Ellen S. Marbach, Ph.D., Associate Professor of Early Childhood Education, The Pennsylvania State University, University Park, Pennsylvania

Carolyn C. Maurer, Ph.D., Assistant Professor of Education, College of Education, North Texas State University, Denton, Texas

James J. Muro, Ph.D., Dean, College of Education, North Texas State University, Denton, Texas

Edward H. Plimpton, Ph.D., Child Life Program, Downstate Medical Center, Brooklyn, New York

Joseph Sayles, Division of Teacher Education, Wayne State University, Detroit, Michigan

Norma Gayle Schmidt, Ph.D., Associate Professor, Department of Health and Physical Education, Texas A&M University, College Station, Texas

Lynne S. Schneider, M.S.W., Clinical Practitioner in Social Work; Doctoral Candidate, Columbia University, New York, New York

Phyllis L. Schneider, Ph.D., Lecturer, Faculty of Educational Studies, State University of New York at Buffalo, New York

Arlene Seguine, Ed.D., Associate Professor of Health and Physical Education, Hunter College of the City University of New York, New York

Anneliese Sitarz, M.D., Associate Professor of Clinical Pediatrics, College of Physicians and Surgeons, Columbia University

Robert C. Slater, Director, Department of Mortuary Sciences, University of Minnesota, Minneapolis, Minnesota

Elvira A. Tarr, Ph.D., Professor, School of Education, Brooklyn College of the City University of New York, New York

Irene Trowell, R.N., M.P.H., Misericordia Hospital and Medical Center, Bronx, New York

William Wertheim, Poet-Consultant and Teacher, New York, New York

Rev. James Zimmerman, Pastor, Christ Lutheran Church, East Northport, New York

Preface

Helping children comprehend the mysteries of our world and helping adults comprehend the mysteries of their world are most challenging twin tasks for educators, parents, and caregivers. One of the mysteries is the encounter with death that awaits us all and unites us all, the young and the old. We hope to protect children from danger but we cannot always conceal from them the fact that life is fragile, that they will at some time suffer losses, including that of a loved one, or even that they themselves may be threatened by a serious illness. However, it is possible to offer children a healthy perspective on living and to create an environment that will foster appreciation of life's enriching aspects. Those who nurture children can impart knowledge that relates to more than the chapter and verse of academic facts.

Children must be prepared to cope with the trauma of life events. And death, unfortunately, can present as one of these traumas. Children are exposed vicariously to death on television; they feel threatened by it when an older relative dies; and they fear it when illness alters, even temporarily, the normal pattern of their own lives or the lives of those near to them.

The contributors to this book cover these aspects of "death education" for children from the perspectives of many disciplines. Their goal is not to implant seeds of morbidness into a child's mind but to encourage communication that will relieve anxiety, fear and suffering and that will foster an increasing understanding of life's stages. Educators, parents, and caregivers address and are addressed by other educators, parents, and caregivers. Guidelines are proposed, practical learning exercises are suggested, and illustrative experiences are utilized to substantiate the positive consequences that can result when children learn whatever can be taught or shared of the facts of life in appropriate ways.

The Editors

PHILOSOPHY OF EDUCATION AND TEACHING ABOUT DEATH
Elvira A. Tarr

"The function of reason," Whitehead (1929) said, "is to promote the art of life." Not to prolong life, for as he well knew, "persistence is to be dead." Only inanimate objects persist through long periods of time. What we human beings are concerned with is, in fact, the art of living, the quality of that lived life, the values we hold, and the societal supports that undergrid those values.

The question may be asked about whether educators, qua educators, are proper professionals to discuss these ideas. Perhaps social philosophers, historians, cultural anthropologists — or maybe a public policy committee in Washington — ought to be considering how we promote the art of life. While I would not deny the valuable contribution those groups can make, I believe that educators have a special, unique role to play in the discussion and the implementation of decisions about how to promote the good life. In fact, this question, expressed in different ways, has been of traditional interest to educators, and it has been assumed as one of our responsibilities. However, we have not lately or in the recent past discussed this topic. As private citizens we are no doubt caught up in the myriad activities and problems that beset members of society. However, it is as educators that we must join an examination of what has been taught about the good life and what we find is actually happening in our society. In so doing we may reformulate our own position and consider ways of changing the curriculum. It was Plato who said that the unexamined life is not worth living, and we might add that the unexamined curriculum is not worth teaching.

What I hope to show is that our philosophy of education is deficient in that it does not attend to a vital aspect of the affective domain. In the absence of education about death, loss, grief, and mourning we cannot, I maintain, teach an appreciation of life or develop the art of living in a way that invests that life with value and significance. Most of us would agree with Holderin, who said, "He that has thought most deeply loves that which is most alive" (Sneler, 1962 p. 87). We enjoy and celebrate the dynamic and exciting people and events in our life. We actively engage in those experiences that make us feel part of the flux and change in the world. And so, one might correctly ask, why include ideas about death and loss in the curriculum? I hope to show that if we do not teach about these feelings, we are ignoring an important part of human experience and one that establishes a necessary tension for an appreciation of life. There have been some sensitive teachers who have used various experiences to teach about death and grief, but what is here being proposed is that these ideas be deliberately and systematically incorporated into the curriculum and taught from the earliest years.

Justifications for curricula decisions have always been rooted in conceptions of the world, the nature of human beings, and the function of reason. When Plato proposed the system of governance in *The Republic*, he rested it on an educational scheme. He did so because he believed that an education prepared one to engage in those activities for which one was suited. The various educational hurdles were designed to identify those men or women who were most capable of using reason to contemplate the truth. These capable people would do so and then inform those less able to reason about how to live a just life. While we do admire the use of the socratic method — and most of us employ it — we know that Plato used it not to discover new ideas but to reason to the eternal verities that he believed were fixed and permanent for all time.

The medievalists in turn were doing no more, when they set their curriculum, than to say that only those people who knew certain subject matter were to be considered educated. Not only was the socratic method used, but men like Loyola employed fierce competition in order to identify those youths who were capable of carrying the true message of the church.

I am sure most of us recall Descarte's tortured reasoning to his own existence. And there are still those who believe that knowledge of the truths that can guide our behavior is attainable only through retreat to the contemplation of the mysteries of the universe.

In short, the belief that the proper function of reason was to discover the truth that was already known had guided educators for about two thousand years. It has only been in the last few hundred years that we have looked to some other ways of arriving at the truths, or verifiable statements.

The empiricists were most influential in shaping our philosophy of life and education. It was their ideas that the Puritans brought with them from England. Of course, they had hoped to establish a theocracy in the New World because they saw themselves as "protectors of the true doctrine" (Werkmeister 1949, p. 21). Their bigotry led to the Salem witchcraft trials. But what really ended their hegemony were the social and economic conditions of the early colonies. It was difficult to maintain the original harshness of the doctrine of the "necessary depravity of human nature" when one saw so many unskilled laborers rising to the ranks of the prosperous burgher class. This is not to say that life was easy. The harsh life of the Puritans was responsible for early deaths — only 50 percent of the children born lived to be five years old. What was in the beginning seen as God's grace was gradually shifted to be viewed as the typically American conception of the self-made man. We will return to the Puritans later on, but it was on this conception of the self-made man on which transcendentalists relied for the apprehension of absolute goodness, truth, and justice. They spoke of the eternal verities that could be comprehended and incorporated in one's life. The social and economic transformation that later culminated in the Gilded Age was accompanied by still newer trends toward materialism.

It was the publication of Darwin's *Origin of Species,* however, that marked a watershed in American thought. It saw the beginnings of a new science of mind that elevated consciousness, habits, and morals in terms of their survival value for the human race rather than in terms of their religious meanings. In the later decades of the nineteenth century there were many crosscurrents of ideas concerned with individualism vis-a-vis industrialism. Along with the praise of the self-made person that we find in Carnegie's idea of the Gospel of Wealth, we also have Veblen's trenchant criticism of the modern industrial state. He saw that society as spawning the type of individual who must cultivate his predatory instincts, be unscrupulous in the conversion of goods and people to his own ends, and be callous in disregard for the feelings of others. In other words, he must become what we would call an "ideal delinquent."

There have been others who were critical of our society's values. Men like Josiah Royce and Charles Peirce called for the development of a sense of comunity. Dewey was familiar with their work and many of his ideas show their influence. We have as guiding principles the following: people learn by doing, the scientific method is the paradigm for the development of a critical intelligence, and school and society should be treated as interdependent. These ideas have not only provided the subject matter for our schools but they have molded our public behavior as well. We have learned the pragmatists' lessons well. We have opted for experience as a way of knowing, and in so doing we have escaped from the solopsistic world of pure reason and the fanciful flights of idealism. We have chosen the concepts of growth, change, and progress — the big, booming, buzzing confusion of a real world. One might think — given what seems like a positive philosophy of openness to experience, the acceptance of change, and the valuing of the individual — that we would have an optimistic, dynamic, and supportive society. Unfortunately, we know that this is not the case.

What do we find as we briefly survey the American scene? We find the acceptance of moral decay as part of the fabric of our daily lives. We find elections determined not by the merits of the candidates but by the slick public relations campaigns of David Garth. We find large corporations using the media to sell junk foods and dangerous toys to children. Politicians lie and steal, and multinationals evade the law.

We know about these conditions, but we have been taught to ignore them. We have indeed lost the capacity for righteous indignation, and so the American public can be counted on to accept quietly the decline of our values. Barely a mutter is heard when we are told that a disgraced ex-president has been invited to the White House. We casually read about dinners that cost hundreds of dollars and then turn the page to just as casually read about the rise in unemployment and the fears of the elderly.

We have been trained, in short, for a life as consumers, and we have accepted the built-in obsolescence of objects. We do not regret their loss or absence. We just go out and buy another one. But now we find that not only are objects expendable but people are too. Alienation and inauthenticity are the stigmata of our society. Even the family, as Christopher Lasch (1977) has so eloquently stated, is no longer a haven in a heartless world. We have all allowed, permitted — even encouraged — the gross exploitation of human beings, and only recently are we becoming aware that feelings of resentment, a mean-spiritedness are eating away at our body politic. We are told to buy books that teach us how to find the vulnerable points in other people and how to use them to make them do what we want them to do. Whatever became of Immanuel Kant's dictum that we treat people not as means to our ends but as ends in themselves? When we raise a generation on what Dostoevsky called "bread and circuses" can we then wonder that they become narcissistic?

What has gone wrong? Is it that we did not take seriously the lesson that Dewey taught? He wrote about educating the whole child, but I believe that we have been educating only a part. We have allowed the pressures of our industrial society to focus on the child as a future worker and consumer and we have developed those skills that are needed in the marketplace. We teach them to control their emotions, to be on time, and to cultivate what we call "true grit." We do not teach them to give expression to their feelings of joy or of pain. We concentrate on building vocabularies but not on helping children to build a repertoire of responses to feelings of loss and grief and happiness. Charles Silberman has correctly described our classrooms as joyless places. And they are joyless. How can they be otherwise when the affective domain is relegated to a minor position in our curriculum. If we had been taught to value people, I doubt that so many of us would have been able, during the war in Vietnam, to watch men being blown to bits and then continue to passively watch the weather report that followed.

Many years have passed since Americans have considered their philosophy of education. In the early part of this century we were concerned with developing the skills necessary for participation in a democratic society. We saw as our goal the teaching of skills and the development of critical thinking. While we gave lip service to the idea of the whole child, we neglected to concern ourselves with the range of experiences and meanings that that idea implies. Perhaps before the century closes we will begin to pay attention to the totality of the child. We know that education cannot solve the problems of our society, that education, the formal education that goes on in the classroom can help children feel and make judgments that are informed by those feelings.

There have been critics of society who have described the anomie that pervades our society. Camus, in *The Rebel*, tells us we must begin to form communities in order to develop a sense of worth. Others have also suggested that small is beautiful as an antidote to the overpowering control of mass society. It is not surprising that we find a resurgence of ethnic communities and a powerful impetus to go back to one's roots. We are urged to return to religion or to give up our possessions and join one of the proliferating cults that continue to emerge.

While some of the suggestions are well-intentioned we know that most are inadequate and some are dangerous. All of them, however, are trying to respond to the need for people to experience a sense of self-worth, the worth of a full, feeling human being. We have seen how distorted these attempts become. The *New Times,* in an article entitled "Decadence" (1979), described the cultists as follows: they have a contempt for ordinary life, for the ability of individuals to make rational decisions. They become humorless, fanatical "saviors" of our souls. It finally doesn't matter if they claim to be of the Left or the Right, for Christ or against him — they are inevitably the destroyers of life (p. 14).

What, then, is the role of education? I propose that we accept as our first guiding principle Dewey's (1934) statement about intelligence. He said, "Intelligence . . . is inherently involved in action. Moreover, there is no opposition between it and emotion. There is such a thing as passionate intelligence, as ardor in behalf of light shining into murky places of social existence, and as zeal for its refreshing and purifying effect" (p. 80). As a second guiding principle I propose that as educators we assume the responsiblity of converting the classroom into an exciting place where real experiences are allowed to be examined in the full range of their emotional and intellectual content. Each human being feels joy and pain, loss and bereavement, and they must be incorporated into the curriculum in appropriate ways. If we just think of the social studies, there are innumerable instances that lend themselves to discussions about death and dying. The feelings and values attendant on those instances are almost never talked about. Instead we engage in the recitation of lists of battles and wars that were fought. Can we teach about the value of life if we do not talk about its cessation? We can no longer afford to treat children as objects by refusing to deal with their feelings of loss and sadness, and we must begin to help them cope with their responses to major events in their life.

Many years ago death was seen as a fit subject for discussion. The Puritans kept reminding themselves that life was not supposed to be pleasant and that it was "only a journey to the grave" or "an error to be rectified" (Cable 1972, p. 156). And as late as 1800 there were still the use of hellfire and damnation preachers who, Cable tells us terrified childish hearts with pronouncements like, "Before the next Sabbath you may not only be taken sick, but taken away; and your tender bodies covered up in the cold and silent grave" (p. 67).

No doubt our reluctance to teach about death is partly in reaction to what had been done to children. We have no intention of using threats of death to gain conformity, nor is it being suggested that we return to or reconstruct the past. Our *Weltanschauung* has radically altered in the ensuing years. We have, however, begun to think seriously about the quality of life, and it is in this regard that we must begin to prepare children who value that life. One of the ways to teach about an idea is to talk about what it would be like if the opposite were the case.

Educators are aware of curriculum development and how flexible curricula can be. Changes are made by people who think that there are valuable ideas that ought to be incorporated into the work they do. I urge consideration of some of the ideas that have been discussed and resolution to find them important enough for inclusion in the curriculum. There is no more appropriate time than now.

REFERENCES

Cable, M. 1972. *The Little Darlings: A History of Child Rearing in America.* New York: Scribners.

Camus, A. 1954. *The Rebel.* New York: A.A. Knopf.

"Decadence." 1979. *New Times* 12 (Jan. 8).

Dewey, J. 1934. *A Common Faith.* New Haven: Yale University Press.

Friedenberg, E. 1976. *The Disposal of Liberty and Other Industrial Wastes.* Garden City, N.Y.: Doubleday.

Lasch, C. 1977. *Haven in a Heartless World: The Family Besieged.* New York: Basic Books

Sheler, M. 1962. *Man's Place in Nature.* New York: Farrar, Strauss and Giroux.

Werkmeister, W.H. 1949. *A History of Philosophic Ideas in America.* New York: Ronald Press.

Whitehead, A. N. 1929. *The Function of Reason.* New York: Macmillan Co. 1929.

GUIDELINES FOR DEATH EDUCATION FOR YOUNG CHILDREN
Dixie R. Crase and Darrell Crase

An overview of child development suggests that the discovery of loss begins during infancy. Toward the end of the first year of life the young child has become attached to significant people and, consequently, develops two universal fears—fear of strangers and fear of separation. Even temporary loss of the familiar person is fear producing. Learning to let go of the known and facing the unknown is not accomplished without a struggle at any age.

The most significant element in the development of a healthy personality may be the sense of trust established during the first year of life, and yet, as early as the second and third year of life, the toddler strives toward a sense of autonomy—he is learning to let go of his total dependency on others.

Children's bedtime rituals are often prolonged (another drink, another bedtime story, another kiss) because separation from favorite people is not welcomed. Even exhausted babies on occasion won't give in to sleep.

One of the first games children play is Peek-A-Boo which stems from Old English words meaning "dead or alive." The child in the highchair delights in an adult retrieving a dropped toy. As a child's interest in games of disappearance and return develops, he gradually comes to suspect that some things do not return. They may instead be "all-gone."

Children's language reflects their interest in separation, loss, and non-being. "All-gone" often becomes a pivot word. A toddler who washes his hands may say, "All-gone sticky" or when he comes indoors he says, "All-gone outside." The two-year-old's fascination with the toilet is, in part, due to the possibility of all-goneness.

Piaget's work suggests the significance of the attainment of object permanence. Newborns react as though an object that disappears no longer continues to exist. By 18 months of age, babies behave as though objects are "permanent"; that is, they continue to exist though they are out of sight. The child's discovery of nonpermanence may be as significant a developmental milestone as the grasping of object permanence.

Babies learn to wave and say "Bye-bye" long before comparable greetings are verbalized. Olds (1978) quotes psychologist Diane Papalia-Finlay as saying, "From the time I was a little girl, I could not say 'goodbye' because that was too final. That implied death" (p. 48). When continuity is built into an ending (See you later. Take care.), the basic fear of separation is easier to handle.

Young children continue to play out their developing concepts of life and death. The preschooler reacts as though death were reversible or simply "less alive." Chasing games during childhood are sometimes interpreted as death being "it," with the child trying to escape death. Not until most children are about nine years of age do they understand the irreversibility, universality, and inevitability of death.

If separation tolerance develops from handling the many losses that punctuate life, how should children be prepared for losing? Can children be "immunized" to protect them from significant losses, particularly a loss associated with death? If happiness in childhood is the best preparation for withstanding possible future unhappiness, should awareness of death be avoided as long as possible? Is death education for young children to be interpreted as a buffer against the pain of loss and grief?

The challenge of providing developmentally appropriate death education experiences is an immediate concern of many professionals. Some observers are convinced that more is known about the mishandling of death than about how to treat it openly (Koch, 1977). The controversies surrounding death education at any age level become more intense the younger the age group being considered. Many parents as well as some professionals question the advisability of confronting young children with death-related experiences. Direct, first-hand experiences with death may be delayed for many of today's children because death has been taken out of the home. In the past, parents had difficulty discussing the beginning of life but could handle the ending of life. The situation may be somewhat reversed today because urban living, nursing homes, hospitals, and funeral homes have helped create a death-denying society. Even as society makes it easy for families, particularly children, to avoid real experiences with death, young children may be routinely faced with death as it is portrayed on television. A typical child may see as many as 13,000 deaths on television by the time he is 15 years of age. A two-year old who discovered discarded flowers in the trash asked his mother why they were there. When his mother replied they were dead, he wanted to know, "Who shot them?"

Given the limited exposure to real experiences with death on the one hand and the variety of vicarious experiences with death on the other, what is the young child's perspective of death? And, what are the implications for parents and professionals who work with young children? Just as preparation for life cannot be taught in one single attempt, neither can death education be accomplished in one neat, concise package. Appropriate death education experiences should occur throughout the development of individuals whenever relevant issues arise. Thus, the following section identifies practical guidelines for those in a position to respond to children's needs as they experience loss.

Confrontation with One's Own Feelings and Thoughts about Death and Death Education

Although adults may not have finalized their personal attitudes toward death, a developing understanding of death as a part of life promotes positive responses to children's expressed needs. Hawener's (1975) study indicated that teachers are in a unique position to assist children in facing issues related to death and dying. If a teacher is in the classroom for as many as five years, there is a 95 percent chance his students will be confronted with the death of a classmate, the death of an immediate family member of a classmate and/or the death of a national figure who is meaningful to the children. Hawener's study indicated that in 75 percent of these instances, teachers chose to ignore death, at least in part because of their own inadequate preparation for death education.

A more recent study (Crase and Crase, 1978) confirmed that early childhood educators are generally convinced of the need for self-development and understanding of death education although they are not universally comfortable with this role. They are not convinced that teachers should feel free to share personal beliefs about death with children in the classroom. However, a sensitivity to children's feelings, a willingness to listen to questions and/or concerns, an insight into a child's behavior, and at times the initiation of a conversation may speak to the needs of a child experiencing loss.

Parents have difficulty communicating about death with their own children. Children are too often given little information or assistance in expressing their feelings partially because of parents' limited understanding of death education. Furman (1974) reports research indicating 41 percent of the bereaved parents studied told their children under 16 little about the other parent's death. Although children should not be subjected to continuous emotional outpourings, they need to see surviving parents grieve. Thus, children understand that they too can express their feelings about the loss.

Understand the Child's Level of Comprehension

Just as adults differ in response to death-related issues so do children's responses vary. Note the children's reactions in the following situation described by a teacher of three and four-year-olds:

> I arrived one morning to my classroom to find our pet bird lying dead on the floor of his cage. Some children said he was sleeping. One child announced, "Throw him in the garbage can . . . he's dead." One child said, "I'm sorry he is dead." Another child wanted to bury him in the ground. This idea upset a child who said, "But what will he do when he's not dead anymore?"

Children's responses to death vary in part because of their different experiences. However, there are some general characteristics of young children that adults may find helpful as they attempt to communicate about death.

Obviously, children under two or three years of age will remain primarily dependent on non-verbal forms of communication for reassurance and comfort when faced with a significant loss. Older preschoolers will on occasion have difficulty verbalizing their fears, anger or frustration and their behavior may be inappropriate and require redirection. The sensitive adult may be able to help the child confront his difficulty in a more direct, verbal and appropriate manner.

The egocentrism of young children is well documented. When a child asks, "What will happen if Mommy dies?" he may in reality be concerned about, "Who will take care of me?" One child suggested his grandfather did not die and go to be with God. Rather, God had come to Texas to be with his grandfather.

Since children are egocentric, they have difficulty comprehending a differing point of view. Children's ability to develop an ecumenical understanding of and respect for conflicting beliefs about death may await a later age.

Young children communicate primarily in terms of concrete, real, tangible experiences. Experiences with death confront the child with intangible, abstract and spiritual concepts which may perplex young children. Even so, adults should try to lay a framework that forms the foundation for later concept development. When basic concepts are "retaught" at various age levels, children may begin to question the adult's authenticity.

Truthfully Answer a Child's Questions about Death

Questions in sensitive areas often tempt an adult to protect the child from unpleasant or possibly disturbing answers. A child who is aware of inconsistent or incomplete answers by the adult is more unsettled by this misrepresentation than by the truth he is seeking. In fact, the child's imaginative answers to his own questions that are not handled satisfactorily by the adult may be far more disturbing than an appropriate answer. At the same time, there may be questions in relationship to a violent or sudden death which require a basically true answer without all of the grim details being shared with a young child.

In answering children's questions, try to make sure you understand what the child is asking. The child who asks, "What's it like to die?" may be seeking an opportunity to explore his own thoughts. Sometimes to reverse the child's question is helpful. Try asking the child, "What do you think it's like?" This offers an opportunity for the child to clarify his specific concern. In some situations, acknowledging the mystery or uncertainty of specific aspects of death is the only true answer.

When an adult is emotionally overcome, he may honestly say to a child, "I can't talk about that now, but we'll talk soon." Children are sensitive to adults' true feelings and will differentiate between being "put off" and being invited to share in the adult's grief experience.

Acknowledge the Child's Perception or Reaction to Death

On occasions, the child's response to death-related experiences may seem unfair, unkind or inappropriate. The tremendous value of message acknowledgment becomes evident when dealing with sensitive or controversial areas. To accept as valid the child's interpretation of a death-related experience seems essential to keeping open the lines of communication. In a classroom of young children, a twin died after the Christmas holidays. When the surviving twin and her mother returned to school, they attempted to briefly explain the death of the twin sister. One child asked, "What did she get for Christmas?" Responding to a child by saying, "You shouldn't ask that," or "You shouldn't feel like that" is to deny the child's feelings. When a child's perceptions are consistently denied, he begins to question the validity of his own reactions. Acknowledging, not necessarily agreeing with, the child's perception or reaction seems to be a prerequisite for the adult to be in a helping position.

Avoid Confusing or Fear-Producing Explanations

Young children may find simple, clear answers regarding the cause of death (illness, accident) more helpful than general philosophical or religious explanations. A recent study (White, Elson and Prawat, 1978) confirmed the child's willingness to view death as a form of punishment for wrongdoing. In fact, 22 percent of the subjects felt that an unkind woman's death was caused by her bad behavior.

Using symbolic language ("He was chosen to be a flower in God's garden") may be misinterpreted by children. A child may feel he is unacceptable since he was not chosen to be in God's garden.

Equating death with sleep may be fear-producing. A child who knew very well the fate of the family pet being "put to sleep" wanted no part of being put to sleep in order to complete a battery of medical tests.

Introduce Children to Beginning Concepts of Death in Objective, Relatively Simple, Everyday Experiences

A dead bird in the park or a dead fish in the aquarium may be ignored, disposed of or replaced without children's awareness of death. However, such experiences may be utilized to introduce children to beginning concepts of death. Children may begin to understand that the dead bird does not fly; the fish does not move; that animals die when their bodies are old and worn out or when they have a serious illness or accident.

The death of a pet is often the child's first real experience of personal loss. Wishing to "spare the child," well-meaning adults may consider quickly replacing the pet. Most authorities recognize the value of the child having the opportunity to openly grieve the loss. The support of understanding adults will enable the child to positively and therapeutically express his real feelings. Replacing the pet immediately may repress this expression or suggest that pets can be easily and painlessly replaced.

A discriminating concept of death may be initiated from an early age. Not all death is the same. Colorful autumn leaves die and fall off trees. Discussions of sources of food reveal that some plants and animals serve as food for other animals or for people. From a relatively early age, children may be introduced to the cycle of life. After the Halloween pumpkin has been enjoyed, it may be planted (or buried) in the garden. The old plants enrich the soil for new plants. As children grow older, this discriminating concept of death is expanded to include discussions of abortion, suicide, murder and war.

Recognize That Television and Literature Influence Children's Understanding of Death

As indicated earlier, today's children are regularly confronted with television's presentation of death. Some researchers are convinced that the more violence and aggression viewed by the child, the more likely he is to feel violent and aggressive. If he doesn't act out his feelings, he is at least likely to become more insensitive to pain and suffering of others.

Television and fairy tales may reinforce misconceptions about death. Cartoon characters are regularly blown sky high or flattened and promptly return to normality. Death in folk tales is the customary end for the various creatures of evil. Death is quick, extremely tidy, and once accomplished, usually forgotten. The heroes and the good guys are rewarded and live happily every after. The good grandmother in some versions of Little Red Riding Hood steps out of the wolf, hale and hearty representing complete denial of death.

In recent years, more appropriate presentations of death have appeared in several books for young children. Early childhood educators in one study (Crase and Crase, 1978) noted the greater ease in reading about and discussing the death of pets as opposed to reading about and discussing human loss.

Invite Children to Participate in Family Rituals Surrounding Death

Children's experiences with human loss take on a special meaning beyond the death of plants or animals. Philosophical and religious belief of parents and professionals define their reactions to death and thus their interpretations shared with children. Traditional ceremonial events surrounding death give a child a chance to ask questions, make comments, and act out real feelings. Although no child should be forced to participate, most authorities suggest that children can understand their inclusion better than they can understand their exclusion from such family events. Being aware of the parent's pain and grief may be more distressing than the loss of a grandparent for a young child. Helping him understand his parent's feelings reassures a child that he is not the cause of his parent's unhappiness. Opportunities to share mutual grief can strengthen family relationships. The wise management of grief in children revolves around the encouragement and facilitation of the normal mourning process while preventing delayed or distorted grief responses.

Conclusion

The ability to cope with loss seems most directly tied with one's concept of self. According to Satir (1972), those who know how to handle life's "downs" and emerge from crises as whole persons have positive concepts of themselves. One significant element of a healthy self-concept is the individual's feeling of control or power over his own life. The learned-helplessness theory proposes that persons give up in despair not because of the actual severity of their situation, but because they feel they can have little or no effect in changing it.

Encouraging children toward the establishment of a positive and realistic self-concept may be the single most significant stabilizing factor in their young lives. An unconditional acceptance of each child, an awareness of individual differences with the emphasis on each child's unique strengths, and acknowledgment of weaknesses are positive and realistic. Preparing children for the future has always been the challenge of parents and professionals. With the future fraught with change, the challenge of coping with loss seems upon us. If the ability to handle loss is indeed linked with self-concept, programs and policies affirming the significance of a healthy self-concept for each child must be consistently supported.

REFERENCES

Crase, D. and D. Crase. "Attitudes Toward Death Education for Young Children." *Death Education,* in print.

Furman, E. 1974. *A Child's Parent Dies.* New Haven, Conn.: Yale University Press.

Hawener, R. 1975. "Understanding Death." Paper presented at the Annual Conference of the National Association for the Education of Young Children, Dallas, Texas, November.

Koch, J. 1977. "When Children Meet Death." *Psychology Today,* 11, 64-66.

Olds, S. W. 1978. "The Long Goodbye," *Family Health,* 10, 47-49.

Satir, V. 1972. *Peoplemaking.* Palo Alto, Calif.: Science and Behavior Books.

White, E., B. Elson and R. Prawat 1978. "Children's Conceptions of Death."

DEATH EDUCATION:
Some Issues and Suggested Practices
Carolyn C. Maurer and James Muro

The topic of death is a prominent subject in the national media, but few individuals in our society react to the subject on a personal level. The inevitability of death, and perhaps a fear of dying, clouds the topic with an almost Victorian point of view that precludes its discussion except in very generalized abstract terms.

The somewhat phobic reaction to personal discussions about death and dying is strange when one considers the voluminous amount of literature on such topics as avoiding probate and references to the fact that highway deaths in the United States annually exceed the total number of casualties suffered in Vietnam. Most individuals buy life insurance and cemetery plots; few, however, make any preparation for grief. The nature of the human personality is to delay the discussion of a separation and the accompanying personal loss.

The contradictions about death outlined in this article are also very much in evidence in the public school curriculums throughout the land. Society, its social conscience piqued by endless tales of tragedies, supports and even demands that the curriculum include drug education, sex education (in some communities), affective education, and nutritional education. Moreover, in a field that is by its very nature, labor-intensive, specialized personnel are provided to be the vanguards of these curricular innovations.

The relative dearth of death education programs can be traced in part to the lack of strong advocates for such study. Unwanted pregnancies, child abuse, drug abuse, highway accidents, and health concerns do not suffer from the lack of vocal and persuasive individuals to support a particular cause. Concerned parents readily accept drug education, and issues such as the misuse of drugs have not gone unnoticed by the legislators and agencies that have the power to fund such programs.

Within the last decade, there had been a modicum of support for programs of death education in the schools; most support, however, has originated with psychiatrists and ministers who deal with the issue because of their vocational role. Except for a smattering of interest among school counselors, the topic of death education is not deemed to be important enough to incude in an already cluttered curriculum of public education.

The fact that schools are populated by the relatively young does not help promote the cause of death education programs. As has been noted in numerous professional and commercial publications, the process of aging in America is a difficult and painful experience. In our culture, unlike some Oriental cultures, we worship youth. Physical attractiveness, skill, and the ability to accomplish the difficult are percieved to be qualities that we correlate with youth. Television commercials and newspaper and magazine advertising constantly bombard the viewer and reader with the message that young is beautiful and old is ugly. When age is advertised, if it is at all, it is discussed in terms of how to avoid the appearance of having lived beyond forty or fifty years. Gray hair, mature figures, toupees, and face lifts all suggest that the aging process, if not reversible, can at least be delayed and substantially modified. Small wonder that there is little room for death in our culture.

Even those who support death education in the public schools do not speak with a single or unified voice. The issues are broad-ranging and at times fraught with controversy. Diverse opinions imbedded in divergent value systems do not readily lend themselves to cohesion and consensus in the educational community. Some of the more common issues deserve further elaboration:

Who Should Enroll in Death Education Programs?

Are discussions of death and factual materials related to dying necessary for all children? There are those who contend that death discussions and the counseling of grieved individuals are best reserved for those who have experienced or probably will experience a personal loss. Moreover, many contend that the historical role of the public school is deeply rooted in the development of the intellect in the basic areas of reading, mathematics, language, history and science. Given this assumption, the introduction of any new areas of study that seem to infringe on the time allocated for the basics is suspect. Death education is frequently perceived as less important than numerous other traditional topics.

Who Should Provide Death Education Programs?

Perhaps no professional in America is expected to be as flexible and knowledgeable in so many areas as is the public school teacher. While the general practitioner in medicine has lost status and numbers to the various specialities, the teacher has not been allowed to move in the direction of specialized practice. This condition is particularly apparent in the elementary school, where the predominance of the self-contained classroom dictates that a single teacher be competent in all the academic subjects while he/she still must contend with the emotional and physical needs of developing young people.

The fact remains that relatively few teachers are prepared to deal with death education, even if they deem it important enough to be considered for curriculum inclusion. Most teachers begin their careers after completion of the baccalaureate degree. At the elementary school level, this preparation includes study in general education and a professional or pedagogical sequence of experiences that include student teaching. At the secondary level, prospective teachers enroll in a general education sequence and an in-depth study of a single area, generally social studies, mathematics, English, or science. There is probably not a single teacher's college in America that prescribes a required course for teachers that deals with death. Can one teach what one has not studied and does not know? Perhaps, but this is akin to allowing an airline pilot to fly a 747 jet plane without prior instruction. The results in both examples would be highly predictable and the consequences disastrous. Death education, if it is to appear in public schools, will require a massive retraining of practicing teachers and the introduction of appropriate courses and experiences in the undergraduate curriculum. Without such effort, programs must be left in the hands of doctors, psychiatrists, and ministers. Since most of their efforts would be offered on an ad hoc basis, if at all, this does not appear to hold promise as a long-term solution.

What Are Children's Needs in This Area?

Mosley (1976) has provided empirical data with respect to children's needs and beliefs about death. In her study of 125 rural and urban children in a Southern city, she found that the vast majority of the elementary school children surveyed believed that all individuals will die at some time; moreover, most believed that any single individual can meet an accidental death. In addition, the majority of respondents to her Death Belief Inventory noted that the chief reason children fear death is that they do not want to leave loved ones. Most children in the survey also believed that death is not punishment, although over 68 percent of those responding believed that death is the end of all life. Younger children are more likely to believe that every person is afraid to die, and nonurban children tended to express the opinion that death is similar to sleep. Most elementary school children experience some contact with death — seeing a corpse, visiting a funeral home and cemetery, and observing the regret of their parents over the death of a loved one.

While the schools the children attended did not have formal education programs related to death and dying, there was also evidence to suggest that the topic was rarely discussed at home, church, with friends, or at Sunday school. Almost one-third of the respondents indicated that they had never had a discussion about death in any of these settings.

The results of this and similar investigations suggest that children's needs with respect to learning about death are not systematic and that the knowledge gained about the topic is more likely to be obtained from indirect sources. While direct contact with death appears to be related to the children's learning, most children's beliefs are probably classified as more immature than one would expect.

What a child believes about death in an abstract or theoretical way is not always constant. The cognitive, affective, and behavioral components of death beliefs are not fully developed. The public school, if conceptualized as a social agent, must do significantly more if it is to become influential in helping children learn about death.

Can a School Curriculum Be Adequately Planned
in the Area of Death Education?

The writers believe that the public schools and the institutions that prepare teachers can meet the needs of children in the area of death beliefs if the issues noted in this paper are vigorously confronted. Cognitive understanding can be increased, affective understanding can be clarified, and the resulting behavior can be understood *if* death education becomes a vital part of the school's planned curriculum, and if teachers are prepared to deal with their own beliefs about death. While awareness of death results from a personal experience with the events that surround a funeral or loss of life in a pet, one finds it difficult to argue that a child's initial encounter with death should be so harsh. Little is to be gained if the child must face death to understand its nature. Honest dialogue among children and teachers in a relaxed atmosphere could be extremely beneficial in the elimination of fears and misconceptions.

To assist in cognitive understanding, teachers can create opportunities such as reading stories or discussion of television stories to promote questions and open responses. The death of a classroom pet, current events (death of a national figure), and units in science, social studies, and fine arts can provide informal approaches to continue informative discussions. Death education need *not* be material that is foreign to the basic curriculum. The objectives of such experiences are to provide vicarious participation with themes like Dignity in Old Age, Death Is a Natural Phenomenon, Euthanasia, and The Wasting of Lives in War, Poverty, and Accidents.

The effective component of children's learning about death must be elicited by teachers who are understanding and reflective listeners. Basic counseling courses introduced into the preservice curriculum should provide teachers with the skills to clarify, empathize, reflect, summarize, and understand the emotional reactions of children. Children can be helped to understand that crying, fear, and other grief-related reactions are both natural and acceptable to friends and relatives of the dead individual. The major task of the teacher in this context is that of assisting the child to develop and understand his or her own values and not that of imposing the teacher's beliefs on the child. Such a process is not only more psychologically sound, it is infinitely more acceptable to concerned parents and communities who fear some form of religious indoctrination. Rather than express personal views, the teacher can respond to questions with a simple "What do you think?" or "It's important for me to know what you believe."

With a combined cognitive-affective program of death education designed to provide factual information and help children reach a personal understanding through a clarification of their feelings, the schools could assist children in ways that are educationally sound and minimally controversial. An outline for such programs is presented in the remainder of this paper.

Developmental Concepts Related to Death and Dying

The period of middle childhood is characterized most often as a period of latency or a time of continuous yet quiet growth. During this relative calm before the storm of adolescence, the children nonetheless still experience the range of emotions typical of human beings and direct their interest toward such affect-laden areas as politics, religion, social relationships, and death. With this perspective in mind, we can see that it is important to address affective as well as cognitive domains of learning in the elementary school years.

The child's concept of death has been described as following an age/stage developmental pattern closely related to the stages of cognitive development explored by Piaget (Gardner 1978; Koocher 1973; Ryerson 1977; Zeligs 1974). Before the age of six, children most often adhere to an unrealistic concept of death, characterized by fantasy and magic, animism, and egocentricity. These conceptualizations relate closely to the cognitive expectations of a child in Piaget's preoperational stage of development. Preoperational children are unable to think abstractly, and so they cannot add structure to an abstract concept such as death through fantasy and imagination. A distinctive feature of children in this stage is their inability to comprehend the permanence and irreversibility of death. Until the skill of reciprocity, present in Piaget's concrete-operational stage, is mastered, children are unable to utilize the experiences of others to explain abstract concepts. Hence, young children cannot construe the permanence of death from the fact that no one within their experience has actually returned from death.

Sometime during middle childhood (ages seven to eleven), the child enters the stage of concrete-operations, distinguished most acutely by the ability to conserve. The skill of conservation demands that a child deal realistically with operations performed on physical elements. In this stage, a child is able to comprehend that though these elements may change in appearance, they are the same after the operation as before. Thus, the concrete-operational child can appreciate the permanent quality of matter as well as grasp the permanence of such phenomenal events as death. In addition, this child begins to generalize from experience to experience and thereby comes to recognize the universality of death and other events.

With their ever more realistic view of the world, elementary school children concern themselves with the causes of death and also demand explanations of what occurs after the physical event of death. Without adequate and truthful explanations of death and dying, fears regarding one's own impotence in the face of death can develop during these middle childhood years and persist into adulthood. Therefore, the case for early intervention concerning death becomes significant if, as adults, people are to possess the ability to understand and deal with their own inevitable demise.

Death Education in the Elementary School

The elementary school setting is particularly suited to the process of preventive, early intervention in that children within that setting range in age from about five or six years through ten or eleven. Such intervention programs are considered developmental in nature because they are geared to answer the needs of the child during the time that those needs are experienced. Therefore a developmental death education program in the elementary school would focus first on the fantasy associated with dying for preschool children and would incorporate increased personal, concrete experiences with death and dying for intermediate (fourth grade to sixth grade) children.

Since death and dying are relatively new issues to be dealt with on an educational level, it can be assumed that many of the adults present in the child's world may be in need of remedial education in order to help them cope adequately and properly with the educating of children along those same dimensions. For this reason, death education for the school-aged child must also incorporate educational experiences for the adults in the child's environment. A program of teacher-in-service and opportunity for parent education would be integral to the success of any comprehensive approach to death education in the lives of children.

Programs and Activities in Preschool and Primary Grades

The young child approaches the issue of death and dying from a vantage point of fantasy and imagination. Although not developmentally able to comprehend death and its consequences, the preschooler nonetheless must be able to deal with such issues not only as they arise but also as a means for establishing the foundation for future learnings. Much of the young child's experience with death occurs through the death of a pet and through children's stories and fairy tales in which good triumphs over evil, life over death. The effect of such stories in the face of the reality of death, as in the death of a loved one, is to enable the child to cope with fears and also to reassure the child of the unreality of those fears (Moller 1967, p. 149). From a developmental approach therefore, death education for young children would incorporate the use of stories and fairy tales to teach that death, though presented as a fantasy, is an event that occurs as a part of living and is not a result of evil forces to be faced with fear by the dying or deceased.

Capitalizing on the young child's penchant for fantasy, the use of puppets would facilitate the expression of feelings associated with loss and death. Many preschool and primary age children do not yet possess the verbal repertoire for expressing feelings, and puppets therefore can serve to elicit words to enable the young child to express his or her feelings (Maurer 1977). Puppets and puppet plays would provide young children with positive sources of identification through which to experience fears of separation and loss. In addition, puppets may be used as a resource through which a grieving child could express the shock, loneliness, anxiety, anger, and guilt associated with such a loss.

During the primary grade years most children can be expected to enter, at varying points, the concrete-operational stage of development. With this disparity in entry point, it is imperative that the educator stress transition, rather than entry, defining activities and competencies in a manner that reflects the skills of both the old and new developmental stages. In the issue of death and dying, the child in transition may be expected to exhibit traits from both developmental stages, fantasy and imagination enjoying an interplay with reality and concrete experience.

It would seem appropriate, therefore, for the teachers of upper-primary grade children to provide experiences wherein students could utilize their fantasy-level creativity to approximate concrete-level reality. For example, children could be encouraged to fantasize the answers to such questions as those explored by Koocher (1973):

> What makes things die?
> How do you make dead things come back to life?
> When will you die?
> What will happen then?

All alternatives presented would be considered "correct" at this level. The more concrete and reality-based alternatives would then be explored further, through concrete and reality-based experiences, such as a dead plant or classroom pet that might be buried in the playground (with appropriate ritual and mourning), group sharing of personal experiences with death and dying, a field trip to a hospital or a party held for children in a hospital ward. The impact of such transitional experiences would be to expose both the fantasy and reality associated with death.

Programs and Activities in the Intermediate Grades

As with other affective areas, the process of death education in the intermediate years is best accomplished as a part of the total school curriculum. Integration of death education activities with other curricula keeps such activities among the usual, the expected, such that the taboo experience related to the concept is minimized. The question of how and when to integrate death education can only be resolved through the creativity and ingenuity of the school staff.

Mueller (1973) reported the integraton of death and dying experiences with subject areas constituting fifth-grade curriculum during a three-day unit of study. Spelling words dealt with death concepts and were utilized not only as test items but also as vocabulary for creative writing exercises. Math exercises presented death-related problems; social studies also focused on death and dying. Guest speakers and a field trip to a mortuary and cemetery highlighted the course of study. The author reported the unit to be a success, basing this evaluation on student reactions during the experiences and transfer of learning to events that occurred in their lives late in the year.

During the intermediate school years, most children are cognitively able to comprehend the concrete events associated with death and dying and can integrate these within their own perceptual framework to formulate some sense of personal identification with the concept as a fact of living. In the realm of social development, intermediate children are in the process of discovering themselves in relation to their peer group; and, although not as yet so strongly aligned with their peers as the adolescent, in a social context these children learn most effectively from interaction with their peers. As an intervention strategy, therefore, peer group experiences offer a powerful medium for the presentation and discussion of such affectively-loaded issues as death and dying. Berg (1978) reported the success of group counseling as a strategy for the discussion and exploration of death. The students, preadolescent boys, were self-referred, recognizing their own needs for answers and insights into the death phenomenon. The success of this counseling group experience led Berg to conclude that group counseling from a developmental point of view that is, addressing the needs prior to a crisis event — provided effective learning within the school setting.

In a review of the case notes from his work as consultant to a large Midwest school district, Danto (1978) discussed the need of children who had witnessed the homicide of their teacher to support one another during the court trial of the accused. Within the crisis orientation of the consultation, Danto rushed to meet the immediate needs of the children, parents, and staff while recognizing the long-range impact of the crisis and subsequent interventions for the children. Strategies of intervention therefore had to include direct remedial procedures (psychotherapy) and developmental activities aimed at establishing a foundation for future growth in the integration of death-related experiences. As an intervention during a crisis situation such as this, group counseling and group discussion experiences would afford children the opportunity to share the grief and fears surrounding the trauma of violence and a courtroom testimony.

The inclusion of concrete experiences with death and dying for intermediate grade children can be accomplished through the use of simulation and instructional games, role-playing, and field trips. Simulations are group activities that simulate real-life events and processes through a game-like atmosphere in which roles are taken on, problems posed, and alternatives explored (Muro and Dinkmeyer 1977). These differ from general role-playing activities in that directions for playing are described initially and at each phase of the game, with details of events being left to the spontaneity of the players. Thus, a simulation for death education might focus on the death of a family member, with roles of other family members, doctor, mortician, clergy, friends, probate judge or attorney, and even the deceased being filled by group members. The tasks of the group would be to grieve, plan a funeral, hold a wake, gather for the reading of the will, and resume everyday living in the aftermath. General role-playing situations, on the other hand, focus on a microcosm of the above experiences, such as role-playing the feelings the deceased's widow might experience. As another experience within the concrete, realistic arena, field trips for this group of children might be planned to a local mortuary, cemetery, or nursing home for instance, to acquaint children with the visible realities of the dying process.

As related earlier, all of these and other death education activities would be integrated with the on-going curriculum. As opposed to the three-day unit approach used by Mueller (1978), true integration of a focal topic with the rest of the established school curriculum occurs when the topic permeates other school activities throughout the school year. Although concentrated focus on a given topic may take place for a given amount of time, opportunities for discussion and further exploration must be provided. The alert teacher is acutely aware of the developmental needs of the students, individually and as a group, such that further experiences are timely and relevant for the children.

In addition to the role of the classroom teacher in death education experiences, many of the activities explored in the above sections would require the involvement of a qualified professional, such as a school counselor, social worker, or psychologist. The very assumption that adults in the child's world may themselves be in need of death education indicates the need for a skilled mental health professional not only to introduce and coordinate experiences for children and adults, but also to intervene directly in the educational process. The suggested group counseling, psychotherapy, and simulation-games are sufficiently intense to warrant careful, skilled handling by trained personnel. The increase in the numbers of elementary school counselors, employed throughout the nation over the past decade, speaks to the recognized need of elementary administrators for personnel with specified training in the behavioral and social sciences. Although in the past teachers have been delegated the sole responsibility for cognitive as well as affective development of school children, affective experiences are now most usually implemented and/or coordinated by the school counselor as the most highly skilled mental health professional at that level.

Programs and Activities for Parents and Teachers

As noted earlier, parents, teachers, and other adults in the world of the child are likely to be in need of education regarding death and dying in relation both to their own knowledge and personal experience and to methods for aiding the understanding of the child. Danto (1978) noted that children whose parents were able to cope effectively with the trauma and tragedy of the homicide and explain the event directly and fully to them experienced fewer problems in coping with the event. On the other hand, children who were highly anxious during the court proceedings appeared to have parents who were also highly anxious (p. 84). The responses of parents to this event exemplify the need of the adult population for exploration with death prior to the actuality of the event for themselves and significant others. The work of Kubler-Ross has served to amplify the fears and accompanying emotions with regard to death experienced by adults. Group experiences that provide a nonthreatening atmosphere for sharing concerns, fears, and feeling as well as questions about death are very much in order for all adults involved in the lives of children.

The reality of such group experiences directed by a counselor or skilled professional in the public elementary school setting is that usually only a small percentage of the parent population becomes involved. With teachers, the percentage stands a better chance to be inflated, for such experiences can be offered as a part of in-service education components and workshops where attendance may be required. For those parents, teachers, and other adults not to be reached through group experiences, opportunities for education in death and child development must be afforded. These may occur in the form of school newsletters, parent-teacher association programs, parent-teacher conferences, local newspaper and other media coverage, community education course offerings, and other resources.

Perhaps most generic to the whole arena of programs and activities for parents and teachers is educating them to communicate effectively with children. Communication skills are an important component of any parent and teacher intervention program, because such training serves to enhance the adult-child relationship and create a basis for mutual understanding. Wittmer and Myrick (1974) have suggested a continuum of verbal response patterns that are related to effective modes of interaction. These include asking open-ended questions, clarifying what another has said through restatement, and responding to the feelings either expressed by or apparent in another. A vast amount of the counseling literature reports that these kinds of responses tend to create an atmosphere of understanding and acceptance conducive to self-exploration and personal growth (Carkhuff 1969; Rogers 1957;

Wittmer and Myrick 1974). Studies of training programs in communication skills for parents and teachers indicate that these skills can be learned and integrated in a relatively short time period (Carkhuff 1969; Carkhuff 1971; Maurer 1979). Parents and teachers utilizing such facilitative skills in their interactions with children will promote openness, freedom, and clarity of communication about death and other issues.

In all these strategies for reaching the adult population, current cultural taboos must be recognized and examined from an objective stance, tempered by the subjective experience of the culture at that given point. For example, examination of the effect of euphemisms to describe death — "passed away," "lost," "gone to the Great Beyond" — brings to awareness the need to mystify a very human phenomenon and at the same time dispels the very mystery thus created. In these instances and others, such as forbidding attendance at the funeral of a loved one, the adult population, in its effort to protect the younger population, shield children also from pertinent knowledge of life and from experiences that, if experienced openly, would aid in normal, healthy development. Therefore, in working with parents and teachers, recognition of their good intentions, while explaining the restricting impact of those intentions, is as important a component of the intervention process as information regarding developmental needs, sharing of concerns and feelings, and training in communication skills.

The Grieving Child

In the elementary school, the greatest focus of a developmental program of death education will be each and every child's growing awareness of death as a part of living a preventive, before-the-fact approach. Within the school population each year, however, there will be children who face the actuality of death within their families. For these children, the need for immediate intervention is acute, and the role of the school in such intervention must be clearly delineated (Danto 1978). Perhaps the first person to be made aware of such an event in the life of a child will be the classroom teacher. This teacher — in collaboration with the school counselor, principal, and other support personnel — can offer support for the grieving child by providing means and opportunity for the child to express grief and its accompanying emotions.

Understanding the process of grieving is crucial to the success of all interventions, because the grieving child is likely to experience not only the expected sadness, but also anger, fear, loneliness, and anxiety (Uroda 1977). The primary age child is most likely also to experience guilt, as the death of a parent or other loved one is often associated with fantasies and wish-fulfillment (Anthony 1971; Ryerson 1977). These children may view themselves as personally responsible for the death of another, a "wish-you-were-dead" come true. Thus, intervention with such children must focus first on their feelings, to be followed by experiences to differentiate reality from fantasy — such as finding a dead bird that no one wished dead, or a dying plant that had made no one angry and yet is dying.

Intervention strategies suggested for developmental death education programs are applicable for grieving children but are presented on a more intensive, personal level and in a more tightly compressed time period. The school counselor can aid greatly in the implementation of such immediate intervention, providing opportunity for counseling using puppets and other play media and peer support through group counseling. The counselor may also work with other bereaved family members so that they will be able to offer the support needed by the child at this time.

REFERENCES

Anthony, S. 1971. *The Discovery of Death in Childhood and After.* London: Penguin.

Berg, C.G. 1978. "Helping Children Accept Death and Dying Through Group Counseling." *The Personnel and Guidance Journal* 57: 169-71.

Carkhuff, R. 1969. *Helping and Human Relations: A Primer for Lay and Professional Helpers. Vol. I: Selection and Training.* New York: Holt, Rinehart and Winston.

Danto, B.L. 1978. Crisis Intervention in a Classroom Regarding the Homicide of a Teacher." *The School Counselor* 26: 69-89

Gardner, H. 1978. *Individuality: Developmental Psychology.* Boston: Little, Brown.

Koocher, G.P. 1973. "Childhood, Death, and Cognitive Development." *Developmental Psychology* 9: 369-75.

Maurer, C. 1977. "Of Puppets, Feelings, and Children." *Elementary School Guidance and Counseling* 12: 26-32.

Maurer, C. In press. New Dimension in Interpersonal Skills for Teachers." *The Humanist Educator.*

Moller, H. 1967. "Death: Handling the Subject and Affected Students in the Schools." In Earl A. Grollman, ed., *Explaining Death to Children.* Boston: Beacon Press, 145-67.

Mosley, Patrica A. 1976. "Developing Curriculum for Death Education: How Do Children Learn About Death?" Paper read at AFRA Convention, San Francisco, April.

Mueller, J.M. 1978. "I Taught About Death and Dying." *Phi Delta Kappa.* 60:117.

Muro, J. and Dinkmeyer, D. 1977. *Counseling in the Elementary and Middle Schools.* Dubuque, Iowa: William C. Brown.

Rogers, C. 1957. "The Necessary and Sufficient Conditions of Therapeutic Personality Change." *Journal of Consulting Psychology* 21: 195-203

Ryerson, M.S. 1977. "Death Education and Counseling for Children." *Elementary School Guidance and Counseling* 11: 165-74.

Uroda, S.F. 1977. "Counseling the Bereaved." *Counseling and Values* 21: 185-91.

Wittmer, J. and Myrick, R. 1974. *Facilitative Teaching: Theory and Practice.* Pacific Palisades, Cal.: Goodyear.

Zeligs, R. 1974, *Children's Experience with Death.* Springfield, Ill.: Charles C. Thomas.

DEATH EDUCATION — FROM THE BEGINNING
Robert C. Slater

"Man is born to die," and "It is appointed once to die." Without regard to the source of these quotations, all of us recognize the frequency with which we hear them and the basic meaning to be found in each of them. They are not restricted to any age group, but will permeate the thinking persons of any age when they are capable of reason. This is especially true of children. We do not need to read the authorities but only to have had the experience of parenting to know that children determine their own readiness to accept or understand certain basic truths and to interpret attitudes.

Francis Bacon, in his essay, "Of Death," said, "It is as natural to die as to be born, and to the little infant, perhaps the one is as painful as the other." This statement sums up my concept of "death education from the beginning" for the child. The child early in his existence realizes that death is natural. It is only when we as adults begin to pervert their sense of values and place upon them our own anxieties and concerns that children will begin to look upon death as unnatural; and as Bacon proceeds to say, the infant, and perhaps the child of any age, finds both birth and death very painful experiences.

However, those charged with the education of the child, either as a parent, an educator, or a friend, must realize that pain in and of itself can have therapeutic value and, when placed in proper perspective, can be endured. Even as the child experiences pain in being born, we can lessen that pain by quickly cradling the child, either by placing it in warm water or wrapping it in warm blankets and holding it. The same is true when the child approaches death. Regardless of age, children need to be cradled and coddled. The actual manifestations of cradling and coddling should be adapted to the age of the child. To say that a child does not learn early about death is a misstatement. The nursery rhyme familiar to almost everyone deals with Solomon Grundy. It treats death so candidly, so succinctly, and in such sharp and clear focus.

>Solomon Grundy,
>Born on Monday,
>Christened on Tuesday,
>Married on Wednesday,
>Took ill on Thursday,
>Worse on Friday,
>Died on Saturday,
>Buried on Sunday,
>And this is the end of
>Solomon Grundy.

To those who remember nursery rhymes, this is not the only one that speaks from the beginning ot the child's learning process of death. More than 10 percent of the 500-plus rhymes in the Oxford Book of Nursery Rhymes deal directly, not indirectly, with the subject of death, and some of them have become the favorite nursery rhymes of our childhood memories. Who cannot recite, even yet, Old Mother Hubbard? And we must not forget that when she came back, "the poor dog was dead." The child learns early on the four-letter word *dead*.

I would like to speak to the child's education concerning death from the standpoint of three perspectives: those of integrity, involvement, and information.

First, we must deal with integrity — our own and that of the child. We have no right to begin to share with a child the verities surrounding life's great experience — death — until we have adequately dealt with our own anxieties associated with it. To do otherwise places the child in double jeopardy by adding our own anxieties to the child's. Integrity is basic because unless we can deal with the reality of death, we are not ready to share its meaning with children. We have no license to lie or to be less than wholly truthful with children.

Second, without our creating it, there is already involvement for the child with death. At an early age a child learns that living things die and thereby becomes involved with death. We have seen children exhibit an innate reaction to death when a pet animal dies. We can share with a child the deep and meaningful experiences that surround death by involvement in post-death activities. They, too, learn by doing and participating.

Lastly, we come to the fundament of our process — information. Facts are basic to understanding. The child's readiness for facts, based on his level of comprehension, must be evaluated. Authorities on the subject have indicated that a child up to the age of three is concerned with death as deprivation of a lost love object; from age three to age seven or eight, with the biological impact of death; and from age eight to early adolescence, with the sociological concept of death. The adolescent child thinks in terms of the theological/philosophical concept of death. Therefore, the teacher/parent must determine "where the child is" in terms of readiness for information.

Let us direct our attention now to the matter of integrity. Dr. Edgar N. Jackson has often made the statement that children have built-in lie detectors, and here again those of us who have parented in our lifetime realize the truth within this statement. Inasmuch as children are very perceptive to parents' avoidance of facts, we realize the importance that all education with children should deal with truths, and lies or half-truths are foreign to the process.

The child is already threatened by the fact that a loss has occurred — in this instance, that loss by death. The young child will often ask the question as stated in the book *Should the Children Know?*

(Rudolph 1978), in a single chapter heading, "Who Deaded Him?" To the child, not only is an act learned early but it is an overt act, and death is caused by something or someone. Even though the child may grow in stature and vocabulary, and though the question may change from "Who killed him?" to "What happened?" the basic search and cry for information is the same at all ages. Even adults can acknowledge asking in our own grammatical style – "Who deaded him?" – upon being apprised of a death.

Child psychologists and psychiatrists tell us that children are much more capable of handling the truth than they are handling half-truths, particularly when they realize that the truth is being avoided. Following the death of President John F. Kennedy, child psychiatrists dealt with numerous instances of chilren who not only saw the assassination but also watched in uninterruped awe during the days of the funeral. They came with questions to the psychiatrist, the psychologist, the pastoral counselor, or any other clinician; they sought truthful answers and not the avoidance techniques and half-truths offered by parents and others. When we think in terms of death education, we must realize that it will deal with one of life's anxieties, even as sexuality and chemical dependency deal with life's anxieties. We have learned from the early fifties on that we must, in the educational process, deal with sexuality and dependency in a forthright manner and with facts, not fallacies; with understanding, not avoidance; and with caring, not indifference.

It is apparent when reading the vast literature in this field that the child must be handled with the utmost integrity because basic foundations are laid on which the child will build a sense of values. If these foundations are not solid, the child's sense of values can easily crumble and bring on manifestations not only of physical disabilities but of mental instability as well.

As we proceed with our concept of the development of the child in education relative to the matters surrounding death, we find that inasmuch as death is going to be a natural part of the child's existence, it is extremely important that the child be involved with death.

A corollary that I would like to draw here is the one of children who are born with a lack of natural immunological protection. When this is discovered, medical science has made it possible to raise that child in virtual isolation, often in sterile, germ-free rooms. Parental and other contacts with the child are through glass partitions; or, at best, if the child is physically exposed to others, they are dressed in astronaut-like protective clothing. Some of these children live like this for years. As we read about them, we find our sensitivities being pricked and our reactions bordering on disgust that a child should be subjected to such cruel and inhuman treatment in order to continue to live. Isn't the way some people deal with children and death similarly inhuman?

There are those who believe that they can shield forever a child from the experience, the hurt, and the crisis of separation and loss caused by death. Here again the experts in the field have indicated that this is not possible, but yet there are parents and other well-meaning adults who will attempt to shield the child from all exposure to death. If it is cruel to deny a child a normal life because of physiological infirmities, is it not likewise cruel to deny a child the knowledge of death because of misguided psychological misunderstandings and/or parental personal anxieties? It is not necessary to emphasize that a child will see death, hear death, smell death, touch death, and in many instances attempt to taste death very early in his existence. Is it not the better part of prudence, then, that regardless of what our role as educators might be, to exert every effort to make sure that the education is adequate and will assist the child in the very process of maturation and development?

To involve a child in death obviously means that we will use the very highest degree of discretion in determining a child's readiness for involvement based on his own development and not our anxieties. To force a child into death-related activities or atmospheres is as cruel as to deny that child that experience. Readiness as far as parents are concerned is almost an innate concept. Those of us in education have a myriad of studies and literature to help us determine levels of readiness. The criteria and methods are available. It remains for us to create the involvement.

Even as we must involve a child in the process of dying and death, it is equally important that we involve the child in postdeath activities, not limited to but certainly beginning with the funeral. There are those who seem to possess some unearned wisdom that categorically denies the child involvement in the funeral. As a practicing funeral director, I have seen children of all ages involved in the funeral, and those children who are permitted to participate in the funeral will do so at their own level. They usually will show anxiety and reluctance only when such attitudes are conveyed to them by adults. Children are fascinated by the funeral. To them it is a ritual involving many people whom they love very much and they want to be involved in what is going on too.

Jackson (1965) referred to earlier, has described the funeral as a parade, from the point of death to the point of final disposition. Need I tell anyone how much children love parades? Children not only love movement, but they are also intrigued by progressive movement from one stage or level to another.

There are those who would deny the child the value that can be obtained in viewing the dead body and participating in the funeral and being involved in the family rites and rituals that surround the funeral and postdeath activities. I would ask them to consider what sort of impressions and fantasies the child will create if he is denied such participation. If the child is "sent away to be with a friend," what will be the child's fantasies as to what is happening in the place and with those whom he loved so much who at a time of obvious crisis have denied that child participation therein? We have again but to ask our psychological and psychiatric associates about the problem of dealing with childhood fantasies, especially when they are negative, over against dealing with the child who has been permitted to be involved in actual experiences.

In the process of death education for the child, as far as I am concerned there is no substitute for involvement. I would run the risk of those limited instances in which damage may be done rather than run the much higher calculated risk in which damage would be done if the child is prohibited from participation.

Perhaps it is summed up best by Jackman in a book entitled *The Child and Death* (Sahler 1978), when he says, "When dealing with the unknown, children are often bewildered by the fact that their parents do not know all the answers. Parents, in turn, compound this uncertainty by ignoring their children's questions or by giving long, complex explanations that do not satisfy their children's wishes to know and understand. Children are people with needs, emotions and individual personalities." If we agree with this excellent statement, then certainly it is logical to comprehend and to recommend the involvement of the child in postdeath activities.

Finally, we must confront the fact of the education of the child surrounding death with information. For some of us, it is easier to think in terms of information as dealing with facts.

Although the child does not understand the process between birth and death — namely, that of copulation or procreation — the child understands both ends of that continuum or cycle and will soon enough realize that one is the cause and the other is the effect.

Facts are basic to understanding. The child's readiness for facts based on his level of comprehension must be evaluated. As stated earlier, authorities on the subject have indicated that a child up to the age of three is concerned with death as a deprivation of a lost love object; from age three to seven or eight, with the biological impact of death; and from age eight to early adolescence, with the sociological concept of death. The adolescent child thinks in terms of the theological/philosophical concept of death; Therefore, the teacher or parent must determine "where the child is" in terms of readiness for information.

It is not the intent of this paper to discuss each of these levels of readiness. Educators realize how crucial it is to deal with children "where they are" in the process of education.

In terms of determining the level of the child's readiness, I am concerned when people will tie this to a specific chronological age. All of us, whether we are parents or educators, know that the chronological age is sometimes quickly blurred when we consider the maturation level of the child. B.J. Kennedy, the chief oncologist at the University of Minnesota, has sharpened for me the focus of readiness as well as anyone. Dr. Kennedy was asked by a sophomore medical student how old a child should be before the child was told that he had a life-threatening illness. Dr. Kennedy was not stymied for a second by the question. He said, "It is impossible for me to tell because any child who has cancer and has a limited life span is sitting in my lap when I tell the parents."

It seems to me that what Dr. Kennedy has said is important for everyone dealing with children. We state the facts, we share the facts, and the child's level of readiness will accept them for what they are. It is only when we distort the facts, withhold the facts, or ignore the facts that the child becomes threatened.

Helen L. Swain (1979) summarizes this approach when she concludes as follows:

> Despite the fact that parents and professionals may be quite hesitant to discuss the subject of death with children, it appears that death is a topic that can readily be discusssed with children. It is a subject best dealt with by open and honest discussion. It is important for children to learn that death is something all people think about and that they are not alone in their thoughts. When parents and professionals understand this along with their understanding that death is a natural component of life, they will be better able truly to encourage children in their attainment of an understanding of death and a personally significant philosophy of life.

Death education for the child begins as early as comprehension is evidenced, and those who deal with the child and these attitudes need parameters with which to accomplish this goal with sensitivity and perception. I am suggesting that as our guideline we deal with *integrity, involvement,* and *information.* After all, as we seek the wisdom of educators who for years have established goals and objectives, will not these be basic to any education?

According to Jordan Smaller,

> It was a brisk, sharp January, just nine years ago.
> I was six years old, but not too young to know
> what piece of my life had been torn from the whole
> by this tragedy which would torment my soul.
> Still, I giggled when first told the news;
> It had to be a trick, a thoughtless ruse!
> But in a few lonely days I learned to lose.
> It had happened — and that was how life had to be,
> Yet I cried for days, for I believed that he
> had died not of illness, but of me.

Death education for the child from the beginning asks of those of us who will be the purveyors of that education the very best. Can we afford to give less?

REFERENCES

Bluebond-Langer, Myra. 1978. *The Private Words of Dying Children.* Princeton, N.J.: Princeton University Press

Grollman, Earl A. 1976. *Talking About Death: A Dialogue Between Parent and Child.* Boston: Beacon Press

Jackson, Edgar N. 1965. *Telling a Child About Death.* New York: Channel Press

Pincus, Lily. 1974. *Death and the Family: The Importance of Mourning.* New York: Pantheon Books

Rudolph, Marguerita. 1978. *Should the Children Know?* New York: Schocken Books

Sahler, Olle Jane Z. 1978. *The Child and Death.* St. Louis: C.V. Mosby Company

Swain, Helen L. 1979. "Childhood Views of Death." *Death Education 2* (Winter).

EDUCATION FOR LIVING (INCLUDING DEATH)
Norma Gayle Schmidt

There are two questions that strike fear in the hearts of most parents and educators. These are "Where did I come from?" and "What happens when you die?" Both precipitate that familiar combination of symptoms: sweaty palms, dry mouth, darting eyes, and chronic stammering. Very few adults are able to handle either question with any degree of ease or expertise. Unfortunately, as the child matures and reaches adolescence, the situation does not improve. Rather it seems to degenerate. Somewhere, some way, most will find answers to vital questions related to how life begins, but few learn much about how life ends.

Today many schools have some form of education about sexuality. But most of the curricula seem to assume that once the child knows where he came from, that is all that is necessary. What is needed is life cycle education. This is not found in today's school curriculum. Most growth and development courses end at the conclusion of puberty. There are child and adolescent psychology courses, but few go beyond that. It is as if when one is old enough to vote, one is equipped for life. Yet where, and when, does one learn how to get beyond the twenty-ninth birthday, that you *can* trust people over thirty, that life neither begins nor ends at forty, that you don't put off everything until you retire at sixty-five or seventy, or that you won't live forever. It is time for educators to explore the possibility of a new thrust — that of education for life. So much of our education about life is compartmentalized. We have prenatal and early childhood development, child and adolescent growth and development, sex education, death education, and so on. The attitude seems to be that if we avoid tying these together, life, growth, development, maturity, and death will have no relationship. All of this may be just one more way of postponing the admission that death *is* a part of life.

If we assume, and we must, that life and death are interrelated, then it behooves us to educate for the total of life, which includes death. To be effective, this education should begin early. But many adults cannot accept the fact that children are able to comprehend the basic concepts of the life cycle. Many believe that this is protecting the child from painful experiences that should be avoided until the child is old enough to handle his or her own emotions.

This belief is contraindicated, however, in most homes and classrooms. Pets and plants are a routine part of virtually every child's existence. Aquariums, gerbils, guinea pigs, hamsters, rabbits and so on are frequently part of the decor of both the home and the school. The fish and the animals reproduce and die during the course of a school year. Both situations must be handled realistically and tactfully. Just as a birth to a classroom pet is a time for joy and excitement, the death of a pet is a time for sadness and mourning. Questions related to both events must be answered honestly and openly. Equally important is the need to provide opportunities for children to express their feelings, especially when a death does occur.

Education about death can no longer be avoided. This premise is supported by the large numbers of students enrolled in courses offered in colleges and universities. Ninety percent of all accredited 4-year colleges have courses related to death education. It has been said that two of the most popular courses at universities today are those related to sex and death.

But what about the child? Why should the child have to wait until college to learn about death? There are many reasons, most of which are the same ones given for not teaching about *any* controversial topic. Some of those included are: "The elementary student isn't ready for the topic," "It's the responsibility of the parent," "I would have to include my religious beliefs and I can't do that," "It would frighten the children," and "The parents wouldn't approve." Some of these are not justified. Any child who has watched television has had at least a vicarious experience with death. Many fairy tales, children's stories, movies, and books include death as a major theme, and most children are able to accept this without being frightened. The reluctant attitudes may really be based on the feelings and fears of the individual teacher. This is not an acceptable reason for omitting such a vital area from the curriculum.

Just as every teacher (or parent) cannot or should not teach about sexuality, neither can they or should they all teach about death. There are certain feelings and attitudes that must be worked through before one is comfortable talking about death. First, one must acknowledge — internalize if you will — that no one is immortal. The next step is to include oneself in that category. And this is not an easy task. One does not like to admit that someday one will no longer be able to hear the birds sing, smell the flowers, feel the warmth of the sun or another human being, or experience the joy of loving and being loved. Life is too precious to dwell on such "creepy" or morbid thoughts. But death must be accepted.

Another required change is to be able to talk openly and honestly about death. It is difficult for many to say the words *die, dead,* or *death*. It is more comfortable to refer to "the Grim Reaper," "passing away," "going to the Great Beyond," or some other comfortable euphemism. But when the teacher is able to use proper terminology, he or she is one step closer to teaching acceptance.

It is also important to be able to articulate to others the need for death education in the curriculum. Many administrators and parents feel that children will not experience death until they are adults. This just is not true. Accidental death statistics alone should indicate that some children will die, and not all will die before entering school. Therefore, entire classes may experience grief and mourning and require assistance in working through their feelings. Avoiding death education is not protecting the child; rather, it is depriving the child of needed information.

Improvement of the quality of life is one of the goals of education. For this to occur requires education for living throughout the entire life cycle. Each child must learn not only how to read and write but also how life begins, is, and ends. Not just the mechanics but how it really is and how important it is to make the most of each moment of each day.

DEATH AND THE CLASSROOM TEACHER
Louise Bates Ames

When there is a death in the pupil's family, what does an elementary school teacher do? What does she say? Fearing to add to a child's upset or confusion, afraid of contradicting something the child may have been told at home (perhaps the teacher is not even sure how she feels about death), many teachers do nothing. And so the helping hand that could have been held out is not offered, and a child whose family may have fumbled the subject of death finds no more help at school than at home.

There is no sure-fire recipe for dealing with this problem. Nobody can tell a teacher exactly what to say about death any more than one can tell exactly what to say about sex. Perhaps the best one can advise is that it is what teachers *think* about either subject, their general attitude toward either subject, more than any pat verbal formula that they may prepare for an emergency, that determines how helpful they can be to their pupils.

Rabbi Earl Grollman, editor of *Explaining Death to Children* (Beacon Press) suggests that if we as individuals and as a society could ourselves come to terms with death, we could do a better job of telling our children about it. He also suggests that to be truly helpful *we must tell children things that are rational.* In fact, there is a rather general agreement that regardless of a parent's or a teacher's personal beliefs, a child should not be subjected to theological assumptions having to do with revenge and punishment.

Though one hesitates to make capital of a national tragedy, it's true that a teacher's best opportunity to help pupils come to terms with and accept the notion of death occurs when a public figure dies. Even though the public figure may be much loved, the personal loss, the emotional sensitivity suffered, cannot be as great as when it is a family member or close friend who has died.

Thus in such a circumstance, a teacher can as the psychiatrists put it, thoroughly "ventilate" the topic. Children can be encouraged to ask whatever questions they like. Teachers can feel themselves on a pretty firm ground in answering these questions or even in suggesting others. Their answers, of course, should always be based squarely on fact, so far as we know it. Thus the loss of a public figure can be made a theme for a general discussion about the inevitability of death and for placing the end of life in the context of a person's growth and accomplishments.

Too specific questions, which teachers cannot in good conscience answer, can quite fairly be replied to by saying that there are many things about both life and death that we do not know. Any promises about the future should, ideally, be made in terms of "some people believe" rather than as definite promises. Comparisons to natural events are, of course, helpful — flowers die, leaves fall from the trees, but next year other flowers, other leaves appear. Or the very bold teacher can venture into the animal kingdom — old pets (dogs, cats) die but their place is taken by puppies, kittens.

If a good, satisfactory, and reasonably clear discussion has been carried on at the time of death of a national figure, it will serve as a home base to which teacher and pupils can return if and when death strikes nearer. Children can then have the comfortable feeling of being back on familiar ground.

Another excellent preparation for any necessary discussion at the time of a family death would be to have some of the new kind of discussion that some teachers are now recommending — group discussions of *feelings*. Most teachers have mastered the necessary facts. Feelings are sometimes considered outside their domain. Yet a child's feelings can be as important in the way he or she develops as the facts that are mastered. In a general group discussion of feelings, a teacher could boldly introduce the discussion question, "Has any one of you had somebody in your family die?" A grandparent might be suggested as such a possible person. And then feelings about this death could be discussed.

Such a discussion should come at a neutral time when, so far as the teacher knows, no child has recently been bereaved. This sensitive subject could first be discussed at a nonsensitive time and then later, when an immediate death has occurred, perhaps be referred to.

According to school psychologist Hella Moller, teachers should not avoid the subject of death by rationalizing that they are thereby "sparing" the child grief. Total avoidance of the topic can lead a child to believe that knowledge is dangerous or that the subject is just too dreadful for the teacher or other adults to discuss in the child's presence.

Children from six to nine may at times be able to acknowledge verbally that they are unhappy about death; those from nine to twelve hardly ever so. Regardless of age, in most cases the aftereffect of the shock of a death is such that the child does need help from a teacher.

As Dr. Moller points out, since the school is the child's natural habitat outside of home, the school situation usually becomes the main focus of the displacement caused by grief, so that more often than not, as the child suffers, schoolwork suffers as well. But direct help needs to be given to the child, not to the schoolwork.

What the child may need more than anything else is a chance to talk about his bereavement and bafflement. It is not so much what the teachers say to the child about death as what they allow, even encourage, the child to say about it in either class or more likely to them personally. It is not so much verbal assurance that such children are seeking as a chance to express their own grief, their own uncertainty, their own questionings, and finally the assurance that they gradually feel able to give themselves.

In addition to providing opportunities for discussion — either at times when no immediate death in the family is upsetting a child or, if need be, even at the sensitive time — teachers need to be aware that many children who have experienced a family death may for a while need to receive a great deal of personal attention at school. They may feel the need to relate incidents that have happened at home. Some teachers have found that negative personality traits that were prominent before the loss of a parent tend to be exaggerated afterward — for instance, a shy child might become even more withdrawn. Such reactions can last longer than the teacher would ordinarily expect, for months or even for a year or longer.

There are instances when a classroom teacher should not be expected to handle the situation herself. If a child seems unduly disturbed, or mildy disturbed but over an unreasonably long time, she should seek the help of the school psychologist or guidance clinic. There are those children who need special help in the time of any crisis. There are those who harbor guilt feelings, especially if they have been angry at the deceased parent just before the parent died, who clearly need the help of the specialist. There are others who quite normally feel anger as well as grief — anger at the loved person for leaving them. This feeling, too, may require the help of a specialist before the child can come to terms with it. It is only after the child has come to some kind of terms with death that the emotional capital invested in a lost love object can be withdrawn and reinvested where it can produce a healthy response.

Either the school psychologist *or* the teacher, according to Dr. Moller, can become an important source of strength during a crisis situation and can help the bereaved child to overcome any fear of abandonment and to vent any despair over the loss of a loved person.

Thus there are many things that classroom teachers can do to help any child faced with the problem of death. They can have built up in the classroom a background of discussion about the topic to which a child can refer in time of need. They can, within reason, provide answers to a child's wonderings and questionings. More than that they can try to provide an opportunity for the child to express his own thoughts and feelings. They can for a time be people to whom the bereaved child can specially relate. And they can, if the need seems evident, see to it that the help of a specialist is made available.

Sometimes by just being there with felt emotional support, teachers can do more for a child than by anything they say. In fact, as always, it may be their attitude quite as much as anything they do or say that can give the grieving child the needed support.

THE DEVELOPMENTAL APPROACH TO DEATH EDUCATION FOR CHILDREN
Ellen S. Marbach

And always understand that your real challenge is not just how to explain death to children, but how to make peace with it yourself.
Rabbi E. A. Grollman,
in "Explaining Death to Children,"
The Journal of School Health, June 1977

* * * * * *

Death education may become a part of the school curriculum, although the issue is still controversial (Wass and Shaak, 1970). Even if the controversy were removed and death education became part of the school curriculum tomorrow, there would be many unresolved issues:

1. whether death education should begin in kindergarten or later;

2. whether death education should be developmental or not;

3. whether death education should be learned vicariously through children's literature about death (Swenson, 1972) or integrated into existing school subjects (Stanford, 1977) or by some other method;

4. whether all aspects of death should be taught or only certain personally relevant aspects; and

5. whether every teacher is able or willing to teach death education effectively (Zazzaro, 1973).

Thanatology experts are and should be concerned about the real possibility that death education in the schools may result in a superficial or an excessive treatment of death (Zazzaro).

In this paper I take the position that death education is a necessary part of the school curriculum because it is an important part of the child's development in both the social as well as the psychological parts of personality. Since death education is truly developmental and lifelong (Reisler, 1977), even the teacher is still in the process of understanding death through life experience and a continuing thought synthesis concerning its meaning.

Both child and teacher are in the process of learning about death. They can learn together and from each other (Grollman). In the developmental approach to death education, the learner deals with death at his own developmental level with the amount of life experiences acting as a resource and a method for growth and understanding.

The teacher as well as the child must be viewed developmentally. The traditional concept of the adult being at a higher level of development than the child does not apply in this approach. Consider that some teachers may deny the existence of death and wish to avoid talking about it (Schwartz, 1977). The child who has accepted that death exists and is willing to talk openly about it could be at a higher developmental stage than the teacher. The developmental approach can explain these differences in terms of levels of understanding and provide the basis for a dialogue between learners (teacher and children) for determining curricular content.

The curriculum for death education needs to be based on an understanding of the developmental stages that occur in children and perhaps adults. This paper will define those stages and relate them to curricular content.

The Developmental Stages in Understanding Death

Understanding terms such as *dying, death,* and *dead* is not like learning the eight basic colors or the ABCs. The terms surrounding death are very abstract and frightening to children. Understanding them occurs in stages. These stages appear to be related to the age of the child.

Stage One: Denial of Death as Final

From birth to about five years of age, children conceptualize death as going to sleep or taking a trip (Reed, 1970). Death is not permanent because a person wakes up after sleeping and usually returns from a trip. Death is a lot like the game peek-a-boo, which in Old English meant alive or dead (Cook, 1973). Around three or four years of age a child might say that *dead* means you cannot hear (Formanek, 1974). This type of reply indicates that the child is unclear between the meanings of *dead* and *deaf*.

The young child is egocentric and has just as much difficulty understanding what is alive as what is dead (Formanek). This age child (zero - 5 years) might think that plants are not alive but a doll or toy is alive. Egocentric children are handicapped in that they can focus only on self and on momentary concrete perceptions.

Often the young child thinks that people die because they did something wrong, something their parents would not approve of. Even the toddler has mixed feelings toward death (Furman, 1974). Perhaps the child's mother dies. The child grieves and longs for her but is also angry that she left. At as early as two and a half years of age the child must experience a period of identification with the dead parent before the parent's death can be accepted (Furman).

Identification might take many forms. Some children relive, act out, or constantly express verbally the experiences shared with the parent before death.

Since 80 percent of children's fears center around "death," or the fear that the caregiver will die and the child will be abandoned, it is not surprising that the Stage One child would prefer to deny the existence of death (Reed). Some adults, too, feel that they can deny the existence of death by not talking about it (Schwartz).

Stage Two: Denial of the Universality of Death or One's Own Death

From five to nine years of age, children achieve the understanding that death is final or permanent. This finality is understood about particular friends or relatives who die (Reed). *Death* is understood better as a word (Formanek). The Stage Two children do not believe that everyone will die, and certainly not themselves (Reed). Death is not seen as universal. Although the Stage Two children are less egocentric than at the previous stage, they still are having problems with generalizing about death. Death is still only a part of particular situations and happens only to particular people.

The Stage Two child sees death as a person or being (Reed). Death might be a man or a ghost who catches you and takes you away somewhere. Some children at Stage Two will still deny the finality of death by saying that if the ghost catches you, you can try to get away.

Death can be interpreted as going into the hospital, being in a funeral, or going to visit the angels (Formanek). For the Stage Two child death cannot only be a person who spirits you away but also an unusual place where some people go. Death can be something that happens to you such as shot with a gun, taking dope, having cancer, eating poison, or old age (Koocher, 1975).

Death, to the Stage Two child, is still not very real. It happens only to certain people or animals. Death is a special person, a strange place, or a peculiar happening surrounded by mystery and fear. There are words or labels associated with death that people use, such as *funeral*, that are only partially understood by the child. The Stage Two child is still unable to come to terms with much of the reality of death.

Stage Three: Acceptance of Death as a Part of Life

Around the age of ten, children begin to believe that everyone dies, including themselves (Formanek). Death is universal and inevitable. To the Stage Three child death can be thought of as part of life. Going to school and dying are both parts of life (Reed). If the parents and the culture believe in an afterlife, the children can understand that to die means the end of this life and the beginning of a new one (Reed).

In Stage Three, children are less egocentric than in the previous stages. They do not see death as centered around certain people, places, or happenings. They can generalize enough to be able to view death as happening to everyone at some time. To conceptualize death as universal requires abstract thinking and thinking that is flexible enough to lead to generalizations. In one study only 20 percent of the seven-to-nine-year-olds were at Stage Three (Formanek).

Relating the Developmental Stages to Death Education

One type of approach that is being suggested for death education is the "teach-everything" approach. This involves teaching the student everything surrounding death, such as the decay of the body, what is done at the funeral parlor, and the life cycle of plants and animals (Stanford). Usually this approach is accompanied by the idea of integrating death education into the existing subject matter areas. For example, science becomes body decay, math becomes measuring for casket size, social studies becomes studying how to grieve and attend funerals. This grisly approach is criticized as being a fast shot at death education, too shallow to lead to learning, too morbid to be accepted—and too watered-down, because death education is lost in preference to the other subject matter areas (Freeman, 1978).

The teach-everything approach is unacceptable also because it does not fit either Stages One or Two in the development of children, as described in this paper. Neither level would be ready to accept all the aspects of death. It could be argued that even the Stage Three children would be taught little using this approach because of its shallowness and morbid nature.

Another mode being considered for death education is the children's literature approach. It is thought that children can be prepared for the reality of death by reading or hearing about death through literature (Swenson). Since the trend in the seventies toward presenting death in books is toward realism and sensationalism (Carr, 1973), the children's literature mode would appear to be unacceptable for children in Stages One and Two. The Stage One child by denying the finality of death would only enjoy the literature if it had the "good fairy" bringing grandmother back from her long sleep. Snow White dies only temporarily until the prince can come. The Stage Two children can benefit from a literature approach if it deals with death as a bird or creature from whom some could escape.

The current realism in the children's literature on death makes it appropriate for only the Stage Three child, who has accepted the finality and universality of death. The children's literature approach to death education becomes acceptable only if it is matched to the child's developmental level rather than to the reading or grade levels. Even so, the literature approach, because it is vicarious, may be more appropriate for some children than for others. Each child has his own style of learning. Whether vicarious learning is the best route for all children is debatable.

The spontaneous approach includes children's questions about death and role-playing of death ideas as the bases for death education. The children, rather than the teacher, introduce death into the curriculum.

An example of a program that appears to be using the spontaneous approach quite effectively is the one in Gainesville, Florida, for seven- and eight-year-olds. The children visit regularly (three to five times a week) their adopted grandparents at a nearby nursing home (Whitley, 1976). When an adopted grandparent dies, the teacher helps the children to share their grief and their questions. Often the children write letters to members of the dead person's family telling them how much that person had come to mean to them. The program stresses understanding of death as an ongoing process.

The spontaneous approach would be a more appropriate curriculum for death education because it allows the children and their environment to be the initiators of education in a school setting. Children at each developmental level can fit into the spontaneous approach. However, this approach does involve some teacher planning of the environment, or death education might never occur.

The Developmental Approach to Death Education

The developmental approach to death education could have elements of many of the approaches just discussed, but its focus would always be on what the child is ready to understand about death. The process of death education would not be forced or presented superficially but would be matched to children's developmental levels. Death education could begin in the preschool and extend throughout life. Children's literature might be selected as one learning method, if the literature matched the children's developmental levels and learning styles. Only those aspects of death would be taught that children at a certain stage could understand. The teacher and the students would both be learners about death.

The goal of death education should be that each student will learn to make peace with death. Death education requires the developmental approach because death is such an abstract and frightening concept for children to understand. Making peace with death is a long learning process, unlike learning the alphabet or the multiplication tables.

Developmentally, death is a series of personal denials before understanding and acceptance can occur. Education is important because it reduces some of the trauma associated with death and promotes an adaptive process in children and adults (Berg and Daugherty, 1973).

REFERENCES

Berg, D. W., and G. G. Daugherty, 1973. "Teaching About Death." *Today's Education.* NEA Journal, March, pp. 46-47.

Carr, R. L., 1973. "Death as Presented in Children's Books." *Elementary English*, May, pp. 701-5.

Cook, S. S., 1973. *Children and Dying.* N.Y.: Health Sciences Publishing Corp.

Formanek, R., 1974. "When Children Ask About Death." *Elementary School Journal*, November, pp. 92-97.

Freeman, J., 1978. "Death and Dying in Three Days?" *Phi Delta Kappan.* October, p. 118.

Furman, E., 1974. *A Child's Parent Dies: Studies in Childhood Bereavement.* N.Y.: Yale University Press.

Gordon, A., and D. Klass. 1977. "Goals for Death Education." *The School Counselor,* May, pp. 338-47.

Grollman, E. A. 1977. "Explaining Death to Children." *The Journal of School Health,* June, pp. 336-39.

Koocher, G. P. 1975. "Why Isn't the Gerbil Moving Anymore?" *Children Today*, January/February, pp. 18-36.

Reed, E. L. 1970. *Helping Children with the Mystery of Death.* Nashville: Abingdon Press.

Reisler, R., Jr. 1977. "The Issue of Death Education." *The School Counselor,* May, pp. 331-37.

Schwartz, S. 1977. "Death Education: Suggested Readings and Audiovisuals." *The Journal of School Health,* December, pp. 607-9.

Stanford. 1977. "Methods & Materials for Death Education." *The School Counselor,* May, pp. 350-60.

Swenson, E. J. 1972. "The Treatment of Death in Children's Literature." *Elementary English,* March, pp. 401-4.

Wass, H., and J. Shaak. 1976. "Helping Children Understand Death Through Literature." *Childhood Education*, November/December, pp. 80-85.

Whitley, E. 1976. "Grandma—She Died." *Childhood Education 5.* (November/December), pp. 77-79.

Zazzaro, J. 1973. "Perspectives on Death." *Nation's Schools*, May, pp. 39-42, 102.

CHILDREN AND DEATH—A BIOPHILOSOPHICAL PERSPECTIVE IN DEATH EDUCATION
Arlene Seguine

Death is one of the few universal experiences of human existence. It is the most predictable event in our lives, one that is to be expected with absolute certainty. Yet the nature of death is immersed in deep mystery. The enigmatic nature of death opens a wide range of possibilities for individual and collective imagination (Grof and Halifax 1978).

In retrospect:

When we look back in time and study old cultures and people, we are impressed that death has always been distasteful to (the average) man and will probably always be (Kubler-Ross 1977).

Within the context of the human life cycle, death marks the final rite of passage into another dimension—a still largely undefined location sometimes called "the beyond." Our ambivalent attitude toward death—that is, our curiosity coupled with our fear about death's mystique—has emerged and expressed itself more formally in the form of death education. Yet, while the subject of death itself is sensitive enough, infant/child death often seems to evoke its own unique grief.

Furthermore, the growing interest in thanatology in the United States today has naturally generated concern about the even more taboo aspect of children in relation to death. One of the factors that has probably traditionally separated the mention of children in conjunction with death is the difficulty in accepting the "unexpected reality" of death at an early age. This last notion has a multifold connotation. In terms of the children themselves, how do they perceive death in general, and, on a still more personal level, their own imminent premature demise? On the other hand, how do their parents (and other closely involved adults) deal with these varied dimensions of death? These questions are reflective of a biophilosophical approach to death education within a pediatric context.

This theme purports to discuss death—the final stage of growth—and the five stages of the dying process of the life-death cycle as they relate to the involvement of children, either as witnesses or as subjects themselves. Generally speaking, while the idea of one's own death is subjectively inconceivable, it is even more unfathomable in the case of the child's very own expiration. In essence, this "untimely event" is naturally construed as "out of order" with the line of succession in terms of family heritage. Within the course of this discussion, therefore, recent touchstones in thanatology pertinent to the pediatric aspect will be explored.

More specifically, this includes addressing the American culture's attitudes toward the prospect of death in conjunction with the child. Particular focus is directed toward identifying the appropriate coping mechanisms in response to the death process for the child both as observer and as the actual victim. In addition, this exploration encompasses the entire spectrum of death—for instance, the natural, accidental, and suicidal causes.

Only recently have we begun to see death as a part of the process of living, and to learn something of the myriad of attitudes and responses to this ultimate phase of life. "To study dying is to fear it a little less" (Gross et al. 1978).

And like all human situations, it has an existential dimension—it changes the individual's relationship with time and therefore his relationship with the world and with his own history (de Beauvoir 1973).

Moreover, with regard to the heightened consciousness revolving around death education in our society:

. . . the new open curiosity about death, the new techniques and skills aimed at helping the dying to the "good" death, far from constituting a resigned acceptance of mortality, is actually another show of human heroism, another way of overcoming death (Powledge 1978).

Though there are many levels and facets to this revolutionary shift in death-consciousness, the overall meaning is probably one of gain and health and not of decadence and morbidity. Only in a mature culture can death come of age and be received and accepted as a natural companion of life (Maguire 1974).

Since no mortal has ever pierced the veil of mystery surrounding death, the teacher and particularly the parent are frightened at the thought of finality. Perhaps for this reason many adults try in every way to keep children from the idea of death. . . . Death touches the ebb and flow of the deepest feelings and relationships. . . . There are no simple, foolproof answers to death, the most difficult of all questions (Grollman 1967).

Because death is naturally viewed as a formidable topic, it is understandable that the American culture has been a death-denying society. Yet:

In the decade since Kubler-Ross first gave her seminar on

dying, the taboo has weakened. Death is in vogue as a topic of books, seminars, scholarly articles, and classes at every level from college down to elementary school. There are two professional journals devoted to the study of death, dozens of volunteer groups working with the dying, and one or two medical facilities geared solely to helping people die with dignity (Goleman 1976).

But still another dimension of thanatology evolves:

> Therapists are beginning to realize that the subject of death should be faced and discussed in order to deal with death as part of life. Some books have been recently published on the subject relating to adolescents and adults, but very little attention has been focused on death as children experience it, how they understand it, and how they are emotionally affected by the way parents and other authoritative figures deal with it (Zelig 1974).

Apropos of these observations, John Birtchnell, et al. in their article "The Possible Consequences of Early Parent Death" (1974), provide this reasonable explanation:

> It should be emphasized that our society has never had much in the way of identifiable guidelines to follow in dealing with children's confrontations with death. . . . They (parents) tend to conceal their own grieving, feeling that it would be upsetting to the child. . . . Thus the child's unwillingness to accept the event of death and to grieve over it is reinforced by the protective attitude of adults.

According to Gibney (1965):

> Like adults, children can best recover from loss when they are encouraged to face the fact and express their feelings openly. . . . Grief is a useful friend and mourning a process of healing which helps us face and recover from loss.

Since death is a universal phenomenon, it is only fitting to frame this discourse in a multidisciplinary context. Consequently, the various perspectives expressed will be drawn from and interfacing from among sociological, biological, anthropological, philosophical, and educational viewpoints. Such a multi-faceted approach permits a greater opportunity for gaining a more in-depth comprehension of child-related death issues.

> Children's concepts of death tend to reflect those of the society in which they are reared. They learn much more than they are intentionally taught. . . . The way the child conceives

of death depends largely upon his age and maturity level as well as on what he is taught (Anthony 1972).

While the child's conceptualization of death is largely determined by these factors, it also provides the foundation for developing the child's coping mechanisms in response to death in its various guises.

If death is, indeed, the final rite of passage, then what are the periods of transition that lead to this culmination? Elisabeth Kubler-Ross has identified five stages in the dying process: denial, rage, bargaining, depression, and finally acceptance, all of which are intended to serve as rough guideposts for following the dying person's relationship with the people around her or him (Goleman 1976a). And of even more significance is her contribution of finding "new life in the subject of death" by providing insight into transcending "the conspiracy of silence" (Kubler-Ross 1969) that often naturally surrounds the dying child. Relevant to this:

> To help a child face and master loss, even smaller losses than death, is to help him master a most important job in life. . . . In a severe crisis, such as death, a very little help can go a very long way, and if we support children's realistic efforts at compensation, they often find highly creative solutions which last them for a lifetime (Gibney 1965).

Since coping with death is a very subjective experience, a particularistic approach is appropriate when exploring reactions to this final event of the human life cycle. In his book entitled *Help Your Grief* (1977), Freese suggests that grief can be turned into a process of growth. In an interview with Elisabeth Kubler-Ross, Daniel Goleman addresses her:

> "You've said we treat grief and pain in life as bad, but that these experiences are really gifts. What is the gift of pain?" The famous Swiss psychiatrist and pioneer in the realm of thanatology responds:
>
> When you look back at the anguish, suffering and traumas in your life, you'll see that these are the periods of biggest growth. After a loss that brings you dreadfully painful months, you are a different man, a different woman (or child). But many years later, they will be able to look back and see . . . the togetherness . . . that came out of their pain (Goleman 1976b).

This, of course, is one of the paradoxes of life — to grow from a negative experience and thereby become more in touch with oneself and others. Evolving out of this lesson in living is the realization that:

> In the course of (facing death), we can give up, de-

mand attention, scream, we can become total victims long before it is necessary. We can displace anger and a sense of unfairness onto others, and make their lives miserable. Or, we have the choice to complete our work to function in whatever way we are capable and ... touch many lives by our valiant struggle, and our own sense of purpose in our existence (Kubler-Ross 1978).

Whether the child is the victim or more particularly the witness to death, it is important for the adult guardians in his life to be cognizant that:

> Until children are about six years old, they can't conceive of the finality of death. They think of it as a sleep from which people awaken or a trip from which the person will return. But this doesn't mean that they aren't deeply affected by the separation (Gibney 1965).

Pertinent to this is Freud's theory of cathexis/decathexis, or:

> "Grief work" ... is the process of gradually detaching our emotions from the person who has died and re-attaching them to others. It is often a lengthy process — for most adults it takes a year or two, for children, usually longer. ... However, if we don't allow ourselves to experience this relinquishing sorrow, we may remain emotionally tied to the dead person and be unable to establish other ties. Children particularly, may have a hard time recognizing and working through a feeling of grief, unless we help them (Gibney 1965).

Consequently, then, parent(s) play the crucial role of providing careful guidance to their children with respect to helping them come to terms with death — their own or another's — in all its stages, thus ultimately reaching a sense of resolution or realistic acceptance. This, of course, marks a critical phase in the healthy maturation of the child. Herein lies the value of ritual or religion in the case of grieving either by children or with them. These provide the necessary vehicles or contexts for searching out the appropriate behavior patterns commensurate with facing death as a natural part of life.

With respect to the psychosocial dynamics involved with the event of a death, it is vital to encourage an honest interfacing between the dying person/child and the companion survivors (other adults/children). Only then can a child and, indeed, any other person, experience a valid confrontation with this final rite of passage. From a biophilosophical viewpoint, this is the viable difference between living a life that is real versus one that is counterfeit. An important component in the child's learning progression is the enviromental setting in which death is encountered:

> In the old days people were more likely to die at home rather than in the hospital. When a person is home, he's in his own familiar environment with his family and his children around him. Dying under these circumstance is not only easier and more comfortable for the patient, but it also does something for his family — especially the children, who can share the preparatory grief for a person who is dying in the house. Such a child will grow up and know that death is part of life (Kubler-Ross 1971).

While the child does not always have the advantage of the circumstance just described above, it is nevertheless, incumbent upon the parent(s) to foster positive dynamics in terms of the child's social organization of death.

> Trying to help the children see death as an inevitable human experience and in sharing grief with them, the parents may be able to diminish in the process their own bewilderment and distress. Instead of feeling inadequate because they do not know what happens after death, adults should welcome their children's questions as occasions to explore the problem with them (Grollman 1976, p. 4).

> It cannot be precisely determined what concepts of death can be understood at a given age. . . . Age is but one of the factors affecting an understanding of death to be contrasted to the unique religious, political, and social attitudes of the (child) and his group's cultural life (pp. 4 — 5).

> (For these reasons parents should) . . . sit down and watch the youngsters while they work and play . . . observe them in action and hear the tone and timbre of their voices. Let the youngsters tell the adults how they feel about death, what they think, what they know, where they want to go (p. 4).

In the course of explaining death to children, parents can draw from two main bodies of knowledge in regard to the cognitive dimension: the interpretative, or the religious concepts; and the "factual," or scientific sources (Grollman, p. 8).

Within the purview of formal pediatric education, the prominent educator Jerome Bruner, Director of the Harvard Center for Cognitive Studies, promotes the hypothesis that:

> any subject can be explained effectively in an intellectually honest form to any child at any stage of development. Understandably, the knowledge may be imparted with

symbolic imagery or intellectual reasoning (Grollman, p. 4).

But one must be careful to explain the difference between "sleep" and "death"; otherwise, he runs the risk of causing a pathological dread of bedtime. There are children who toss about in fear of going to "eternal sleep," never to wake up again (p. 12).

While the exploration of the cognitive domain is essential in the child's death education, the actual determinant is the emotional, or affective, influence, transmitted by the tenor of the parent's/adult's teachings. And certainly it is the level of the adult's emotional maturity/degree of wisdom that ultimately governs the extent to which the child adopts a realistic perspective of death with its multiplicity of characterizations. In the final analysis, the parents should make it clear to the children that with death, life stops (as far as the physical body is concerned), and the body is actually buried. Given this frame of reference, the child will be better equipped to deal with the various mantles of death (natural, accidental, suicidal, etc.), even though each one is a unique tragedy unto itself. Without this precaution, the inherent danger is to mislead the child into thinking death is just a temporary "time out" or rest period.

If the adult establishes a close interfacing from the point of anticipatory grief, then this can set the stage and tone for the child to cope with the subsequent stages of the dying process. But more important, it will help to preclude the "conspiracy of silence" identified by Kubler-Ross by establishing a bridge of communication between parent and child within the parameters of death. Ironically, but realistically, the grief and loss experienced from a death can be the touchstone for both individual and mutual growth between parent(s) and child. In fact, the psychosocial dynamics generated may create a heightened awareness of life's meaning for them and the recognition of death as an integral part of the maturational process.

These same psychosocial elements are clearly described and interfaced with the approximate time frame in the booklet entitled *The Foundation of Thanatology:*

Emphasizing life and living (even in the presence of death and dying), the broadened perspective of thanatology includes . . . the stages of psychosocial evolution related to death "events" that are designated as follows:

(1) anticipatory grief — that is initiated by the unfavorable diagnosis of the patient's illness and that continues through the pre-death period.

(2) dying and death — the actual processes.

(3) acute grief — that is precipitated by the death of the patient and that can continue for a period of two to three weeks (or longer) after death;

(4) bereavement — the period during which grief symptoms are present among survivors and when the multitude of practical and emotional adjustments to the loss are begun; and

(5) closure/adjustment to the loss — a time when the bereaved individual has been able to complete the work of mourning and re-establish a stable and productive pattern of living.

While this sequence is framed in a medical context, it has equal validity and applicability to other kinds of death (excluding anticipatory grief in the case of suicide). Whatever the circumstances governing or precipitating a death, it is essential to avoid the mistake of attempting to fit the individual's response to fatal illness into a preconceived pattern. This is clearly illustrated by Leyn (1976) in two case studies of families, both of which had a daughter (one a toddler, the other a teenager) with leukemia. The family dynamics preceding each youthful death and the grief reactions following both fatal events are examined for their uniquely different nuances. Moreover, it cannot be accented enough that grief is a normal reaction and therefore a healthy psychophysiological outlet. This is highlighted by Eells (1977) in her clarification of the natural human need for open expression of grief as a prerequisite to realistic acceptance of death.

With respect to the phenomenon of grief, there are certain points the parent should be cognizant of when the child is the griever. According to Bowlby (Grollman, p. 13), the average child experiences three phases in the natural grieving process. The first is protest or refusal to accept the reality of the death. The second is despair coupled with disorganization, at which point the child begins to accept the departure of the loved one. And, the third is hope, when the child starts to reorganize his or her life without the lost person. In addition, the parent should be prepared to expect some alternative expressions of grief, or reactions to death: denial, bodily distress, hostility (toward the deceased/living persons), guilt, replacement, imitation (of deceased), idealization, anxiety, panic, and so on. As a word of caution, it is necessary to mention that any one of these behaviors in and of itself is not a distorted grief reaction unless the child exhibits it to an excessive degree. A truly wise parent will provide the comforting attitude necessary to help the child sort out his or her feelings in the process of discovering that life is a series of reintegrations. Such a role model will serve to furnish the child with the positive perspective that out of pain grows wisdom, and that the business of life is living. All in all, these guidelines provide an appropriate conceptual framework for the parent to help the child as griever come to terms with death as an integral part of the life process. And equally important is the fact that this relationship is tempered by the humanistic concern of the parent(s) for the child to develop a realistic perception of life's dynamics.

On the other hand, facing the painful reality that the child is the victim rather than the witness to death is perhaps an even greater test of the parent's measure of emotional maturity. In conjunction with this speculation, reference is made once again to Daniel Goleman's (1976) interview with Kubler-Ross when he inquires of her:

> "But death is so final, the separation so complete. Don't people naturally fear death?"

She responds:

> Grownups make such a nightmare out of death, but very young children are not afraid of death. They pick up the fear as they get older.
>
> (In case of child death:) The child will always be there. Real love doesn't die. It's the physical body that dies. Genuine, authentic love has no expectations whatsoever; it doesn't even need the physical presence of a person. . . . Even when he is dead and buried that part of you that loves that person will always live (p. 52).

How poignantly true her remarks are, especially the last one. Clearly, the parent's threshold of maturity bears a large influence on the child's attitude toward his own impending death.

This, in turn, suggests the importance of the coping mechanism known as adaptation, in which one strives to establish an equilibrium not only within oneself but also in one's interaction with the environment (Goldfogel 1970). This coping behavior embodies the three phases: initial, intermediate, and terminal. The initial stage is dominated by feelings of denial; the intermediate characterized by recognition of the reality; and the terminal marked by acceptance of the forthcoming fatality. This sequence of events provides the necessary time-cushion during which the emotional interplay between parent and child serves as the bridge of mutual courage connecting the realm of life with the domain of death. This interrelationship not only furnishes the appropriate comfort with respect to a predictable death (i.e., terminal illness), but also posthumously in the case of a sudden one (i.e., accidental, suicidal).

> . . . it's most difficult for people whose loved ones die suddenly. They can't finish unfinished business. They can't tell their lost one, 'I love you.' What I try to teach people is

to live in such a way that you say those things while the other person still can hear it. What do you think dying people teach you? *THEY TEACH HOW TO LIVE* (Goleman 1976b).

Implicit is the lesson in living — that is, to convey to people "in person" that you love them before death intervenes. Since death is everyone's heritage, why not acknowledge this universal brotherhood together by becoming attuned to the reality that while death is inevitable, it can, ironically, provide new insight for the personal renewal of the survivors? In essence, death is the mentor who guides us to sharpen our perceptions about life.

It is clearly evident that much remains to be done in terms of shedding more light on the still largely shaded gray area of pediatric-oriented death:

> The study of bereavement and post-death patterns of interaction is sadly in need of concrete research, and while difficulties of observational access to such a domain may be great, they do not seem, at least on the basis of my experience, insurmountable (Sudnow 1967).

Finally, further exploration of this death-related behavior may illuminate a new "landscape of learning" replete with profound lessons "of living, for the living!"

REFERENCES

Anthony, S. 1972. *The Discovery of Death in Childhood and After.* New York: Basic Books.

Birtchnell, J., I.C. Wilson, O. Bratfos, et al. 1973. *Effects of Early Parent Death.* New York: MSS Information Corporation.

deBeauvoir, S. 1973. *The Coming of Age.* New York: Warner Paperback Library.

Eells, J. 1977. " In Time of Grief." *Journal of Religion and Health.* 16 (April): 116-18.

Foundation of Thanatology, The. *The Foundation of Thanatology.* Booklet. Address 630 West 168th Street, New York, N.Y. 10032.

Gibney, H. 1965. "What Death Means to Children." *Parents' Magazine and Better Homemaking* 40 (March): 64 – 142

Goldfogel, L. 1970. "Working with the Parent of a Dying Child." *American Journal of Nursing* 70 (August): 1675–79.

Goleman, D. 1976a. "We Are Breaking the Silence About Death." *Psychology Today* 10 (September): 48–52.

–. 1976b. "The Child Will Always Be There: Real Love Doesn't Die." *Psychology Today* 10 (September) : 48–52.

Grof, S., and J. Halifax. 1978. *The Human Encounter with Death.* New York: Dutton.

Grollman, E.A., ed. 1967; *Explaining Death to Children.* Boston: Beacon Press.

Gross, R., B. Ross, and S. Seidman, 1978. *The New World: Struggling for Decent Aging.* Garden City, N.Y.: Anchor Books.

Kubler-Ross, E. 1971. "What Is It Like to Be Dying?" *American Journal of Nursing* 71 (January): 54–59.

–. 1977. *On Death and Dying.* New York: Macmillan

–. 1978. *To Live Until We Say Goodbye.* Englewood Cliff, N.J.: Prentice-Hall.

Leyn, R.M. 1976. "Terminally Ill Children and Their Families: A Study of the Variety of Responses to Fatal Illness." *American Journal of Maternal-Child Nursing* 5 (Fall): 179–88.

Maguire, D. 1974. *Death by Choice.* New York. Doubleday.

Powledge, T. M. 1978. *"Death as an Acceptable Subject."* In R. Gross et al., eds, *The New World: Struggling for Decent Aging,* Garden City, N.Y.: Anchor Books.

Sudnow, D. 1967. *Passing On: The Social Organization of Dying.* Englewood Cliffs, N.J.: Prentice-Hall.

Zeligs, R. 1974. *Children's Experiences with Death.* Springfield, Ill.: Charles C. Thomas.

"SOMETIMES I THINK ABOUT DYING": HELPING CHILDREN WRITE ABOUT DEATH
William Wertheim

As a poet-consultant and teacher, I had three years experience in 35 schools trying to devise ways children could learn about their feelings through the writing of poetry. Rather than use an intellectual-didactic technique for each short-term involvement (six sessions over a period of three weeks in each school), I decided to appeal to the children's active participation in the world as the source for their writing. These young people, by reaching into their already-rich experiential lives, could share the myriad events that made each life both ordinary and unique.

I was contracted as a consultant by Poets-in-the-Schools, Inc., which had arranged with the New York State Council on the Arts and the local schools where I taught. The classroom during each residency became a place where children could express their feelings about crucial or commonplace events in their lives. I interpreted my job as being a guide to the unearthing of deeply repressed feelings and to controling and forming these feelings through the craft of writing. I will try to show how in relating the results of this experience, how adults in authority can begin allowing those they deal with permission to express buried feelings about loneliness, separation, dying, and death.

My status as "professional poet" could have cut off sensitive communication between the students and myself, so my first move was to invite them to call me by my first name. Then I shared with them something about myself and about my attempts to write about feelings I had toward others and the world around me. There was no hint of anything resembling disintegration resulting from my decision to give up the formal title and mode of address. On the contrary, the mood was relaxed, and the children, still highly structured in their response to adults, authority, and the generally controlled atmosphere of the classroom, behaved responsibly.

I think that doctors, because they have the same natural authority and respect, can allow themselves to become more human and vulnerable with their patients. As doctors acknowledge their own struggle to deal with and accept the confusing paradox of life and death, they enter into a new relationship with their patients; instead of being the terrifying harbingers of bad news, they can present themselves as another participant in the human drama.

The focus on relationship between myself and the students developed an atmosphere of trust and sharing, so that as we progressed over the first four days, talking and writing about parents, friends, and others, an intimacy developed in which all of us acknowledged a wide range of feelings, including doubt, anger, and loneliness. We wrote about death during the fifth session, saving the last session for a free-associative fling. It is still amazing to me to read the intense poems concerning the subject of death even after such a short period. It seems that the children were longing to find some outlet for their hopes and fears, and a creative environment in the classroom allowed them to write these thought down.

Since I concentrated on honest expression during each session, I requested that they abandon rhyme and meter. In doing this, I was removing the constraints imposed by traditional methods of writing, which can hinder the free expression of the emotions in poetry. Similarly, I stress the word "I" and the five senses as the vehicles for establishing a relationship between themselves and the world. My familiarity with them, from the first moment of meeting to the last, enhanced their attempts to reach deep down inside of them to pull out the tender, powerful feelings that informed all their work.

Dying
by Margaret Tamas (sixth grade)

Up in the room he lays while I sit down here
waiting to see him.
After midnight, I feel very weary.
I know how he feels, even though I've been that way.
What am I going to do when I see him?
God, please be there to help me.
It's my turn, I feel so scared.
Why? I don't know. I've seen him so many times.
I'm going to cry, I know it.
Hi grampa, are you O.K?
Is it O.K. if I cry?
Why are you going to die? Good-bye Grampa.
I cry and cry. I cry so hard I can't breathe.
It happened a few years ago, but I love him
more than ever.

Another poem, **"When He Died,"** *by James Sickinger*, a fifth-grade student, is similarly haunting:

When he died
It was like nothing I had ever experienced.
He, he was so motionless
He was lying there
in his best clothes
The flowers
of so many different types
Red, violet and yellow.
But
But when I touched him

He was so tender, soft
and he looked so pale
his mother in her black dress
was weeping a lot
when they took him away
and he was buried.
I couldn't help crying myself
It was like the world turned upside down.

Margaret's poem, she tells us, is about something that happened "a few years ago," yet the immediacy of that experience still lives with the impact of the moment. It is a clear and simple poem, and expresses its genuine feeling through direct language. Perhaps being able to write about this event gave this young girl the permission she needed to "give up" the harbored pain. In the second poem, the tender evocation of attending a friend's funeral, and the frightening moment of identification, expresses a moment of recognition common to many of us on an unconscious level.

Other poems that came out of the classrooms I taught were concerned with what happens when one is presented with the inevitable end of growth even as one begins to sense growth beginning in one's consciousness. These pieces tended to fall back on the support of a familiar set of people, usually family, to help the writer through the absurdity of death. Poems like **"When I Think of Dying"** show how important a connection with caring adults can be, when death anxiety shakes the foundation of self:

When I Think of Dying
by Patricia Manning (fifth grade)

When I think of dying
My heart sinks low
My mind gets boggled
Because I'm afraid of dying

When I think of dying I get very sad
Because I think of never seeing the
lovely roses around my house again
Never walking through the fresh morning dew
Never again seeing, smelling or tasting
what life has to offer

But then I think of my lovely family and
friends and all the good things I have
Then I'm not scared anymore.

The doctors, like the poets, can reach others through reaching their own feelings. I worked at touching my own fears and shared them with the class; during the preliminary moments before writing about death, the children learned that my father had died, that I had had pets that had died, that I had moved and lost friends, the I had nightmares and had wondered what life was all about. An adult professional's caring, my personal caring, opened up and helped release fears that, seen retrospectively, were much more significant when repressed. To close off someone from expression denies them the comfort of sharing and finding that they are not alone. *Sofia Hubschner,* a fifth-grade student, writes of her experience of isolation when not told of her grandfather's death:

When Someone I Loved Died

When my grandfather died
I felt like dying myself.
Why didn't my mother tell me sooner?
They called up in the early morning
when I was asleep.
My father cried my mother cried
and if they both cry it must be bad.
I cried.
My parents tried to think of happy things
and so did I but it didn't work,
everything I thought of
I got off the topic.
When I asked myself, "Will he ever come back?"
I knew what the answer was, "No."
The confusion, anger, pain and loneliness
was too much for me.
When my parents held discussions about it
and didn't let me in on them
I felt so left out.

In each of the 35 schools where I taught, a community of feeling developed as a result of the persistent and courageous exploration of death and dying. Poems concerning the death of relative or pet, the fear and loneliness of the night, the leaving of old neighborhoods — all of these were written about in direct, evocative language that came from an honest confrontation with deep feelings. My place as a concerned professional who offered to share his own feelings and to grant permission for others to do the same helped create an environment of trust among all of us. Some children had expected further isolation and bitterness by writing about death; they found, instead, solace and support. At the end of most of my short visits, I had the feeling that a large percentage of children, joined by their peers and made stronger by that knowledge, had learned to express hidden parts of themselves in a natural, open language. They had gone into an area of concern that had little precedent in the past and now had been brough into the open; this seemed to show me that by encouraging repressed fears to surface, with the guidance of a professional who had admitted his vulnerability and willingness to grow, a new spirit of community could develop.

FACTORS TO BE CONSIDERED IN DESIGNING A PROGRAM OF DEATH EDUCATION FOR TEACHERS
Rudi Alec and Joseph Sales

Many writers feel that in addition to the home and the church, the school has a responsibility to help children learn to accept death as an integral part of the cycle of life. They argue that death occurs in the lives of children, but the taboo nature of the topic in our society forces educators to ignore its reality and the possible impact of death-related experiences on student behavior in the classroom. They argue further that the often cursory treatment of death in such courses as literature and biology is insufficient to be considered a systematic approach to the subject.

The recognition of this need by colleges and universities that prepare teachers often generates a temptation to implement a program of death education immediately. A review of the literature in the field, however, suggests that a number of factors should be taken into consideration in the design of such a program: Should the program consist of a single course or a series of courses, or should it become an integral part of existing courses? Are there special personality characteristics that should be specifically associated with the teacher of death education? Who should be involved in designing the program? Are there particular cautions or dangers associated with the inclusion of death education in the K-12 school curriculum?

In order to gain a better understanding of the kinds of factors involved in designing a program of death education for teachers, a series of questionnaires was developed and administered to a cross-section of people involved in teacher education. Table 1 shows the types and number of people who responded to the various questionnaires. The teachers and administrators represented both urban and suburban schools and grade levels from kindergarten through high school. The undergraduate students were either juniors or seniors, and all were enrolled in some phase of their teacher preparation program that involved actual work in school settings. The college faculty represented instructors of basic foundation courses (such as educational psychology) and specialists in teaching methodology. In addition to the questionnaires, informal discussions were held with respondents and others associated with teacher education.

TABLE 1
Respondents to Questionnaires

Type	Number	Percentage of Total
Classroom teachers	57	40
School administrators	30	21
Undergraduate students	45	31
College faculty	12	8
TOTAL	144	100

Are Teachers Confronted with This Problem in the Classroom?

The teachers were presented seven types of situations related to death and dying in the classroom and asked to identify those that represented their own experiences. As shown in Table 2, over half indicated that they had experienced a situation in which there was a student in class who had a terminally ill friend or relative (54 per cent) or had lost a friend or relative through natural causes (79 per cent) or an accident (51 per cent).

The following statements are representative of the kinds of comments made by teachers:

> "The children I teach are between 9 and 12 years old. They don't seem to think that death is a permanent thing. It seems they always speak of the dead as though he or she were alive."

> "It is very difficult to help small children in these cases. I really don't know if I can help."

> "I did have a student who was murdered on a family outing. It was a difficult experience for the class."

> "The child had leukemia and was a real fighter—he wasn't told but I'm sure he knew."

> "Sometimes you are at a loss at how to respond."

A closer examination of Table 2 shows that approximately one-third of the teachers had been confronted with a situation in which a student had lost a friend or relative through suicide (35 per cent) and through murder (33 per cent). Almost one-fifth had worked with students who were themselves terminally ill. An analysis of the results of similar questions to the other categories of respondents established that: (1) Preservice teachers perceive that they need assistance in these situations that teachers have confronted and (2) school administrators and college faculty feel that teachers are not adequately prepared to handle these situations. These and related findings tend to provide support for the argument that death education should not be ignored by schools.

TABLE 2

Teacher Classroom Experiences with Death

Situation: Student Who...	Percentage of Teachers Indicating Experience*
1. Lost a friend or relative through natural causes	79
2. Had a terminally ill friend or relative	54
3. Lost a friend or relative in an accident	51
4. Had a friend or relative who committed suicide	35
5. Lost a friend or relative through murder	33
6. Lost a friend or relative in a war	28
7. Was terminally ill	19

Totals are over 100 per cent because some respondents checked more than one situation.

Is There Support for Including Death Education in the Teacher Education Curriculum?

The recognition that a problem has manifestations within the school setting does not in itself mean that educators will feel an obligation to deal with it. Thus, to determine the degree of support, all respondents were asked to indicate their agreement or disagreement with the idea of incorporating death education into the teacher preparation curriculum. Table 3 shows that there was strong support for including death education as a component of teacher education (76 per cent of all groups agreed). The highest level of support was among undergraduate students and the lowest was among college faculty. Representative comments from each group included:

Classroom Teachers

"We can never be sure that we won't have a child who is in a situation like this. Through understanding their thought processes, we can help them feel more comfortable."

"It would give teachers a few guidelines they could follow when necessary. Sometimes, well-meaning intentions can be handled in the wrong way when an unexpected situation occurs."

"This as well as many other topics should be covered. There are many natural events in life that are almost totally ignored, yet they must be dealt with. The more you understand the more effectively you can deal with them."

School Administrators

"It should be considered important enough to be included—each school should have resources available to assist students who need such help."

"It would make it easier to handle the situation if it should arise instead of just ignoring it or expecting the student to react 'normally' and get over it rapidly—especially in high school, where 'homework' has such a high priority."

"Teachers need help in coping with children's emotional needs, mainly because it may not be provided in the home. Death is an experience that is difficult for adults as well as children. The teacher needs to know techniques of dealing with students who experience death of relatives or friends. An example: a child's parent is accused of murder. The child is faced with guilt and peer pressure. How can a teacher help?"

Undergraduate Students

"Death is a reality that we all have to face. Why not teach it?"

"This is especially needed in large cities, where the chance of death from unnatural causes is higher."

"I feel this subject would be a very valuable asset to teacher preparation in general. Effective learning cannot take place if the student is overwrought due to the death of a family member or pet (I have experienced this firsthand). Therefore, I feel that it is a part of the teacher's responsibility not only as a teacher but as a *person* to help this student through the crisis in whatever manner he can. Naturally, some training in this would greatly facilitate matters."

College Faculty

"Like sex education, it is part of what children face, live with, and must learn about."

"The subject should be included in courses or a course at both the undergraduate and graduate programs."

"The subject should be included, but time is a problem. Perhaps death education could be incorporated in the context of handicapped education as a broad context for dealing with differences and emotionally difficult situations."

TABLE 3

Respondent Reactions to Including Death Education in Teacher Education Curriculum

Respondent Type	No.	Agree	Disagree	Undecided
Classroom teachers	57	72%	17%	11%
School administrators	30	77	7	16
Undergraduate students	45	84	7	9
College faculty	12	67	33	0
TOTAL (all groups)	144	76%	13%	11%

What Should Be the Content of Death Education?

A review of related literature and the outlines of courses about death and dying provided a broad cross-section of what could be included in constructing the curriculum for death education. The respondents were presented a list of thirteen topics, based on this review, and asked to indicate those that they felt should be included in the teacher education program.

The results, presented in Table 4, show that more than 50 per cent of the respondents in all groups agreed that the curriculum should include the topics "Knowledge of Various Religious Views of Death," "Philosophies of Death," and "The Sociology of Death." At least three of the four groups agreed that the curriculum should also include the topics "Suicide" and "The Medical Definition of Death." Except for administrators (and in one case, college faculty), there was little support for including euthanasia, war and violence, and the historical and anthropological perspective of death.

The respondents were given an opportunity to suggest additional topics that could be included in the curriculum. The following are examples of the types of suggestions given:

Coping with long-term illness

Hospices: Places reserved for the care of dying patients

Death etiquette

Helping youngsters deal with death

What children learn about death from television—the nonreality element

How to work with parents in this area

TABLE 4

Respondents' Selection of Topics to Be Included in Death Education Curriculum*

Topic	Teachers	Administrators	Students	Faculty
Knowledge of various religious views of death	56%	63%	60%	67%
Euthanasia	30	53	27	17
War and violence	33	50	44	17
Philosophies of death	56	57	51	50
Medical definition of death	56	70	38	58
Legal definition of death	49	63	31	58
Historical and anthropological perspective of death	28	43	20	42
Suicide	49	83	67	50
Burial customs and cultural differences	40	53	38	42
Biological life cycle	51	43	31	42
Sociology of death and dying	56	60	60	50
Process of dying	37	50	47	50
Economics of dying	33	50	20	42

* *Totals are over 100 per cent because some respondents checked more than one situation.*

Who Should Be Involved in Designing the Curriculum?

The nature of death education suggests that a variety of professionals could be involved in designing the curriculum. In order to determine the type of representation needed on a curriculum planning team, the respondents were presented with a list of eleven professionals and asked to check those they felt should be involved in the development and implementation of a death education program. The list included the following professionals:

Teacher/educator	Nurse	Psychologist
Mortician	Doctor	Psychiatrist
Pathologist	Coroner	Sociologist
Priest/rabbi/minister	Social worker	

Although the rankings of the various groups differed, Table 5 shows that all groups agreed on the same five types of professionals: Teacher/educator, priest/rabbi/minister; doctor; social worker; and psychologist. It was interesting to note that the three types of professionals that were mentioned least by all respondents were pathologists, coroners, and nurses.

TABLE 5

Respondents' Highest Ranking of Professionals to Be Involved in Designing Death Education Curriculum*

Rank	Teachers	Administrators	Students	Faculty
1	Priest/rabbi/minister (75%)	Teacher/educator (84%)	Psychologist (73%)	Teacher/educator (82%)
2	Teacher/educator (73%)	Priest/rabbi/minister (84%)	Doctor (71%)	Psychologist (73%)
3	Social worker (67%)	Doctor (77%)	Teacher/educator (67%)	Social worker (64%)
4	Doctor (61%)	Social worker (67%)	Priest/rabbi/minister (67%)	Priest/rabbi/minister (55%)
5	Psychologist (54%)	Psychologist (67%)	Social worker (64%)	Doctor (45%)

Totals are over 100 per cent because some respondents checked more than one situation.

How Should the Curriculum Be Presented?

Two questions were included to elicit opinions about the methods to be employed in presenting death education. The first concerned the preservice teacher education program. Respondents were asked to indicate whether they felt that death education should be incorporated as a separate course or a program consisting of a series of courses, or be infused into the ongoing program. Although there was some support for providing a separate course, the greatest majority of respondents in all categories would rather have death education infused in the ongoing preservice teacher education program (Table 6).

The second question concerned the in-service teacher education program. Respondents were asked to check their recommended method for preparing practicing teachers (in-service teachers) to deal with death education in the classroom. The results in Table 6 show a strong preference for workshops and in-service activities. It was noted during some of the followup interviews that many of the respondents checked both terms on the questionnaire because they considered them to be synonymous.

TABLE 6
Recommended Methods for Presenting Death Education for Teachers

METHOD	Teachers	Administrators	Students	Faculty
Preservice				
Infuse into on-going program	49%	45%	45%	91%
Provide a separate course	27	34	42	9
Provide a program consisting of a series of courses	24	21	13	0
In-Service*				
Provide workshops	47	43	54	90
Provide a separate course	31	27	28	9
Provide in-service activities	27	57	33	67
Provide program consisting of a series of courses	22	13	14	7

* Totals are over 100 per cent because some respondents checked more than one situation.

Are There Teacher Characteristics to Be Considered?

Many writers suggest that the sensitivity and general personality of the teacher of death education are the most critical factors related to the successful implementation of a program. They argue that the teacher's ability to cope with his own concerns about death is a basic prerequisite to success. To determine the degree of concern about death and dying, the respondents were presented four topics and asked to check those that they felt represented their own concerns about death.

As shown in Table 7, there was less concern about the death of self than there was about any of the other topics. Except for college faculty, the greatest concern was in the handling of bereavement and grief. The second greatest area of concern for all groups except college faculty was caring for the dying. This was the greatest area of concern for college faculty (82 per cent).

TABLE 7

Personal Concerns About Death*

Topic	Teachers	Administrators	Students	Faculty
Death of self	44%	40%	47%	27%
Death of family member	65	53	56	36
Caring for the dying patient	70	63	60	82
Handling bereavement/grief	74	67	67	45

* *Totals are over 100 per cent because some respondents checked more than one situation.*

The comments of respondents who were against including death education as a component of teacher education (Table 3) were reexamined to determine if the responses were in any way reflective of teacher characteristics that should be considered in the design and implementation of a program. There were several reasons given for not including death education in teacher education. Some related to the time factor (i.e., the feeling that there isn't enough time to add this topic to a teacher education curriculum that is already overloaded with academic subjects to be covered). Others reflected what appeared to be a sincere feeling that this is a topic for the home, the church, or some social agency but not the school. A few of the comments reflected either strong religious objections or the feeling that it would not be possible to separate this topic from the teacher's own personal religious beliefs. Specific comments from each group included the following:

Classroom Teachers

"I feel it is a topic to be explored and discussed at home with the parents."

"Preparation for death should be a part of everyone's background but not incorporated into the teacher preparation curriculum."

"I don't think any person or book could cover the topic as clearly, truthfully, and simply as the Holy Bible. . . Ecclesiastes 9:5; Romans 5:12 for starters!"

School Administrators

"It is this writer's opinion that death education as such is not an appropriate topic to be included in teacher preparation. Rather, an in-depth preparation in counseling for several areas (including death) seems appropriate. 'Death Education' as such is seen to infringe into a very personal, religious, and moral level."

"We are not really successfully handling the curriculum offerings now. This would be a low priority of mine – I would palm it off into the Department of Social Services."

"I feel that it's a *personal* subject, not another course that students should be subjected to."

Undergraduate Students

"It might be incorporated into existing classes, but for heaven's sake don't invent a new one!"

"The educational system should have trained employees (not teachers) to work in that area if needed."

"If a member of a child's family or a friend of the child dies, it is up to the family to deal with his pain and confusion – not the school's responsibility. The money used to start this course could be used in better ways *I'm sure!!*"

College Faculty

"Not as a separate course. It should be incorporated into psychology/guidance/counseling curricula. There are so many special needs that we cannot have separate courses for each."

"Preservice education has enough to do!"

"Not all children are exposed to the problem of death — therefore, the rest should not have this additional problem to deal with."

Are There Cautions or Dangers Involved?

The respondents were asked to indicate whether they perceive any particular cautions or dangers associated with including death education as a part of school curriculum at the grade levels kindergarten through high school. The results, in Table 8, indicate that cautions or dangers were recognized by all groups. In fact, such possibilities were recognized by all college faculty involved in the survey. The following statements are representative of the areas of concern expressed:

"Like all other topics, expand on where children are — don't overdo it. Don't give too much information at too young an age. Be honest!"

"I would caution against presenting any *one single* approach or set of beliefs or customs."

"Teachers and other support personnel must be adequately prepared to deal with children in this delicate area."

"Families may question this. It is important that any program which is being considered be discussed with the appropriate parent groups in the school."

"It is thought by many to be as sacred as religion or sex. Religion is already barred from public education and people's views on death are just as varied."

"Death education should be taught in a teacher preparation program, but it is too sensitive a topic to be included in the K-12 school system."

"Methodology could be tricky, as religious beliefs might be offended. Also, material to be used might be minimal."

"The teacher should feel *AT HOME* with the subject and feel personally comfortable with the material, otherwise ambiguous feelings and fear will be transmitted to the students."

"Overemphasis of death — taught by an insensitive person."

"I see the danger of present educators causing more harm to children than the experiences of death itself. I do not feel that the educators are prepared to deal with the topic as it relates to themselves. If a program is to be instituted, all teachers need some training."

"Such an addition to the curriculum in K-12 would be 'nice'. However, we are under much pressure to produce kids that can read and write. Perhaps the schools might be taking on an area that they shouldn't be responsible for."

TABLE 8

Respondent Perception of Cautions or Dangers Involved in Including Death Education in K-12 Curriculum

Respondent type	Yes	No	Undecided
Classroom teachers	61%	16%	23%
School administrators	67	7	26
Undergraduate students	49	18	33
College faculty	100	0	0

SUMMARY

The increasing volume of literature in the area of thanatology over the past decade or so has led to increased pressure for schools to assume a greater responsibility for helping children learn to accept death as an integral part of the cycle of life. Colleges and universities who prepare teachers are being called upon to provide leadership in designing programs that are responsive to this need. In order to gain a better understanding of the factors involved in designing a program of death education for teachers, a series of questionnaires was developed and administered to a cross-section of classroom teachers, school administrators, undergraduate students, and college of education faculty. Informal discussions were also held with respondents and others associated with teacher education. The data suggest that a number of significant factors should be considered:

1. **Need.** There is strong support among all groups for incorporating death education into the teacher preparation curriculum. The responses from teachers indicate that they are confronted with a variety of situations in the classroom that are directly related to death and dying. Undergraduate students feel that they would have difficulty handling these situations, and both administrators and college faculty agree that practicing teachers are not adequately prepared to respond in a constructive and helpful manner.

2. **Content.** There appears to be general consensus that the curriculum should include the topics "Knowledge of Various Religious Views of Death," "Philosophies of Death," and "The Sociology of Death." There is also strong support among three of the four groups for including suicide and the medical definition of death as additional topics. There is much less support, however, for including euthanasia, war and violence, and the historical and anthropological perspective of death.

3. **Curriculum Design.** The respondents seem to agree that because of the uniqueness of the content of death education, the traditional approach of making curriculum development in teacher education the sole responsibility of teacher educators should be abandoned and replaced by an interdisciplinary team approach. There is general agreement that religious leaders, doctors, social workers, and psychologists should work with teacher educators in designing the curriculum.

4. **Presentation Mode.** It is not unusual in teacher education to use the "add-on" approach when responding to new teacher needs. In this approach a need is identified and a related course (or set of courses) is developed and added to the curriculum. The results of this survey strongly suggest that death education should be infused into the ongoing preservice teacher education program and that practicing teachers should be provided with workshops and in-service sessions.

5. **Teacher Characteristics.** Most respondents indicate that they have definite personal concerns about death and dying. These would certainly have to be taken into consideration in the design and implementation of a program. Consideration will also have to be given to the reasons why some people are against including death education as a component of teacher education. Concerns and anxieties related to such areas as insufficient time, political pressure, and strong religious objections cannot be ignored.

6. **Cautions or Dangers.** Although it is clear that a large majority of the respondents recognize a need for including death education as a component of teacher education, an even greater number see particular cautions or dangers associated with including death education as a part of the K-12 school curriculum. This finding can be interpreted in several ways. It could suggest a need for developing very deliberate plans for eliciting parent and community support prior to introducing the topic into the schools. It could also suggest a need to focus total attention on preparing teachers to deal with death-related issues when and if they arise in the classroom without introducing it as a specific curriculum topic for children. A combination of the two approaches could represent another option.

The results of this study clearly suggest that there are serious factors to be considered in designing a program of death education for teachers. With the increased awareness of society's failure in this area, there may come increased pressure for schools to respond. We must not allow this pressure to preclude our giving adequate attention to the factors involved.

ON UNDERSTANDING AND COPING WITH DEATH DURING CHILDHOOD

Stephen Viton Gullo and Edward H. Plimpton

Eric Segal began his novel *Love Story* with the question, "What can you say about a 25-year-old girl who died?" His 138 page answer became a best selling book and movie. On a less dramatic scale, death has been a troublesome companion not only for love stories, but for all living beings . . . the 25-year-old, the 80-year-old, and the 5-year-old. While any person's death may bear elements of tragedy, the death of a child is a particularly tragic and often incomprehensible event. This chapter concerns the way children die, or, more precisely, about the way they live while they are dying.

The authors view the child's response to terminal illness in terms of game strategies in which each of the unwilling players — the child, the family, and the medical staff — plays according to unwritten and usually unspoken rules. The term "game" is not used here to diminish the importance of dying, but rather as an analogy which suggests that all social interaction among people is governed by rules. This is most clearly seen in activities such as tennis, but it is also implicit in rules which govern actions, such as the type of permissible conversation, and who opens the door for whom. Unlike ordinary games, however, this one is a serious activity in which each participant attempts to deal with a possibly overwhelming reality. The objective is not to win, but to learn to accept losing with some degree of courage and dignity.

A major focus of our research has been on the child's role in these games — the understanding and the coping styles children, especially the older ones, develop in facing their own death.

The Child and Death

The complexity of the dying process makes any discussion of it appear somewhat superficial. It is important, therefore, to identify the major variables that may influence how a child comes to terms with death. Among the most significant are the nature of the child's relationship with parents and other family members (e.g., siblings), the type of disease and its effects, the modes of treatment required, the child's sex, and the degree of support provided by medical personnel, ministers, and other societal agents. The child's death is also influenced by the manner in which he gains information about his condition. In general, children have difficulty learning about death. In our society, a taboo has traditionally been placed on any discussion of death. Furthermore, death, when it occurs, is usually hidden in hospitals or nursing homes. More specific to the problem at hand, is how the dying child obtains information that he is dying. In those cases where the parents and staff inform the child, there is obviously not the question of where the child received the information. However, in cases where the child is not informed, the question of how a child obtains awareness is a much more complicated one. A partial answer would probably be found in the changes in staff and parental behavior toward the child and in the other non-verbal cues that adults in this situation unknowingly provide.

Perhaps two other factors should be added to the list. The first is the child himself, because the way a child dies reflects the combination of strengths and weaknesses he has developed in the course of living. The other consideration is the child's level of understanding. If a child is too young to understand what death means, then his behavior will not be influenced by attempts to cope with loss of life. The very young child may respond to pain, to hospitalization and the terror engendered by many of the treatments, to separation from parents and home – but he is still unaware of death's approach. A key to the child's understanding of death appears to be his grasp of the concept of time, the ability to distinguish the finite from the infinite. The child who cannot understand that life is finite and that death is an irreversible loss of life and everything that life entails cannot be fully aware of death's threat. It is the child's understanding or non-understanding of the threat he is confronting which will be a singularly important variable in how death is coped with.

Unfortunately, the present status of pediatric research does not tell us to what extent each of the major variables shapes the child's response to dying. Pioneering studies by Jean Piaget, S. Anthony, and M. Nagy do, however, offer valuable guidelines for deciphering the child's understanding and experience of death at different ages. And our exploratory research and clinical observations have enabled us to further refine these guideposts particularly as they apply to the child of ages 10 and above.

In the coming pages we will now focus on two inter-related factors in the dying child's experience: the child's present understanding of death and how this level of understanding influences the games or coping styles developed by the child.

The Early Childhood Years
Infancy to Age 3

While some researchers such as Maurer (1973) suggest that the natural contrast between being asleep and being awake prepares children from infancy for their eventual recognition of death, it is clear that this child is not really able to understand what death is. Indeed, the younger child is typically not even aware of death's existence unless he has experienced the death of a pet or a significant person.

In respect to coping styles, what this child is most sensitive to is separation from parents and familiar surroundings. While intense separation anxiety is caused by hospitalization, it is particularly acute during early childhood. The young child's anxiety and dependence are further increased by pain and the strangeness of medical procedures. The hospitalized child of this age group experiences dying as separation from parents. Because he cannot understand what is happening to him, he reacts to the crises with terror.

The death of such a young child evokes a special sense of helplessness, because there may be little one can do to save his life or ease his psychological and physical suffering. In addition, because of the child's limited mental development, it is difficult to explain medical procedures or to reassure him that he is not being abandoned or punished. Perhaps Dr. John Schowalter of the Yale Child Study Center expressed it best: "The toddler does not know death — only absence. If the mother is not frequently present in the hospital, the dying child experiences only a rotation of nurses, who come, then leave, thus aggravating his terror. It may be paraphrased that toddlers may die many times before their death, while the older child need taste of death but once" (Schowalter, 1970).

The Pre-school Child
Ages (3-6)

During this period, a primitive awareness of death begins to emerge. This early awareness of death reflects both an achievement in the child's thought as well as a new limitation upon it. Perhaps the major achievement of this age level is the developing ability to represent the world symbolically through language. Just as with any other newly acquired tool, the child enjoys the power which language gives. One young hospitalized preschooler found her amusement in a rather macabre way: she would wander up and down the hall during visitation hours and announce to unsuspecting (and horror-struck) visitors, "I'm dying." The child's amusement does not derive from any comic sense of personal mortality, but simply from being impressed with the effect such a statement produces.

This new-found ability to think about the world in symbolic terms poses certain limitations on the child's thought that will only be overcome at an older age. Typically, children at this age level tend to confuse the symbol with the object it represents. Thus, a preschool child will not be able to understand that a word such as "death" can have several different usages and meanings. In a general sense, preschool children reason with a one dimensional type of logic from which it is impossible to consider more than one feature of the environment at a time (Piaget, 1950). Thus, death will be understood by preschoolers in terms of one feature of the situation which they find perceptually most vivid. One young girl who saw her dead cat taken away in a taxi cab thought that "death is going away in a taxi cab." For other children, depending upon the situation, death will mean "to be less alive," "to go away," "to be asleep for a long time" or "to be broken." The hospitalized child might also interpret death in terms of some aspect of the hospital proceedings. Indeed, for many of these youngsters, the "dead" will return after a period of absence.

Despite the advances in the child's level of thought, coping remains characterized by the same separation anxiety, terror and dependence known by the younger child. In addition, guilt is first seen in the dying preschooler, who often interprets illness as a punishment for "being bad" or "having evil thoughts." These children are now old enough to recognize that they are different from other children. They cannot go out and play, they cannot go to many of the places other children go to or do any of those countless activities which bring joy to the life of a child. The recognition emerges that what makes them different is the fact that they are sick and this sickness may come to be seen as a punishment for wrongdoing. While the toddler may die "many times," the preschooler must bear many burdens — not the least of which is guilt born of misunderstanding.

The preschool child's awareness of death has often been misinterpreted. Once these children become aware that they are "dying" (often from overhearing staff and family), they may startle their caregivers with such pronouncements as, "Did you know I'm dying?" Nevertheless, while these children may become aware that they are dying and even refer to the fact in their conversations, they do not fully grasp what death means or the threat that it presents.

The Primary School Child

During the school age years, the child begins to realize that death is final. Unlike the younger child, these children realize that death is not just another form of life or sleep. Death is final and irreversible. In addition, the primary school aged child tends to externalize and personify death. Thus, death is seen as an external agent such as an "angel" or "a very old man with a long white beard." One primary school girl, dying of leukemia, drew a picture of a white blood cell that was eating all the smaller red blood cells as if they were sandwiches; she explained, "that big, bad, white blood cell is death."

The tendency to externalize death at this age level has both an effective and cognitive component. The latency age child is different from the preschooler. The latency aged child realizes that the quantity of something like water does not change because it is poured from a short fat container to a long thin one. The child is able to reason that changes in width are compensated for by changes in height and thus the total quantity is preserved. This ability to simultaneously deal with two perspectives also enables the child to separate a concept such as "death" between a "dead motor" and a "dead person."

On the other hand, the primary school child is not aware that the way he perceives the world is often the result of his own intellectual efforts rather than being perceptually inherent in the environment. As Looft points out,

> When the school child constructs a hypothesis, he naturally assumes this is a product imposed by external data rather than a result of his own thought. If he is challenged, typically the child will reinterpret that data to be congruent with this hypothesis, rather than change his initial stance (Looft 1972, p. 77).

One example of this type of thinking is found in the child's relationship to moral rules (Elkind, 1974, p. 84). Children at this age level often feel that rules and the reasons for obeying them exist outside of themselves. Thus, the only reason for obeying rules is to avoid punishment from adults. This, of course, parallels the manner in which children view death at this age. Death for the latency child is something which is external to himself.

The externalization and personification of death also has an important affective dimension. The Hungarian psychologist Nagy points out that the externalization of death allows the child to cling to a belief that personal death might still be avoided. It may be possible to "run faster than death," "trick him," "lock him out," "hide from him," or protect oneself with magical charms. As Dr. Nagy describes the child's experience, "Death is still outside of us."

This protective mechanism, however, becomes less and less effective in the older children of nine and ten who usually begin to realize the gravity of their personal situation. It is not uncommon for them to ask, "Am I dying?" The older child may now comprehend the significance of what is happening. The realization that he must suffer while other children are out living often gives rise to anger and even rage, especially in those children who recognize that their illness has nothing to do with punishment. Often the pent-up rage is directed at parents, the medical staff or other siblings. One young boy who screamed, "Why me? Why me?" expressed the thoughts of many of these children.

Adolescence

The complementary contributions of emotional and intellectual development can again be illustrated in the adolescent's relationship to death. Let us first consider how the cognitive abilities acquired during adolescence place the individual in a new relationship to death. In contrast to the latency child, the adolescent is able to perform logical operations. The younger or latency child would not be able to conserve matter unless he actually saw water being poured from one container to another. However, the adolescent can understand that the quantity of water will remain the same without having to see the water poured.

The adolescent, as opposed to the latency child, has the ability to deal in what is called "combinatory logic."

When confronted with a problem, the adolescent is able to construct several possible solutions and then accept or reject them according to their tested validity. When presented with four different colored poker chips, the adolescent has no difficulty in thinking of all different combinations which they could be arranged into such as red and yellow, yellow and blue, etc. (Elkind, 1974, p. 100). However, the latency child cannot think in terms of multi-possibilities. The new cognitive abilities of the adolescent, which have only been briefly alluded to here, have several important consequences in how he faces death. It is only in adolescence that an individual is able to think and reflect about himself and in doing so realize that he will die just like any other living object. Not only does the onset of adolescence bring an articulated awareness of personal mortality, but also, in a more general sense, a realization of the subjectivity and arbitrariness of one's own perspective. Thus, the adolescent when faced with the prospect of death feels a particular existential loneliness which younger children are typically incapable of feeling. While older adults will naturally feel loneliness while dying, their experience will be different. Unlike the adult, the adolescent, with an emerging self-concept, has only recently recognized his separateness and individuality in the world. He has not yet had a chance to find solutions to the problems of ego-identity and the loneliness it may entail.

By the time a child is above 10, his understanding of death usually *begins* to parallel that of the adult. He knows that death is permanent and that it touches all living creatures, including himself. Magical thinking with regard to death declines — it is no longer possible to run faster than death, hide from or trick it. Death is no longer an external agent or a person but an inherent part of any life cycle.

The growing intellectual abilities of the adolescent are also accompanied by new emotional issues. While all illness may be inconvenient, it is particularly inconvenient for the preadolescent and adolescent. Anna Freud points out that just as the youngster undertakes a quest for his own identity and independence apart from his parents, he is forced to endure regression, loss of control, and an inability to care for himself. Just as he begins to sense the possibilities and opportunities he can create for himself, he is confronted with the fact that cherished hopes and aspirations may never become a reality.

The next section of this report will describe some of the games which the adolescent develops when faced with the prospect of his own death. While many of the coping strategies may be similar to those of adults (Gullo, Cherico, Shadeck, 1974), the adolescent's response to death is different in one important respect: The adolescent is at a point in time where he is just becoming aware of the possibilities which life offers. (Older adults can at least gain a limited reconciliation with death in that they have had a chance to fulfill some of their potential.) As his friends and peers undertake new ventures in living and plans for the future, he is forced to confront the reality that for him there will be no new ventures, no new plans and, worst of all, no future. Understandably, the youth responds with anger and rage but he often does more than this — he attempts to cope and to "live" in the looming shadow of death.

How these youngsters react to this crisis, how they structure their lives in the face of personal death, and the games they play with themselves, their families and their caretakers has been a major concern of the writers' research. We will focus on the most important player in the triad, the dying child.

As one attempts to decipher the complex patterns of response found in dying children, a number of game or coping styles common to many of these children can be identified. Of course there is no way of presently classifying the entire repertoire of responses to dying, but some of the games children play and the rules which guide them can be outlined as follows:

The Game Plans

The Death-Acceptor

This type of youngster tends to be a realist. He confronts the reality and gravity of his illness and acknowledges (at least to himself) that his life may be in danger. He makes plans to cope with his continued illness and may even speculate about his death and its effects on those he loves. He wishes and hopes for continued life, but he does not lie to himself, even though others may lie to him. He struggles to go on living but when the efforts of the medical staff and his own efforts lead to little progress, he recognizes what is happening and what his fate will be. He does not run from or deny this reality, and when death seems inevitable he grieves for the loss of life and loved ones and from this grief emerges a sense of resignation or acceptance of death.

A young boy, who was a death-acceptor, provided a sensitive insight into the coping style of death-acceptors when he recited his favorite prayer: "Dear God, give me the courage to change the things I can in life; the patience to accept the things I cannot change, and the wisdom to know the difference."

The Death-Denier

These children adopt a coping style which appears to be the opposite of the death-acceptor's: they attempt to either deny the fact that they are ill or, more commonly, they recognize that they are ill but deny the gravity of the illness. As an illness progresses, it becomes increasingly difficult to deny the fact that one is ill; the child can afford this luxury only in the early stages of the illness. What one observes more frequently is an elaborate defense system developed by the child (usually supported by parents and caregivers) which acknowledges that he is sick but denies that it is a serious illness. A classic example can be seen in the handling of an extremely bright and perceptive 14-year-old boy who was dying from an advanced malignancy. In an effort to support the youngster's denial of the gravity of his illness, the parents hired a telephone answering service which was instructed to answer any calls with the greeting, "Hello . . . . Hospital." The child was then given this number, ostensibly the number of the hospital where he was a patient, and the parents urged him to call "Patient Information" and check on his condition any time those "terrible doubts" started to appear. The operator who answered the phone was carefully instructed on the importance of reporting the child's health status as "fair" or "improving." It is interesting to note that this bright and inquisitive child, who always had to prove things for himself, never once bothered to check if the telephone number was actually that of his hospital. Another child in a similarly grave condition reported that his failing health and intense physical suffering was due to "a bad case of juvenile arthritis."

In addition to the child who denies that he is ill, or denies the gravity of his illness, one occasionally encounters a third type of death-denier: this child acknowledges both his illness and its gravity. He insists, however, that he will definitely be "one of the lucky statistics" who survives all obstacles and odds. The youngster is often quite willing to talk about his illness and he may even state that people think he's "on the way out." Yet, he is convinced that "I'll be the miracle worker around here." While most dying patients cling to hope and almost all individuals find it difficult to accept death on a personal level, this child's coping style extends far beyond these considerations. In essence, he cannot accept his own mortality, i.e., that death could conceivably happen *to him*. Like the younger child who believes he can play a game with death and escape its clutches, this youngster nourishes the conviction that death happens only to others. One youngster cited the 23rd Psalm to support her convictions, "Though I walk through the valley of death I shall fear no evil . . ." Denial is certainly present to some degree in all those facing death, but it is only in the case of the death-denier that we find the consistent and all-persuasive attempt to block out the reality of the situation.

The Death-Submitter

In this type of coping style the child recognizes that he has a grave illness and this realization leads to feelings of being overwhelmed, abandoned and completely helpless. Since the feeling of helplessness is such a predominant element in this response style, the patient's efforts will be of little value. Consequently, one sees a quick diminution of the will to live, and such children develop a sense of "being doomed." Nothing can help them; their "fate" is sealed! They frequently reject any favorable information or glimmers of hope as "lies" or "stories" made up by adults to provide some degree of (false) consolation. For these children there is no hope or escape, there is just gloom and pessimism. Unlike the death-acceptor who fights to live and only resigns himself to death when all resources have been exhausted, the death-submitters see themselves as helpless (i.e., passive) victims of fate. They are "doomed" and so it makes little sense to struggle against what they see to be their "destiny." They do not really "accept" the fact that they are dying. Rather, they are overwhelmed by it . . . they do not think in terms of "accepting" or "not accepting," they can only submit!

The Death-Facilitator

The death-facilitators are those children who consciously (or unconsciously) engage in behaviors which will facilitate their own death. The facilitation of death may be indirect as in the case of the youngster who refuses to take medications or undergo necessary treatments, or it may find a more direct expression in those youngsters who attempt suicide. One youth who chose the latter alternative wrote of his decision:

> Dear Mom and Dad,
> You have taught me that life is sacred, but I have learned another lesson. In these long and lonely months when my only constant companions have been fear, and pain, I have learned that being able to walk, to laugh, to hope and just to plan for the future is also sacred. I have learned that the quality of life is more important than its length. If I cannot live with dignity, I can at least choose to die with it. This realization gives me a strange sense of still being free to control my own life. And it gives me courage! The courage to recognize that my fear of death is far less terrifying than my fear of continuing to live in this way.

The words of this articulate teenager express the inner thoughts of many of the children who resolve to take a role in facilitating death. It is not that they do not wish to live; it is that they do not wish "to live in this way."

On a more analytic level, it is important to keep in mind that not all death-facilitators make a conscious resolution to expedite the course of dying. Very often there may be no conscious awareness of a desire to end life. Yet, the child's behavior tells another story — for example, the older child who repeatedly discards his medications even though the doctors have emphasized their importance, *may be* acting out a subconscious wish to die.

The key issue in understanding the dynamics of the death-facilitator is that the child's behavior — whether directly or indirectly, consciously or non-consciously — serves primarily to facilitate death.

The Death-Transcender

The death-transcenders are usually teenagers who have had the opportunity to develop an internalized value system about the existential or religious significance of death. The youth may believe that death will not be the end of life, i.e., life will go on in another form through the intercession of God or some spiritual force. A deeply religious girl spoke of the Catholic belief about death: "Life is changed, not taken away." Another teenager who did not have any religious faith expressed the viewpoint that death is an "integral part of living." He believed that while his personal life would soon come to an end, his spirit would become part of "the unending life force of the universe." One youth who had no expectation of a continued existence after death was still able to come to terms with death in the following way:

> Death is part of life. Just as I was born, I have to die. You may not like the time or the manner, but dying is part of the bargain of living. You can't explain it; it's just part of life. Soon it may be my turn (to die) . . . but that's the "breaks" of life. You don't ask "Why me?" or "Why now?" . . . Life is its own mystery.

The death-transcender does not just accept death, although this is an important element. These young people (and they appear to be few in number) are able to go beyond acceptance to a point where personal death is viewed in terms of a broader context of life. It is not that these individuals do not mourn and grieve for the loss of life and those they love, but underlying their behavior is an ability to integrate the tragedy of death within a transcendent spiritual or philosophic value system.

The Death-Defier

The death-defier is another coping style usually found among older children. The death-defier recognizes the gravity of his illness and the waning hopes for recovery. Yet, he refuses to "give in" or to "surrender" to death. It is not so much that he expects his struggle to save him from death, it is that in continuing to fight he hopes to preserve some semblance of dignity and freedom. Often this defiance of death may serve only to prolong the youth's pain and suffering, but it may be important, nevertheless, in the child's efforts to maintain a cherished self-concept. In addition, the defiance of death provides many young people with a means to express their anger and rage over what is happening to them. This storm of fury is directed at death by the death-defier.

One teenager spoke of Camus' *Myth of Sisyphus* in which,

> . . . a guy keeps on rolling a rock up the hill although the

rock continues to roll back again. The guy knows his efforts are doomed but he continues and in so doing he asserts his own existence and freedom in the face of the absurdity of life. This is the way I feel I would want to die . . . Of course, my efforts may not help and they may prolong the mess, but they would matter to me and that's the one thing I have left.

As if heeding the admonition of poet Dylan Thomas, the death-defiers do not go quietly into that night of death. They rage, rage and rage wildly! In so doing, they hope to preserve that part of themselves which death must not claim . . . human dignity!

* * * * * * * * * *

While different children adopt different coping styles or game plans for living in the face of death, the primary objective is to reduce anxiety and to enable the child to make some form of adjustment to the impending death *(see figure 1)*.

Human behavior is an ongoing and dynamic process and it cannot be divided into "hermetically sealed" categories. It is entirely possible that the dying child may shift from one coping style to another, or may manifest other forms of coping behavior not discussed in this article. Nor is there any intent to imply that one coping style is superior or "morally better" than another, as New York University neurosurgeon Joseph Ransohoff has cautioned:

> This is no place [dealing with the gravely ill patient] to impose our own philosophy on the patient or the family. One patient may function better denying the imminence of death while another may want things out in the open. In essence, the patient has the right to determine the manner of his dying, and we must make every effort to be sensitive and responsive to his wishes.

The Dying Child as Teacher

Invariably, studies on dying raise many questions including the most basic, "Why study death at all since there is nothing we can do about it?" It may seem so futile, and it would be if staff went around sticking their heads into oxygen tents disturbing the child's final hours. The primary concern, however, is not with these individuals but with the vast bulk of terminally ill children, the slowly dying. The patient may have several weeks to several years to live and if he is not managed properly he can become a burden to his family, the medical team and himself. In these situations it is crucially important to look beyond the physical symptoms and complaints to see a youngster in profound psychological suffering. The child may be dying but his capacity to experience fear, despair, and grief is very much alive. Very often the

Figure 1

A Summary of the Child's Conception of Death

Age[1]	Death Concept	Coping Experience
0-3	The child does not understand death except in the sense of being separated from familiar surroundings and significant others.	The emotions a dying child feels at this age are the same as those he feels when separated from familiar people and places: separation, anxiety, terror, fear, and physical pain.
3-6	During this period, the child confuses the domain of physical and psychological causality. He does not understand that death is a physical event which can happen to him. The child often reasons that the two events which are contiguous in time and space are causally connected. Thus a child might believe that a feeling he had at the time of someone's death was the actual cause of it. In a hospital, a child might understand death as part of the physical proceedings he is required to undergo, such as an operation.	In addition to the emotions the child under three years of age experiences, these children may also feel guilt. They may see their illness as a punishment for bad behavior.
6-10	Death is usually understood as an agent external to the self. In the same manner in in which the products of mental operations are seen as perceptual givens rather than self created, they will also see personal death as avoidable.	In this period, the child will also express anger at the fact that he is ill. The child is able to reason that there is no particular reason why he should be singled out for a serious illness, and hence feels angry.
10-+	Death is recognized as final, personal and irreversible.	The preadolescent and adolescent are developing a distinct awareness of themselves as separate and distinct human beings. Hence the prospect of death accentuates feelings of loneliness which the healthy adolescents already feel. The adolescent tries to cope with the tremendous loneliness, anger and fright he feels by several identifiable game strategies: denial, submission, facilitation, transcendence, defiance, acceptance and possible other strategic combinations.

---

[1] The age categories outlined here are intended to be entirely suggestive. There will naturally be a fair amount of fluctuation between the child's response to death and his age.

psychological management of the youngster by the medical staff and the parents will determine not only whether he is a cooperative patient, but whether he will be able to die with dignity.

In terms of the broader perspective, research on the dying child offers the promise of contributing not only to patient care but to other related issues in child psychiatry such as how children cope with severe anxiety and crisis, what is the effect of the death of a child on other siblings in a family, and how do children deal with *loss,* whether it be loss of health, loss of a loved one through physical separation, or even loss of one's own life. These are fundamental questions for which there are few known answers at present, and there are certainly no high-powered textbooks which offer the hope of quick solutions. In the final analysis it is the dying child who is the teacher, from him we are learning not only about his special needs and fears, but the coping styles, the aspirations, and the courage which are shared by all children.

This article has focused on selected clinical observations and exploratory findings which may be of assistance to researchers, physicians and medical staff in understanding the needs of dying children and the games children play to meet these needs. In evaluating such preliminary data, it is important to keep in mind that future research will undoubtedly add new dimensions and modify current ones. For the interim, one must be careful to avoid the error of the proverbial blind man who explored a single part of the giant elephant and concluded that all elephants were no more than this.

REFERENCES

Elkind, D., 1974. *Children and Adolescents*. London: Oxford University Press.

Gullo, S.V., D.J. Cherico, and R. Shadeck. 1974. "Suggested Stages and Response Styles in Life-Threatening Illness." In B. Schoenberg et al., eds., *Anticipatory Grief,* New York: Columbia University Press.

Looft, W.R. 1972. "Egocentrism and Social Interaction Across the Life Span." *Psychological Bulletin,* Vol. 78, No. 2, pp. 73-93.

Piaget, J. 1950. *The Psychology of Intelligence,* New York: Harcourt, Brace.

Schowalter, J.E. 1970. "The Child's Reaction to His Own Terminal Illness." In B. Schoenberg et al., eds., *Loss and Grief: Psychological Management in Medical Practice,* New York: Columbia University Press.

Spinetta, J.L. 1974. "The Dying Child's Awareness of Death: A Review." *Psychological Bulletin,* Vol. 81, No. 4, pp. 256-260.

Waechter, E.H. 1971. "Children's Awareness of Fatal Illness."*American Journal of Nursing,* June, pp. 1168-1172.

Acknowledgment

An abridged report of this research appeared in *Medical Dimensions,* October 1973. The authors are grateful to its editors for permission to include relevant sections of the report in this paper.

JUVENILE CRIME AND ITS RELATIONSHIP TO CONCEPTS OF DEATH
Carin Elin

> To live is by universal consent to travel a rough road. And how can a rough road which leads nowhere be worth the traveling? Mere living, what a profitless performance; mere painful living, what an absurd! There is, then, nothing to be hoped for, nothing to be expected and nothing to be done save to await our turn to mount the scaffold and bid farewell to that colossal blunder, the much-ado-about-nothing world.
>
> Give assurance that what death appears to proclaim is not so, and the scene is changed. The sky brightens, the door is left open for unimagined possibilities, things begin to fall into an intelligible pattern.
>
> W. Macneile Dixon,
> *Gifford Lectures*

Is it possible that only a person like Dixon, who has been called a Confucius for the West, could have pondered such thoughts on the meaning of life? Many people may feel that young children and teenagers are incapable of such cogitations, especially when they are related to death. But to me, as a teacher in a special type of California classroom, it was clearly demonstrated that this is not so.

First I should say that it soon became apparent when talking to the students that up to now no one had ever bothered to ask them, "What does death mean to you?" While they had pretty definite ideas on the subject, as a rule most of the pupils were not optimistic, as Dixon was. In fact, they were particularly obsessed by the thought of hell and that they were going there.

I offered each class I taught this choice: to go on with their regular curriculum or to discuss the subject of death. They unanimously chose the latter. So the assignment was for the students to draw a picture of their concept of death and then elaborate their views in writing. Bob Stone had this to say (students' grammar and spelling used throughout):

Death is . . . What is death. Is there life after death, or do they just put you six feet under. I do indeed sometimes wonder. Is there a heaven high in the sky. Is there even a hell far below. Or do you just go in the ground when you die.

I think there is a heaven and a hell. It depends on whether your naughty or nice or whether you tell lies or the truth. I think I will go to hell. What is hell. Hell is certainly not heaven. I think hell is a bunch of hoods who don't know there if's and but's from their could's. Hell is eternal fire. With all these hoods, gambling, drinking and doing dope. Let's face it, when you die there is just no hope.

At this point you may be wondering where is this special classroom? The answer can be found in these words of Tom Dent:

What death means to me. Death is when your locked up and you don't have your freedom like being here, when you hear that door shut your throat gets dry and you feel like you just swallowed a clump of flour and it won't go down, then you feel like beating your head against the wall wondering why you are here and why you did what you did to get here. Every so often I ask that question and wonder (where) I will go next. To me death does not mean you have to be killed. One person can die many times in his lifetime.

Yes, these students are all in prison and go to the schools of the juvenile court in San Diego. During a limited stay in this area, the writer taught some fifteen classes.

Why do so many of these teenagers feel that life is already over for them? For Clelia Yates (approximate age fifteen), "being locked up is the first step of death. And after that there is no hope."

While excellent work is being carried on to ascertain the social and environmental causes for criminal conduct among young people, little or nothing has been done by way of investigating how crime may be related to a person's concept of death and how this concept may turn a first offender into a second offender and then into a habitual criminal. Many of the crimes take place, as we know, within the public school buildings. According to the National Educational Association:

More than 60,900 teachers were attacked by students last year (1977-78 school year). Since 1972 classroom murders have increased 18%, rapes have increased 40%, and assaults are up 77% (*New York Post*, December 26, 1978).

In contrast, let us go back a hundred years and to another area of the world. In the British census of 1881 covering the population of India, including Ceylon, figures were given of the record of convictions for criminal offenses:

Europeans in India	1 in 274
Eurasians	1 in 509
Native Christians	1 in 799
Mohammedans	1 in 856
Hindus	1 in 1361
Buddhists	1 in 3787

These statistics were reprinted in the leading Catholic organ of the time in Britain, The Tablet, with the comment:

The last item is a magnificent tribute to the exalted purity of Buddhism . . . It appears from these figures that while we effect a very marked moral deterioration in the natives by converting them to our creed, their natural standard of morality is so high that, however much we christianize them, we cannot succeed in making them altogether as bad as ourselves.

It seems appropriate at this point to consider what Buddha taught that could have such a marked and lasting effect on members of that faith. His teachings and the story of his life can be found in the classic poem *The Light of Asia*, by Sir Edwin Arnold. The year 1979 marked the 100th anniversary of its publication. The *British Dictionary of National Biography* says there were sixty editions in England and eighty in America. In a twenty-six page review Oliver Wendell Holmes wrote: "Its tone is so lofty there is nothing with which to compare it but the New Testament." Before quoting from *The Light of Asia*, it is interesting to note that a student under Freud's personal tutelage related that his mentor called Buddha the greatest psychologist of all time (*The Dhammapada*, p. vi). As we shall see later, some of the stanzas that follow were used in my classes in San Diego:

> I, Buddha, who wept with all my brother's tears,
> Whose heart was broken by a whole world's woe,
> Laugh and am glad, for there is Liberty!
> Ho! ye who suffer! know
> Ye suffer from yourselves. . . .
> Within yourselves deliverance must be sought;
> Each man his prison makes.
> Each hath such lordship as the loftiest ones. . . .
>
> The Books say well, my Brothers! each man's life
> The outcome of his former living is:
> The bygone wrongs bring forth sorrows and woes
> The bygone right breeds bliss.
> That which ye sow ye reap. See yonder fields!
> The sesamum was sesamum, the corn
> Was corn. The Silence and the Darkness knew!
> So is a man's fate born. . . .
>
> By this the slayer's knife did stab himself,
> The unjust judge hath lost his own defender,
> The false tongue dooms its lie; the creeping thief
> And spoiler rob, to render. . . .
>
> Man cometh, reaper of the things he sowed,
> Sesamum, corn, so much cast in past birth;
> And so much weed and poison-stuff, which mar
> Him and the aching earth.
> If he shall labor rightly, rooting these,
> And planting wholesome seedlings where they grew,
> Fruitful and fair and clean the ground shall be,
> And rich the harvest due. . . .

> If ye lay bound upon the wheel of change,
> And no way were of breaking from the chain,
> The Heart of boundless Being is a curse,
> The Soul of Things fell Pain.
> Ye are not bound! the Soul of Things is sweet,
> The Heart of Being is celestial rest;
> Stronger than woe is will: that which was Good
> Doth pass to Better—Best.

From the foregoing it is evident that Buddha taught reincarnation and also its twin doctrine, karma, the law of cause and effect, or as expressed by Saint Paul: "Be not deceived, God is not mocked, for whatsoever a man soweth, that shall he also reap" (*Galatians* 6:7.) As to reincarnation, this is not just an Eastern teaching. It is to be found in the Bible and in early Christianity (Head and Cranston 1977, pp. 134-40, 144-56). Many Jewish rabbis have taught it, and continue to teach it (pp. 124-34). The famous Rabbi Simeon Ben Jochai wrote in *The Zohar:*

> All souls are subject to the trials of reincarnation. They know not how they are being at all times judged, both before coming into this world and when they leave it. They do not know how many transformations and mysterious trials they must undergo. The souls must re-enter the absolute substance whence they have emerged. But to accomplish this end they must develop all the perfections, the germ of which is planted in them and if they have not fulfilled this condition during one life, they must commence another, a third, and so forth (pp. 557, 131).

Let us now hear from more of the students in the Juvenile Court schools:

Sam Ackerly: People say when you die you go one of two places: you go to eternal life or eternal darkness, which means you go to hell. Take hell for instence, have you ever been there, no. Nobody know what hell is. Some say hell is full of wicked things like the devil and boiling hot rocks ect. . . . That is what somebody imagines it is but again nobody knows for sure if its with a big bad Devil or not.

Warren Sands: If I were dead I would go to hell and bern at the stake at the fire place.

Ted Blunt: Death is frighting thing for some people. Death is realistic and a lot of people fear it. I think that death is not real because the only thing that floats or supposely floats is your soul and it goes to hevan or hell but your soul is still alive, so you are not really dead, just a part of you is dead.

Roger Lillis: Satin sez: seconds before I was to die—there rose an ear piercing cry. It said "hello my friend, I've been waiting!" as the words roared off the tounge of satin. At the sound of a chuckle, everything became excessively bright, as he proceeded to touch my ear, I realized the end was near, now I had lost my sight, fearing that there was sound and I just couldn't hear.

As he extended his arm he began to say, with this touch on the planet earth, I have deprived (you) of the gift of birth, now you can see what you were once trully worth. And the'll burn your body away. But I my friend shall take your soul, and if you don't believe me ask any who know, eternal peace is out of the world, once your mine you'll never be as free as a bird, because there is no place under the sun to rest your spirit if you run. If you dont stay on the shelf, you'll yearning for an elf, to come and save you from being fried in a pot of stew. If you don't make me mad, you wont ever be treated bad. But every time I yell, it will be to remind you

YOUR IN HELL!

Not all students, of course, thought of death and the afterlife within a framework of heaven and hell, although they all believed that something survives death. The great majority evidenced a concern with a day of final judgment, when they would be doomed to everlasting punishment. The next two students were not so definite on this:

Sid Worden: Death is not really dieing its only being reborn. You haven't really lived until you die. Then you've been born for the first time weather you go to heaven or hell. After you die your soul is still alive with existance but your body is not. Your soul keeps on living. But I guess if you go to hell then you probably will be much more dead than you would if you went to heaven.

Art Perry: My feelings about death is that life here on earth suddenly stop. And some how a new world open up to us. And life for you now is much different from the one we leading now is waiting for us. A place where you find out what this world here is all about.

If there's a God ore if there's a heaven and hell. To find out are purpose for being here. If it was an test of God to see who would believe in him and do his will. And if they all are real. A chance to find out all the answers we long to know all these years.

During the discussion period it became evident that most of the students—whether they had committed serious offenses or minor ones—

had one feeling they could neither draw nor write about, and that was their hopeless conviction that it was impossible for them to alter their own lives. When they were asked, "Do you want to stop getting into trouble?" a mumbled reply so often came: "Why should I change when I'm going to eternal hell anyway?"

Somehow the sense of responsibility for their own life had been taken away from them. Cannot we find a way as teachers, doctors, or social workers to instill some purpose and hope into these students who feel their lives have already ended? There must be a way to implant a new desire in such a student as *Sandy,* who feels:

Your born, you live and you die... what can I say. A lot of people are afraid to die. I'm not afraid to die. I'm just afraid how and when I'm gonna die. I'll admit this though I'm not gonna be a little Angle so that God will look down on me and pull me up to Heaven—cause I already (messed) my life up. Thats why Im in the hall (Juvenile Hall) cause I stabbed my stepdad, and at that moment I felt death for him. Its a (terrible) feeling knowing that you almost killed some one.

In all classes in death education I presented the words of some of the great teachers of humanity, words that are imbued with hope and courage. When I quoted some of the statements from *The Light of Asia* and asked what those words meant, the students replied that it just may pay off to cease a life of crime and drugs. These lines, for example, were read:

> Ye who suffer! Know
> Ye suffer from yourselves. ...
> Within yourselves deliverance must be sought
> Each man his prison makes.
> Each hath such lordship as the loftiest ones

I would then look up to see if the class understood what was being said, for poetry is not an easy thing for young people to take. I was often amazed to observe their faces beaming with hope. "What is meant by 'Each hath such lordship as the loftiest ones?'," I asked. Often the reply came in the form of another question: "Are we divine too?"

> The Books say well, my Brothers! each man's life
> The outcome of his former living is:
> The bygone wrongs bring forth sorrows and woes
> The bygone right breeds bliss.
> That which ye sow ye reap.

> Man cometh, reaper of the things he sowed,
> Sesamum, corn, so much cast in past birth,
> And so much weed and poison-stuff, which mar
> Him and the aching earth.

After hearing this some students asked if the path they had chosen in this life could have been a path they had chosen before in a past life, and so the tendency to repeat was strengthened. I answered that tendencies can be changed with effort, as Buddha states in these verses:

> If ye shall labor rightly, rooting these,
> And planting wholesome seedlings where they grew,
> Fruitful and fair and clean the ground shall be
> And rich the harvest due. ...

The students gradually came to see that the responsibility for their lives is their own, and consequently there is hope for the future; they are not doomed to eternal punishment.

I have found in the anthology *Reincarnation: The Phoenix Fire Mystery* hundreds of statements by noted writers and thinkers that inspire the students who hear them. The book offers a panorama of views expressed through the medium of practically every known profession. This universal approach speaks to each inquirer from his own specific interest and background, whether that be science, philosophy, sociology, music, art, or psychology.

To close, I would like to share the words of one student who was able to encapsulate in his mind and heart the essence of what has been discussed in this paper:

Bert Anthony: With me life is only a testing ground for my basic emotions and if I prove to myself that love, joy, peace and being human is the way to be, then when my existance on this plane is ended I will step to a higher one and after that the next higher one. But if at any time I fail to see myself and those around me as loving beings and hurt anyone, I come back here to try again till I get it right.

I will leave you now, as I left all my classes, with these words of the Buddha, the ideas of which are not unique to Buddhism but may be found in one form or other in all the world's religions:

> Within yourselves deliverance must be sought.
> Each hath such lordship as the loftiest ones.
> Stronger than woe is WILL.

REFERENCES

Arnold, Sir Edwin. 1879. *The Light of Asia*. Los Angeles: The Theosophy Company.
Dhammapada, The 1955. Alhambra, Cal.: Cunningham Press
Head, J. and S. L. Cranston 1977. *Reincarnation: The Phoenix Fire Mystery*. New York: Crown.

THE ADOLESCENT AND DEATH
Lynn S. Schneider

Introduction:

Adolescence is increasingly being seen as a particular life stage in most cultures, as is the period of latency and adulthood. Such a view suggests that there are or may be particular tasks, needs, developmental crises unique to the period. It is a time, at least in our culture, of turbulence and stress. Studies on suicide (Teischer, 1966, Toolan, 1975), illness (Deischer, 1963), and drug abuse (Brunswick, 1969, 1972) highlight the potential fragility of the age group.

This paper addresses the issue of the impact of deaths of close relatives — parents, gradparents, siblings — on the adolescent. Literature is presented in three areas — the particular views of adolescents of death, the impact on the adolescent of an early parental death, and the impact on later life of deaths occurring in preadolescence and adolescence. A critique of methodological problems posed by this research is presented as well. It is hoped that this review will both provide a modest contribution to an understanding of death for teenagers and suggest implications for future research and prevention of dysfunctional reactions.

It is known that a good deal of the psychoanalytic literature covering children's reactions to death of a parent suggests that mourning does not occur in the preadolescent stage for a variety of reasons, one being that the child has not emotionally developed to the point of mourning a lost object. Here, the normal defenses of latency — repression, denial, and reaction formation — may prevent mourning by serving as an adaptive device that lays the base for continued development in latency. It may also be true that the onset of adolescence represents a loss of one's earlier life and, therefore, serves as a grief that reawakens earlier grief. Observations from a study of 42 children and adolescents who had suffered an early parental loss led the investigators to conclude that the necessary developmental conditions for being able to mourn occur in children during the period from latency to adolescence (Wolfenstein, 1966). This then is a particularly important period for the work of mourning and an area of significant research.

Review of Literature

Literature on the topic of death proliferates, but there appears a paucity of material of the adolescents' experience with and perception of death. In a study by Alexander and Olderstein (1958), the affective responses of children and adolescents to ideas of death were studied. The sample respondents consisted of 108 males, ages 5 - 16, 20 percent black and 80 percent white. There was no reported psychiatric disturbance among the youth, who were predominantly of low income families. The instrument used was a word association test of 27 stimulus words to which response time, galvanic skin response, and response words were recorded. The words were divided into three sets — affective, basal, and death. The sample respondents were divided into three groups, 5-8 years (n-29), 9-12 years (n = 48) and 3-16 years (n = 31) based on the development of logical thought. Results indicated the following: that death stimulus words were responded to by total group with increasing latency and decreasing skin resistance and that all three groups responded with more latency to death words than to experimentally equivalent basal words. A weakness of this study is that cultural factors are not reviewed, and the galvanic skin response is known to be more sensitive to cultural differences. A conclusion drawn from this study is that death may have greater emotional significance for teenagers with weak self concepts and since adolescence is particularly noted for its "storm and stress," death may have a particularly painful impact.

In a study by Maurer (1964), adolescent attitudes toward death were reviewed. Here, a thesis was that death of important relations was an integral part of the adolescents' psychic life and correlates with academic performance. An unstructured approach was used, with the following questions: "What comes to mind when you think of death?" and "What comes to mind when you think of loss?" The subjects were 172 high school girls, ages 17-19 with a response rate of 88 percent. This was an integrated school in a major urban area. All the subjects were normal functioning adolescents with college plans. The group was divided into four subgroups based on achievement test scores. One weakness of the study was a lack of information on the number of previous deaths experienced by the subjects. The responses to the questions were coded into 12 categories, e.g., sorrow, fear, loss, etc. Results of the study were the following: loss was quite important for adolescents and differences in thoughts regarding death ranged from childish to mature. Responses to the death question tended to vary with the degree of maturity and academic achievement. For example, poor achievement was associated with greater fear, separation anxiety, etc.; while higher achievement was associated with greater achievement in acknowledging death's inevitability.

In research by Hogan (1970), adolescent views of death were studied. The thesis of this work was to question the notion of a previous study (McClelland, 1964) that death was analogous to a "lover." Three studies were presented as part of the research. In the first study, seven death-related metaphors were presented to 261 subjects, 83 males and 178 females, ages 17-21. The subjects were asked to rank order the metaphors in terms of classifications of death. Both males and females saw death as an unknown last adventure. In the second study, 80 males and 41 females ages 17-21 years were interviewed regarding their fantasies of death under an induced high anxiety state. Few subjects had fantasies related to sexual notions and only two subjects saw death as a "lover." Forty-five percent mentioned death as related to pleasurable fantasies, and thirty-nine percent mentioned painful fantasies. However, the most common response was fear of the unknown. The third study sampled 117 males and 221 females in a psychology class. The subjects were asked to write directly regarding their perceptions and concepts of death. The most frequent response was death as a religious experience, with females more often reporting this response than men. Death as peaceful was more often reported by women. However, the notion of death as a lover went unsupported. Conclusions of this study were that normal adolescents rarely attempt to deny death; the psychoanalytic notions of death are not supported in this normal population; and the notion of death as a lover is culture bound.

There has been some attempt to compare reactions to death among normal and subnormal adolescents. In a study by Stacey and Reichen (1954), attitudes toward death among adolescent girls ages 14-16 were determined. A questionnaire consisting of 36 items tapping a variety of attitudes toward death was employed. Some of the items were drawn from a study by Schilder and Wechsler (1934). The sample respondents consisted of 75 institutionalized girls and 75 normal girls. Religious groups were equally distributed. Fourteen of twenty-five items quantitatively analyzed showed significant differences between groups. Results confirmed the thesis that there are significant differences between subnormal and normal adolescent girls regarding their attitudes toward death. For example, normal girls more often think of death, while subnormal girls more often see death as painful, and more often think of dying from a fatal disease.

The notion or thesis that death of important relations in childhood has an impact on adolescent development has been well documented. Some studies suggest a direct causal relationship between early parent loss and emotional and/or physical illness in adolescence. In a retrospective study conducted by Seligman et al. (1976), 100 adolescents and young adults, ages 12-20 years, were interviewed and 85 cases were analyzed. The population consisted of 31 black and 54 white adolescents. They had been referred for psychiatric consultation to an inpatient and outpatient medical adolescent service during July 1970-June 1971. Parental losses were recorded for everyone. A control group was matched on age, race, and socioeconomic background. This group consisted of 179 school referred subjects (83 black and 96 white) and 186 clinic subjects (141 black and 45 white). Results indicated few significant differences between races. In the study group, early parental loss occurred for 36 percent of the subjects; in the school group, 11.7% reported some early parental loss and in the clinic subjects, 16.6% reported some form of parental loss. Note should be taken that the reasons for referral for the outpatient medical group were neurotic conflicts and for the inpatient medical group, self destructive injury or drug overdose. However, this study does not present any quantitative findings of the correlation between early parental loss and the designated reasons for referral.

In a study by Beck et al. (1963) the relationship between the development of depression in late adolescence and young adulthood to the death of a parent is explored. The sample respondents consisted of 297 patients admitted to psychiatric outpatient department and a psychiatric ward at the University of Pennsylvania. Each patient was studied by a research team and given a psychiatric evaluation, a diagnosis from the 1951 standard nomenclature (APA) and rating on a four point scale regarding the depth of depression. Each patient was questioned regarding age at time of loss of a parent. Nondepressed psychiatric patients were used as a comparison group and matched on selected demographic variables. Results were quite varied and indicated the following--that the patient sample could be divided into three groups based on their scores on the depression inventory: 27 per cent experienced loss of a parent before age 16 and were in the high depressed group; 15 per cent experienced loss of a parent before age 16 and were in the medium depressed group, and 12 per cent experienced death of a parent before age 16 and were nondepressed. Use of clinical ratings of depression showed similar relationships to loss of a parent. For both males and females, the loss of a father was more frequent, and the greater frequency of paternal loss held for both sexes across all levels of depression. Analysis of variance was used to determine the relationship between orphanhood, age and depression, with the depression inventory as the dependent variable. The major portion of variance in the depression inventory scores was attributable to association between scores and orphanhood. The interaction between age and orphanhood was nonsignificant. Regarding the age of patient at time of death, there occurred an overrepresentation of depressed patients in the group of orphans who lost a parent before age four. Of those who lost parents before age 16, three reported periods of symptom free intervals between onset of depression and bereavement. Methodological problems were overcome by use of the standardized depression inventory instrument in lieu of clinical judgments only and the use of a comparison group of nondepressed psychiatric patients. Grouping of patients according to their demographic characteristics showed significant differences in overall rates of orphanhood between certain classes.

In a study by Birtchnell (1970[a]), a comparison of depressed patients, nondepressed patients, severely depressed patients, and moderately depressed patients was conducted relative to early and recent parental death. Information was gathered from case records of 500 admissions to a general psychiatric hospital during the years 1959-1963; all diagnostic groups were included as were first admissions and readmissions.

The diagnosis of depression was made retrospectively on a four point scale including a range from frequently encountered symptoms to extreme symptoms. Early parent death was defined as death of a parent in the first 20 years of life, and recent parent death as death of a parent one to 20 years before admission. In both cases, the 20 year period was subdivided into four five-year spans. Results indicated that death of a parent, recent or early, was more common in the depressed and non-depressed group than in the severely to moderate depressed group, that early death was more common than recent death in the severely depressed group and that the severely depressed group had experienced more maternal deaths.

The notion that loss of a parent in adolescence contributes in an etiological manner to psychiatric disturbance in adulthood has also been well documented by research. In a study by Pitts et al. (1965), an attempt was made to develop appropriate controls for a systematically studied population of consecutive psychiatric admissions, and to simultaneously assess these populations for parental deprivation (by death and separation) and family history of psychiatric illness. The subjects, 748 white patients, were ages 10-89 years and consisted of 269 males and 229 females. The control group (N=250) consisted of 90 males and 160 females. Relatives of the subjects in the patients groups were interviewed for reliability and validity. The study group was divided into manic depressives (366) and schizophrenics (382). The entire patient group was compared to the control population for variables of age at death of first parent, total parental death, loss of both parents prior to age fifteen, cause of death of parent, age at marital separation of parents, number of siblings, cause of death of siblings, and occurrence and type of psychiatric illness of patients and siblings. Results showed correlations between the two major categories—parental deprivation and family history of psychiatric illness in psychiatric patients. Both groups were stratified for variables of age, sex and socioeconomic status, incidence of psychiatric illness, and mortality rates. Marked psychiatric illness in relatives of psychiatric patients was found when contrasted to matched controls. However, deprivation is one environmental factor that plays no independent role in the genesis of psychiatric illness. The high familial incidence of psychiatric illness suggests that environmental or associational and not deprivational factors play a role in such causation. So, this study gives more importance to the associational variables in lieu of deprivational factors in the etiology of psychiatric illness.

In a study by Birtchnell (1970[b]), a comparison is made between psychiatric and normal groups regarding the sex of the parent lost, the sex of the bereaved, the year of loss, the current age of the bereaved, and the age of the parent at birth of bereaved. The psychiatric group consisted of 500 admissions to a hospital 1959-1963, ages 20-59 years.

These were first and readmissions. Some of the categories of disorders were depression (259), schizophrenia (65), alcoholism (68), and psychopathy (44). The control group consisted of 500 individuals in a nearby town, matched on sex and age. The patient and control groups were not matched on social class, as it is difficult to accept the patient's social class as that of the parents. Results indicated one major finding— that parental death needs to be considered in adequate detail. The incidence of parent death before age 20 is higher among patients under 40, but not in patients over 40, the incidence of parent death before age 70 is significantly higher in the patient group. The most marked difference between patients and controls occurs during the 0-4 age span, with loss of mother alone and loss of mother and father most significant. Since it was found that the mean parental age at birth for patients and controls who have suffered early parent death do not differ significantly, it was suggested that parent death and not parental age at birth is the primary phenomenon.

In a study by Munro (1965), the focus is on normal individuals. The thrust is threefold: to study childhood parent loss in a group of normal adults; to demonstrate that parental bereavement is a more common event than suggested; and to suggest that outpatients of a medical or surgical clinic are good sources of data. The sample respondents, 92 males and 118 females, were 16 years or above, with an excess of those in the middle years. Only patients attending by appointment were interviewed as emergency cases were omitted. To ensure the representativeness of the sample, statistical comparisons using x^2 between medical and surgical outpatient department and between male and female patients on 14 sociodemographic factors were done, with no significant differences. Care was taken in the study to provide detailed definitions of some terms. Parental bereavement, parental loss, and parental deprivation were defined as separation of parent and child; parental absence was defined as loss other than by death of three months duration; disturbed relations with parent as occurring during childhood when relationships with parent were consistently strained and unhappy, and childhood as birth to 16 years.

Results were viewed against the backdrop of the annual parental mortality rates which were 19.5 percent by 16 years of age. Thirty-three percent of the population experienced absence of a parent in childhood; paternal absences were higher than maternal at a ratio of 3:1; 50 percent of the population experienced a childhood bereavement experience and 11.9 percent experienced some form of bereavement of both parents. Findings also indicated an association between parental loss and emotional trauma — 62 patients reporting loss of a parent for any reason and about a quarter of these patients regarding it as distressing. In short, this study questions the etiological relationship between parental bereavement and later psychiatric illnes. If the results of this study are typical of other populations, then the numbers of parent/child separations are enormous. As well, it may be that a measure of the amount of parental separation may be misleading, and parental bereavement per se may not be the only predisposing factor in mental illness.

Methodological Issues:

There are numerous published reports of clinical studies in which the frequency of childhood parental deprivation (loss by death) is determined in groups of healthy respondents. Although the above review is at best brief, it presents some persistent methodological problems.

First, and perhaps foremost, it is the unclear definition of certain terms – early parent death, recent parent death, parent loss, age at time of parent death, and so forth. Some of the studies do attempt definitions of these terms, but more probably do not. Without a clear definition of the terms, operationalization of concepts is at best weak. Secondly, there is no consistency of positive correlations, that is, each study may find a particular age at time of loss to be significant for loss of one particular parent in one class of patients, and there is no agreement. Thirdly, and perhaps more important are serious deficits in particular methodology. For example, some studies suffer from comparisons between unlike samples, and samples not representative due to selection processes. Furthermore, some of the studies suffer from the elimination of a significant portion of the index sample because of incomplete records. Another problem quite common in those studies suggesting a relationship between early parent death and some outcome measure is that association through statistical tests does not imply causation and absence of association does not imply alternative causation. Lastly, when the isolation of criterion or index groups depends on the conventional system of diagnosis, many complex problems related to the variability of psychiatric diagnoses are introduced and restrict the generalizability of results. The latter methodological issue may relate to the problem of definiton of terms, which is resolved to an extent in the study mention by Beck et al. (1963).

Conclusions:

In short, it is hoped that this brief review will suggest some of the issues involved in the experience of death of parents and other important relations for the adolescent. Future research in the area will probably need to refine concepts and continue to provide comparisons between normal and disturbed populations. As well, a further thrust of such research might be to begin to delineate the coping attitudes and social supports which normal populations use in response to death(s).

REFERENCES

Alexander, I. and A. Olderstein. 1958. "Affective Responses to the Concept of Death in a Population of Children and Adolescents." *Journal of Genetic Psychology* 93: 167-177.

Beck, A., B. Sethi, and R. Tuthill. 1963. "Childhood Bereavement and Adult Depression." *Archives of General Psychiatry* 9: 295-302.

Birtchnell, J. 1970a. "Depression in Relation to Early and Recent Parent Death." *British Journal of Psychiatry* 106: 299-306.

——————— 1970b. "Early Parent Death and Mental Illness." *British Journal of Psychiatry* 116: 281-88.

Brunswick, A. 1969. "Health Needs of Adolescents: How the Adolescent Sees Them." *American Journal of Public Health* 59: 1730-1745.

——————— 1972. "Adolescent Health in Harlem." *American Journal of Public Health*, Part 2, Supplement 1-62.

Deischer, R. and C. Mills. 1963. "The Adolescent Looks at His Health and Medical Needs." *American Journal of Public Health* 53: 1928-1936.

Hogan, R. 1970. "Adolescent Views of Death." *Adolescence* 5: 56-66.

Maurer, A. 1964. "Adolescent Attitudes Toward Death." *Journal of Genetic Psychology* 105: 75-90.

Munro, A. 1965. "Childhood Parent Loss in Psychiatrically Normal Population." *British Journal of Preventive and Social Medicine* 19: 69-77.

Pitts, F., J. Meyer, M. Brooks, and G. Winokur. 1965. "Adult Psychiatric Illness Assessed for Childhood Parental Loss and Psychiatric Illness in Family Members — A Study of 748 Patients and 250 Controls." *American Journal of Psychiatry*, Vol. 121, Supplement i-x.

Seligman, P., S. Glesser, M. Rauch, and T. Harris. 1974. "The Effects of Early Parental Loss in Adolescence." *Archives of General Psychiatry* 31: 475-78.

Stacey, C. and M. Reichen. 1954. "Attitudes Toward Death and Future Life Among Normal and Subnormal Adolescent Girls." *Exceptional Children* 20: 259-262.

Teischer, J. and J. Jacobs. 1966. "Adolescents Who Attempt Suicide: Preliminary Findings." *American Journal of Psychiatry* 122, 11: 1248-1257.

Toolan, J. 1969. "Depression in Children and Adolescents." In G. Caplan and S. Lebovici, eds., *Adolescence: Psychosocial Perspectives*, New York: Basic Books, pp. 264-69.

Wolfenstein, M. 1966. "How is Mourning Possible?" *Psychoanalytic Study of the Child* 21: 93-123.

MEMORY AND THE CHILD'S ABILITY TO MOURN
Betty Buchsbaum

Mourning is usually defined as the total response of the individual to the loss of a loved person. In reviewing the literature on childhood bereavement, one is struck by the polarization of writers around the issue: is it or is it not possible for a child to mourn. In actuality, the question must be viewed in a less dichotomous manner.

Freud initially established the criteria for successful mourning in his work with adult patients. Since then, the task he defined, i.e., the ability of a bereaved individual to "remove libidinal cathexis from the memories of the lost object," has characterized healthy mourning. The very notion of memory, however, is, we now know, a developing ego function the features of which alter with age (Inhelder, 1969). Furthermore, the removal of libidinal cathexis from parental images may or may not be a suitable goal for a child. Narcissistic retreat and/or identification with some aspect of the lost person are the most common paths taken by the child if a loving parent is unavailable. Without a meaningful anchor for emotional investment, the young child may be overwhelmed by the feelings released. As Furman notes (1974): "For the young child, decathexis of the mental representation of the love object can diminish or even abolish narcissistic satisfactions and prevent their further development." It may be safer for the prelatency child, particularly, to cling to the representation of the dead love object rather than to withdraw his attachments.

For the purpose of this paper, then, mourning is viewed in the manner suggested by Pollock (1978), that is, as a process with its own line of development, beginning in early life and reaching to maturity only after adolescence when the psychic apparatus is fully developed.

Age, as a major variable influencing the nature of mourning, has been examined by many investigators including Anna Freud (1960), Bowlby (1960), Kliman (1969), Wolfenstein (1966; 1969) and the Furmans (1964; 1974). The focus of their work has been primarily on the relevance of object relations and associated emotional responses to the experience of bereavement of childhood. Although the pertinence of age-related ego functions has, of course, been noted, relatively little attention has been given to the role of memory and how its transformations with age can affect the mourning process. This author's experience in treated young bereaved patients has highlighted the importance of memory as a force molding a child's response to loss. As the organization of memory develops, so, it is hypothesized, will there be changes in the capacity to remember and, thus, to mourn, a lost parent.

First, though, let us review some of the pertinent features characterizing maturation and the changing meanings a parent's death brings to a child at different stages of his life. Patterns of attachment and subsequent growth are intricately bound to the nurture, support, and involvement of parents. Such an event as the death of a parent before the child has finished "growing up," i.e., before late adolescence, is not only a fairly infrequent event, but is felt to be even more unusual because it defies what most of us assume is a law of nature: parents are supposed to complete their job of child rearing. As Rochlin has pointed out (1961), the death of a parent upsets the homeostatic balance established by the child, and the resulting vacuum cannot be left empty for long. If separations were not followed by reunions as a predictable sequence, first, survival and then maturation would be endangered. Moreover, not only is the concept of healthy growth bound to a nurturing and loving adult, but the very notion of loss or abandonment is also intertwined with the child's changing experiences, perceptions of, and identifications with a caring person. As observed by Freud (1960), mourning cannot precede the establishment of object constancy. The very capacity to achieve object permanence is predicated on the recogniton of loss and expectation of return. In other words, the development of object relations could not occur without the conviction that what disappears will reappear. One might expect that once the child has reached 18 months of age and has established some capacity to evoke the maternal image, response to her absence would be significantly different from before this time.

The absence of a parent has a different impact at each phase of development, frustrating different needs and stimulating different sets of responses (Nagera, 1970). For example, during the first weeks of life survival requires substitution of an absent parent. However, little more than the change in sensory experiences affects the infant's response. Only after the second or third month of life is the mother beginning to be apprehended as need-fulfilling part-object (still fused with the infant's own representation). Loss at this point would be the deprivation of love and nurturance, associated with a state of helplessness (and a tenuous sense of self).

After eight months of age, object recognition on at least a perceptual level occurs and the baby can begin to recognize what it is missing. With the onset of the individuation-separation phase extending from about two to four years, greater differentiation between child and mother occurs. It is then that a more explicit cognitive and emotional awareness of the self and the other is possible. Before four years of age, however, reality boundaries are still vague and integration of contradictory elements of the object is not yet achieved. Not only would object representations be fluid and idiosyncratic but efforts to retain a missing object would utilize primitive and unstable mechanisms. Introjection, ambivalent identifications, and unreliable reality testing would be characteristic of the child younger than four. Nevertheless, a three-year-old can articulate his sense of loss as well as register some form of hope.

This verbal ability contrasts with the methods used by the young baby, such as Freud's grandson (R. Furman, 1964), where the sensori-motor act of throwing out and retrieving a reel tied to a string signaled the concern about absence and return. I would like to demonstrate how a three-year-old has expressed the same idea. Here is a segment of his play observed during a visit made by the child to a relative's home while his parents were visiting his just widowed grandmother. He had chosen to spend the night away from his parents and knew that his grandfather had died. Before agreeing to go to sleep, he recited the following: "Go away, come back, go away, come back," pretending to be giving orders to a taxicab driver. Repetition of his instructions went on for about five minutes.

During the toddler and oedipal periods the parents serve as narcissistic supports and sources of affectional contact as well as agents of libidinal control. It is a time when loving and being loved become increasing important. The maternal, nurturing figure is no longer as dominant, while the father's role emerges as increasingly significant. Thus, from two years on, there will be differential effects related to the sex of the child and whether it is the mother or father who survives.

From four to seven years (Piaget's pre-operational stage) (Inhelder and Piaget, 1958), object representation grows perceptually more clear and stable although concrete logical relationships are not yet available. Thus, during the oedipal phase and early latency, parental images can be sustained in more accurate and reliable ways than previously. The reciprocity of personal interactions and the integration of different roles are, nevertheless, still lacking. During latency, with the growth of operational thought, a conceptual ordering of one's experiences is more possible and the retention of images through memory would be more successful. Development of sharper, more complex and vivid images continues through adolescence (Blatt, 1974).

Parental functions during latency are less dependent on narcissistic support and are increasingly related to ego and superego functioning. Phase adequate development of object relations during these years still requires interaction and further identification with parents. If a parent dies during latency, the child often idealizes the parent and erects a strongly cathected fantasy life which may even be used for future structuralization. The child may also relate to substitute parents as vehicles for projection of the fantasied parent and they, too, may become hypercathected (Freud, 1957).

Only in the later phase of adolescence, it is thought, can a process approaching adult mourning come about. As Wolfenstein has suggested (1966), achievement of the "trial mourning" of adolescence, with the working through and relinquishing of the earlier parental attachments intrapsychically, permits disengagement from real parents. With respect to the function of memory — one must wait until adolescence before events can be recalled in a decreasingly wish-dominated manner. Furthermore, a conceptual change to hypothetical thinking and abstract reasoning provides another important link to the adult world. The adolescent can now share wth adults in a comprehending way the mythical, philosophical, religious, artistic, and other creative modes of dealing with object loss, allowing the construction of a neutral reparative response to bereavement.

At this point let us consider the developmental implications of the preceding section and observe the forms of object representation that are available to a child after a parent's death. Generally, it is hypothesized, and clinical data suggest, that the experience of loss of a parent encountered before two years would be incorporated into the sensorimotor schema dominant during that period. The ways in which events registered in the sensorimotor terms may be recalled later in life deserve further study. It is proposed that, while verbal constructs or mental images are lacking, automatisms and bodily sensations would arise to represent these early memories.

Between two and four years, object representation begins to emerge but events are incoherently and subjectively organized (Blatt, 1974; Inhelder and Piaget, 1969). Memories would still be characterized by a personalized system of concepts with only fragmentary and egocentric reference to external events. Some time after four years, as conceptual development progresses, perception and speech become increasingly autonomous functions. During this stage thought can be organized with reference to symbols enabling a more discrete and orderly expression of experience. However, these symbols are nonetheless understood with reference to an unreliable, emotionally dominated system of registration and recall. The newly emerging ability to represent events through imagery and speech would be particularly vulnerable to internal pressures and needs. Loss of a parent during this period would enhance the child's tendency for memory of the parent to occur in an intrusive and illusory manner. With the greater stability and objectivity characterizing conceptual development after six years of age, experiences may be more independently and realistically registered. Parental death during a child's latency might be associated with more conscious (but secret) fantasy constructions. It can be speculated that themes related to the family romance and to imaginary companions might assume greater intensity than would be normally expected. At adolescence the yearning for the lost parent might assume a more integrated and realistic quality. One might, nonetheless, anticipate some acting out of unconscious reunion fantasies. Several case reports of Wolfenstein (1969) support this last notion.

The material of three patients has been selected to illustrate the persistence and strength of perceptual (auditory and visual) forms of contact with a longed-for person. Each of the patients was about five years old at the time the loss of a significant adult occurred. Psychotherapy was initiated 3, 10 and 13 years later. During treatment each patient reported an illusory experience associated with the deceased person with whom either a parental or parent-like relationship had existed. One might question the tenacity with which the immature, perceptually dominated mode of recall had been sustained over time.

Several observers, (Deutsch, 1937; Kliman, 1969), have attributed the encapsulation and intransigence of early memories to the individual's defensive effort to avoid being overwhelmed by grief and anger. In addition to the need to maintain affective boundaries, some further pressures reinforcing the static nature of these memories are suggested here.

1. It can be speculated that the memory scheme itself becomes charged with the meanings attached to the lost person. If so, relinquishing familiar modes of remembering would be equated with giving up the loved person. Thus, the development of a more rationally organized but less familiar view of the deceased could destroy the child's sense of comfort and companionship provided by his immature but thoroughly integrated representation.

2. To the degree that the early memory schemes have served as sources of identification, they also share in the structuring of the sense of self. The remembered forms can thus represent not only the internalized parent but also the picture of the self in relation to that parent. An affective connection to this early self must be retrieved and sustained before a new link to a more sophisticated memory can be effected.

3. Turning to an empirical study by Inhelder, there is a further reason for the child's retention of early memory forms. She has shown that memories of neutral stimuli can, in a sense, self-correct over time in the direction of a higher level of organization. However, Inhelder has also found that, when competing arrangements of stimuli are presented, the organization of their recall does not improve. It can be assumed that the events associated with a parent's death would contain an overwhelming number of conflicting and competing elements. It would be highly unlikely, then, for a child to reorder these events in a more rational way without external help.

In reporting the clinical data which follow only those details relating to the patient's primitive mode of remembering the lost person will be explored.

Mary, a pretty 16-year-old girl, sought treatment because of her depressed state; she cried easily and felt that she was supersensitive to criticism. She was quite lonely but while on vacation in Florida had met a boy whom she liked. He had promised to call her after they returned home, but had not done so. When at home alone, she would think of him being in the house and would, as she put it, talk to the four walls as though she were talking to him. Three months later, she reported having fantasies about a second boy friend, whom she had dated but who had not called when she expected. While waiting for his call, she felt her thoughts were like a dream. She imagined him coming into the house and her mother calling to tell her he had arrived. She became excited and, in reality, ran out of her room to meet him. Although she reported no earlier fantasies like this, she associated to an elderly man, John, a friend of her parents, who had been very affectionate and supportive to her in her early childhood. He had died when Mary was five-years-old. At the time, she was told that John had died because God takes the best people. Mary became angry at God but began to talk to John. She recalled no visual fantasy but reported having conversations with John until she was about 12-years-old. Though John's speech came from inside her, she believed it was John answering her. Interestingly, when Mary's grandmother died, Mary (11-years-old at the time) had sad memories but no fantasies or imaginary conversations with her. It is possible that the yearning for her boy friends evoked similar oedipal longings as had previously belonged to John, resulting in similar, perceptually-oriented reactions.

The next patient to be discussed is Richard who was five and one-half years old when his father died of cancer. This patient has also been described in a report by Dr. Gilbert Kliman who had supervised this case (1969). Following Richard's father's death, his brother married and moved out of the state and his sister left for college. His mother was out of the house for longer periods of time than before his father's death because she began to work. Richard was eight-years-old when his maternal grandfather died and a referral for therapy was made. In third grade, he was receiving failing marks and was inattentive and restless at school. Memory difficulties were a prominent complaint and Richard stated that he got mixed-up a lot. He evidenced many slips of the tongue in addition to forgetting school-related material. Those slips tended to be bound to references to illness and death — for instance, he called an ambulance an alabance.

When Richard did recall emotionally significant content, he often did so in a rather primitive and immature mode, i.e., in a visually-oriented context. The phenomenon included relatively benign events such as projecting the percept of a man's arm onto a tree branch outside the office window. Once Richard was momentarily confused when he almost misidentified a man who resembled his father, thinking the man was, in fact, his father. Richard also reported occasionally seeing things as appearing smaller and more distant than they were, as well as larger and closer than he knew them to be. The feeling of distance was associated with the notion of people leaving or dying. When the therapist speculated about his desire for his father to be alive again, Richard went on to reveal that he had once actually seen an image of his father who had appeared as a "very small man in the kitchen cabinet."

The therapeutic task was aimed at supporting Richard in tolerating his fear of being overwhelmed by sadness. By giving him permission to remember the therapist assumed that the visual imagery could gradually be exposed, decathected and replaced by age-appropriate memories of his loss. The fear and guilt associated with losing control over his sad feelings were clearly expressed when Richard told this story:

> A boy began to cry and flood his home with his tears. When he attempted to cover his eyes, the tears escaped these openings but experienced such pressure that he thought he would crack up. To prevent more flooding, the boy left home and cried for 200 years, flooding a complete desert. Finally, an Indian shot the boy for ruining the ground with his tears.

It was not hard to understand why Richard felt that remembering just causes trouble. Though his school work improved, he was reluctant to report more memories during the sessions because doing so would get him down. After 16 months, Richard improved both at school and on the WISC. His progress was understood in terms of his diminished need to use his memory as a wish-dominated vehicle which retained his father's image. Memory, as an ego function, was becoming increasingly autonomous.

Now let us examine some treatment segments of work with a 20-year-old woman whose mother died of breast cancer when the patient was also five years old. Here, too, visual imagery constituted an important mode of yearning, as with Richard, but she also had conversations with her mother that are reminiscent of Mary's talks with John.

The patient, Helen, was admitted to a psychiatric hospital following a suicide attempt by cutting her wrists with a razor. (She was treated by Pam Kingsley who was supervised by the author.) She was the second of three children who, following their mother's death, were cared for by housekeepers for three years, when their father remarried. From ages of 5 to 10 years, she maintained an elaborate fantasy of her mother being with her at all times. She reported occasions when she would ask her friends to leave her alone so that she could be with her mother. Helen viewed her mother as standing on top of clouds from where Helen's every move could be seen and heard by her. Helen further reported that at the age of 18 years, while shopping at a department store, she saw a woman who resembled her mother, walking with a small girl. She followed this woman around the store, believing that the woman was her mother and was raising a duplicate child.

At one time, Helen reported the delusion that her therapist was her real mother. During this period, she would accept food only from her therapist. Thus, we see the projection of her mother's image onto another significant adult.

Helen's regressions into intense anger and paranoia were precipitated most typically by experiences associated with death or departures.

When confronted by the fact that a psychotic episode seemed to have been precipitated by the death of her friend's grandmother, Helen began to discuss the death of her own grandfather (he had died four days before Helen's suicide attempt). With additional work focused on the issues of mourning, Helen emerged from her psychotic state with some distance from and tolerance for the pain and anger associated with loss.

These examples demonstrate some of the pathological consequences of loss in early childhood. Pollock (1961) attributes the persistence of similar illusory experiences to the incomplete identification of the young child with the lost parent. As he points out, "When an object has been introjected without identification, it exists as an encapsulated image in the ego . . . ." He reports that three adult patients, each of whom had encountered the death of a parent before six years had retained the lost parent "as a figure that can be spoken to, and envisioned." Pollock further states that "the denial of its (the parent's) demise interferes with mourning."

Notwithstanding the obstacles to mourning inherent in a fragmentary, incomplete identification with the lost parent, might not the early schemes of remembering contain a facilitating element, contributing positively to the bereaved child's response to loss? It may be hypothesized that prior to latency the child requires a period of affectively bound clinging to sensory images. The persistence of an illusory percept as the only form of memory possible may serve as a necessary step in the identification process. The child may require, to paraphrase Winnicott, "a transitional illusion" until cognitive and emotional developments permit a different form of remembering and grieving. The ultimate work of separating the affective bond from the parental image would be postponed until late adolescence or early adulthood when a neutral, objective cognitive structure is available. The basic requirements for adaptive mourning, noted by Anna Freud and elaborated by R. Furman, include a realistic understanding of the concept of death, ego mastery over aggression, an ability to deal with the potentially overwhelming affects of anger and grief, and a relationship with the parent that is sufficiently loving and stable to be sustained in his or her absence. In addition, it is being suggested here, a child requires permission to retain the representation of the loved person in whatever form or fantasy it emerges.

It is speculated that once the prerequisites for mourning are met and support and empathy from relevant adults are available to counteract a surviving child's sense of guilt and deprivation, an adaptive mourning response may occur. Most likely some form of enlightened, if not professional, intervention would be required under any conditions following the death of a parent. The impact of such a loss, though of necessity traumatic, would depend on other circumstances as well. These include (A. Freud, 1960) the personality of the child prior to bereavement, life circumstances, the child's relationship to the surviving parent, the sex of the parent and the child, the circumstances of the parent's death and the child's comprehension of it. Research with a non-patient population of parentally bereaved children would be extremely valuable in further examining the possibility of adaptive mourning reactions in childhood.

Wolfenstein (1966) has reported the satisfactory development of a 10-year-old boy who, following the death of his mother, was able to transfer his love to an already familiar and loving grandmother. In contrast to the clinical material of the younger bereaved patients described previously, this boy, 10-years-old at the time of his bereavement was at an age when memories can occur in a comparatively coherent manner. More significant, perhaps, is the fact that a loving substitute had been available before his mother's death. The perception of himself could remain more or less stable as the shift in love object occurred. Whether the grandmother may have served, further, as a symbolic representation of the mother or been, in some sense, fused with her is another possible facilitating factor (A. Freud, 1960).

Bettelheim (1976) points the way to a favorable outcome of childhood mourning in his understanding of Cinderella's difficulties and ultimate triumph. He describes a poor girl, living with her father, stepmother and two stepsisters, mourning the death of her own mother as she, Cinderella, lived among the ashes. Finally, with her father's help, she obtained a twig which she planted on her mother's grave, "she wept and thus watered it so that it grew and became a beautiful tree." Bettelheim suggests that through the tree Cinderella kept alive in herself an idealized memory of her mother. This symbol helped her sustain trust and gain support to help her in the worst adversities. Following the expression of sadness and of hope in planting the twig, our young woman conquered the difficulties that stood in the way of her growing up and marrying her prince. It would appear that by preserving the symbolic existence of her dead mother, Cinderella was enabled to leave the ashes and use the magic that granted her success.

Cinderella's story conveys the possibilities that can occur only in the later phase of maturation. In line with this paper's hypothesis, is the notion that memories can be sorted out, objectified and still be emotionally significant only toward the end of adolescence. Modulation and representation of sadness and yearning together with the objectification of memories enabled Cinderella to mourn her mother's death. The patients discussed earlier lacked the emotional and cognitive resources that would help them contain their unhappiness and organize their memories through a conceptual pathway. It is believed that pathological mourning as an adult can be averted only when the bereaved child can tolerate his feeling and face without fear his confusing immature fantasies. Only then can his memory ultimately become a coherent and, even, comforting part of his mental life.

I would like to conclude at this point with a question rather than an answer. It appears to me that empirical studies of the imagery, fantasies, and memories of children who have lost a parent would offer significant clues to the methods of adaptive mourning that are possible for children. Examination of literature and the arts provides ample evidence of symbolic expression and creative resolutions to the task of mourning in adults. How best to describe and facilitate an adaptive response to the death of a parent in childhood remains a vital problem.

REFERENCES

Bettelheim, B. 1976. *The Uses of Enchantment.* New York: Knopf.

Blatt, S.J. 1974. "Levels of Object Representation in Anaclitic and and Introjective Depression." *Psychoanalytic Study of the Child* 29, 107-157.

Bowlby, J. 1960. "Grief and Mourning in Infancy and Early Childhood." *Psychoanalytic Study of the Child* 15, 9-52.

Bowlby, J. 1961. "Process of Mourning." *International Journal of Psychoanalysis* 42, 317-340.

Bowlby, J. 1963. "Pathological Mourning and Childhood Mourning." *Journal of American Psychoanalytic Association* 11, 500-541.

Deutsch, H. 1937. "Absence of Grief." *Psychoanalytic Quarterly* 6, 12-22.

Freud, A. 1960. "Discussion of John Bowlby's Paper." *Psychoanalytic Study of the Child,* 53-62.

Freud, S. 1957. *Mourning and Melancholia.* Standard Edition, 14. 237-258. London: Hogarth Press.

Freud, S. 1955. *Beyond the Pleasure Principle.* Standard Edition, 18. London: Hogarth Press.

Furman, E. 1974. *A Child's Parent Dies.* New Haven: Yale University Press.

Furman, R. 1964. "Death and the Young Child." *Psychoanalytic Study of the Child* 19, 377-397.

Inhelder, B. 1969. "Memory and Intelligence in the Child." in D. Elkind and J. Flavell, eds., *Studies in Cognitive Development.* New York: Oxford University Press, 337-364.

Inhelder, B. and J. Piaget. 1958. *The Growth of Logical Thinking from Childhood to Adolescence.* New York: Basic Books.

Kliman, G. 1969. *Facilitation of Mourning During Childhood.* Draft Presented at American Orthopsychiatric Association, New York, (April).

Lopez, T. and G. Kliman. 1979. "Memory, Reconstruction and Mourning in the Analysis of a Four-Year-Old Child." *Psychoanalytic Study of the Child* 34, 235-271.

Nagera, H. 1970. "Children's Reactions to the Death of Important Objects." *Psychoanalytic Study of the Child,* 360-400.

Pollock, G.H. 1961. "Mourning and Adaptation." *International Journal of Psychoanalysis* 42, 341-361.

Pollock, G.H. 1979. "Process and Affect: Mourning and Grief." *International Journal of Psychoanalysis* 59, 255-276.

Rochlin, G. 1961. "The Dread of Abandonment." *Psychoanalytic Study of the Child* 16, 451-470.

Wolfenstein, M. 1966. "How is Mourning Possible?" *Psychoanalytic Study of the Child* 21, 93-123.

Wolfenstein, M. 1969. "Loss, Range and Repetition." *Psychoanalytic Study of the Child* 24, 432-460.

SOME INSIGHTS FROM COUNSELING BEREAVED PARENTS
James Zimmerman

"I was taught to kill, I was taught to survive, but I was never taught to deal with death. And I did not know how to cope." Those words convey the hurt and the frustration of a man whose teenage son suffered for ten months from a brain tumor — until he died.

Another father said, "We don't teach children to deal with death. People don't die at home any more, so children are pushed away from the reality of death." And he, too, knew whereof he spoke, for his son had lain in a coma for four months before his death.

A mother reported that something happened to her friends from the time her son was pronounced ill and terminal. People would visit him when he was sick, but they stayed away and kept their children away when they were told that he was going to die.

These are comments from parents who had something in common. That commonality was having a child who, either through an accident or through illness, lived for a time and then died from that accident or illness. These parents shared many experiences, both positive and negative, in a group for bereaved parents. The children of these couples included two teenage children involved in automobile accidents — one in a coma for five days before her death, the other in a coma four months before his death. Two of the children, ages ten and seventeen, have suffered from brain tumors. The period of dealing with this reality was ten months with one family and fifteen months with the other. The final child was a young man who, at the age of 20, died following four and a half years of leukemia. Five mothers and five fathers shared several long evening with me, sometimes in tears and sometimes in anger — and sometimes in laughter — reaching back into their personal histories, which contained, as one father stated, the greatest hurt that one can ever know. Their child had died. They shared their feelings because they knew that through their words, their needs and feelings and hurts and hopes could be made known to others who deal with both parents and children in the crises of illness and suffering and death.

When I asked the question, "What was your greatest need during that time when your child was ill and dying?," the answers came quickly. Said one mother, "I wanted to be with my child, so I could talk with him and touch him." Responded a father, "I needed someone to whom I could talk, not someone with a lot of set answers, but someone who could talk with me from the heart." Said another, "I needed strength to lie to my son for four and a half years," and that man later said that he was sorry he had lied to his son, because never before had he done that. "I needed help from my friends, in just small ways," replied the mother, who daily made trips from Long Island to a New York City hospital with her son. "Just someone to offer to clean my house, or to fix a meal for my family, or to go food shopping with me. I needed someone to supply companionship."

Out of that comment came a unanimous agreement that the famous "If there is anything I can do to help, please let me know" offers no help whatsoever, because a parent in such a state of shock needs specific help at that time and is not able to ask for specifics. Most of the parents expressed great disappointment in family and in those considered to be good friends. Often it happened that when the crisis developed, the "good friends" failed to give the support, and it was unexpected people who so often came to be with them to give offerings of love and concern. One parent related how his own parents, brothers and sisters began to complain about lending a hand or doing a favor or even visiting his son in the hospital. The excuse always seemed to be "I can't cope with it." But, as the mother explained, "They knew they did not have to cope with it — we did. He was our child, not theirs."

"People failed us," one parent shouted in anger. "My son's friends used to come and visit him when he was ill, but when we discovered that he had a brain tumor, and that he was terminal, not only did the visits stop, but one of our very best friends, a mother, refused to let her children come to visit our son. And what do you say when your son asks, 'Why don't my friends come to visit me any more?' "

All of this was summed up by a parent who concluded, "You find out who your real friends are, and you discover those who are truly members of the family."

The needs of those parents then began to focus on two groups of people, two professions, who by the nature of their jobs worked closely with the lives of suffering parents and children — the clergy and the doctors.

To the clergy they said, " We look to you at this time in life for strength and support, but so often you do not seem to understand our needs and our hurts." They spoke of clergy who seemed very afraid of the whole death situation, who offered pat answers and worn out cliches, who gave parents the feeling that they were only performing their duties. One couple told of a particularly insensitive comment made by their clergyman when the report came that their child was terminal. He responded, "You should consider having another child." Such a statement totally denies the feelings and the needs of the parents at that moment. That is precisely what they did not need to hear at that time.

It seems that there are many clergy, as there are many medical personnel, who cannot deal with the reality of death. Clergy who see death as a threat and a failure on the part of God to respond to their prayers, and think they must defend Him, are like medical personnel, doctors specifically, who see death as a personal and professional defeat. What do these people want from their clergy? They want them to just be there, to be a friend, to touch them, not necessarily to say so many words — because often words are wrong, and the wrong words only make things worse — but to be there as a friend, to show that they honestly hurt with their people, that they care for them, that they love them and are willing to cry with them.

"Give us hope," cried one man. "Give us the message that the resurrection of the dead and life after death are reality." And how interesting to me that he was an agnostic. To his plea I would personally add that clergy who are desperately needed by these parents as a source of strength and hope had better struggle very diligently through their own theology of death and their own theology of resurrection, for if you have no hope to offer to these people, you have no business attempting to minister to their needs.

That very word *hope* was dominant as the parents talked about the doctors. One couple spoke of their doctor's honesty in telling them that because of their son's brain tumor the chances of his surviving were very slim. "But," he added, "you never know." And for these parents that glimmer of hope gave them time to deal with what finally became a reality to them, that their son was indeed going to die. Another couple shared that their doctor gave absolutely no hope whatsoever for their child, who also suffered from a brain tumor. So they began to manufacture hope for themselves — they convinced themselves that the doctor was wrong. And they said that this approach helped them through that initial period of unbelief and inability to accept, until finally they were able to cope with the reality of their son's death. Another couple spoke of the differing approaches of two doctors who dealt with their son. One flatly said, "There is no hope." The other said, "It's bad, but we're going to hang in there. And when I call you in, and tell you that there is no hope, then you can believe that." And later when he did call them in, they knew why they were going, and they were ready to accept that.

The comments about doctors can be summarized in two main pleas: Number 1, Doctors, please be willing to admit that medicine is not an exact science, which strangely enough is a word of hope for these people. Number 2, Doctors, please tell us the truth, but do it with compassion and do it with understanding. *Compassion* and *understanding,* two words that these parents chose as intensely as they chose the word *hope.* In fact, time after time in our discussions about doctors or nurses or clergy or social workers or friends or family, the same words were voiced: Have compassion. Be understanding. Take the time to listen to our needs. Treat us as human beings. Be sensitive to us. Listen to us. And love us.

How interesting was the comment, accepted by all, that very often the bigger the doctor, the better known, the more important he was, the easier it was to talk to him and the more he talked with them.

One couple shared with me their feelings about and their experiences with a very special doctor. The first statement they made about him was one of the most powerful and beautiful tributes I have ever heard given to any person. They said he was a doctor who started to treat the parents as soon as he began to treat the child. He was a doctor who loved his patients; he was a man who was kind, who had great compassion and understanding. At the end of one or our meetings, those parents showed me a letter written by this doctor to them, following the death of their son. The letter gave them untold strength and peace as he shared with them his humanity.

The plea of the parents to doctors is: Doctors, please take the time to talk with your patients and their families, because they need to hear from you a word of hope, they need to know that you care, and they need especially to know that everything humanly possible has been done for the survival and for the comfort of their child.

That concern also came up in a discussion regarding autopsies. There was a sense of frustration among the parents that it was difficult to get from anyone a final cause of death. The mother of the boy who had been in a coma for four months indicated how important it was for her to know how extensive the damage had been to her son, for in this way she felt that she could be assured that everything possible had been done for him and that indeed there had been no possibility for him to live any longer. Therefore, again, another plea to doctors: Doctors, sit with the parents, explain the autopsy report to them, and through that be able to give them a sense of peace.

There were other parents who had bad feelings regarding autopsies. One parent said, "It's the final abuse, the final insult. After my child had been in two hospitals, after 16 doctors had been involved with him, the final insult was to demand an autopsy." The father added angrily, "When someone requests an autopsy, and the parents say no to that request, it should be taken as the final answer. One doctor replied to that answer, 'Well, it may help someone else's child.' What is being done then is the placement of a guilt trip on the parent." This was a parent who on the one hand would never want to deny another child an opportunity for medical help, but a parent on the other hand who had witnessed the suffering and the agony of his own child, and who wanted not one more thing done to the body of that child, whom he still loved.

And how important is that child even if they have lost all normal functions, as explained by the woman who cried, "I object to the term *vegetable*. My son is not a cabbage, my son is a person, my son is my child, you call him by name, do not call him a vegetable." She told of how she took a sign that a friend had made with her son's name on it, a very large sign, which she put over his bed, so that everyone who entered the room would know that his name was Mark, that he was a person.

And she suggested that instead of calling such a person a vegetable, could it not be said that he is like a newborn baby, who cannot be improved upon, or rather who cannot improve?

The desire to love and protect that child from unnecessary hurt and suffering came out also in the parents' denouncement of what they called the goon squads. "Every day," said the father of a young boy aged six or seven, "doctors and three and four nurses would walk into my son's room. They would stand at his bed and look at him. They would talk for a while and then walk away. Can you imagine what that did to my child? And can you imagine what he thought when one doctor asked the mother, 'How long has your son had cancer?' " Up to that point the child had not known that he had cancer.

A father pleaded, "Doctors, treat my child as if he were your own, become a parent to my child, become a part of me, for I put into your hands my dearest possession." That thought was echoed by the mother who said, "My son had a surgeon who spoke of his spleen, he had a neurosurgeon who discussed his brain, he had a urologist who talked of his urine, he had a lung specialist who reported on his lungs, but there was no one there to treat him as a person or to speak of him as a person – they were just treating his parts."

Perhaps this can be summed up in a rather unique statement by a doctor who years ago practiced medicine in the Midwest, a doctor with whom I was sharing some of the responses of these bereaved parents. He said, "You may remember that some 50 to 100 years ago doctors had digitalis for heart failure, quinine for malaria, and morphine and aspirin for pain, and the rest of their healing they did with compassion, concern, and care." And he went on to say something that I think is not only for doctors but for everyone: "It's too easy for a doctor today, with all the specializing, to become a mechanic rather than an artist." To be an artist to people, to be artistic in the sense of caring, sensitivity, compasssion, understanding, those qualities must be fostered by all people – whether hospital personnel, administrators, clergy, whoever – all people who touch the lives of people who suffer.

Sometimes hospitals have dehumanizing rules. In one hospital's intensive care unit, visitation could be only four times a day, with a maximum of ten minutes per visit. Furthermore, the ruling was that only one person at one time could visit the patient, which meant that the mother and father could never be together with their dying child at the same time. And what happened to a couple when one day they went to visit their child in this intensive-care unit? As the people were being let in, a nurse asked these parents and an elderly gentleman who was waiting there to wait outside for a few moments. Shortly, a nurse came out and spoke to the older man, and said, "I'm very sorry to inform you that your wife has died." And immediately these parents assumed that they had been detained for the same reason. Later it was announced to them that their son was being given a bath, and that's why they were not allowed to enter. The mother said, "A brief word of explanation would have spared us so much panic."

Some parents experienced going to their son's room following his dismissal from intensive care to find it empty. Again the same thought came into their minds: that he had died. Then it was explained that he had been moved to another room without their knowledge. The mother asked, "Could not a note have been put on the door to that effect, telling us the new room number?"

A request was made by these parents that medical personnel not discuss the condition of patients in public — in hallways, in elevators, in waiting rooms — where everyone else can hear. One parent, hearing a gloomy comment from a doctor who had just come from the room of his child, thought the doctor was speaking of his child. It turned out to be about the child's roommate. Another father, following tests on his son, heard a staff member yell across a considerable distance to a colleague that the tumor was twice the size of the one that had been taken out, and this father knew for certain they were talking about his son. and thus the news that his son would soon die came not from his doctor, in the privacy of his office, but was shouted for all to hear in the public hallway.

Additional insensitivity was experienced by these parents with those people who deal with the business side of life and death. "Everyone wants the almighty dollar!" cried out one father, and after he said that, there came the sharing of many common experiences. One doctor announced, "I'm expensive, so if you can afford me I will help you." And the unspoken words that the parents felt ended his sentence were "and if not, then the hell with you." An insurance agent appeared at the home of the family of the teenage girl the day after her auto accident, when she lay in a coma in the hospital, and wanted to make some settlements.

Parents who went for aid to their own religious charitable agency were told they could not be helped, and then were charged $35 for that information. "You have to be flat on your back and stripped of all your dignity before they will help you," lamented one man. "You get the feeling that when your money runs out, you should pack your bags and get out." Most of the parents indicated that never again would they contribute any money to any charities, because so few had helped them. They would contribute only to individuals. One spoke of never again giving blood, because their son had need of 100 pints of blood, which they were required to repay two for one. They repaid through donors, and they were charged $3000 in "blood-processing fees."

"We need help at this time of our lives," pleaded a father, "for we are in a state of shock and have difficulty in thinking clearly." And he gave some suggestions. A need for a reference book of all the organizations that might help them. A need for hospital social workers to come and clear up confusion for them. A need for a clergyperson to help them and their child and the children at home to face the reality of death. Basically, what they were saying was that they had a need for people to care abut them as people.

But there are many people who do care for them. They spoke of the nurses stopping in after hours to talk with them, taking their own time to let those parents know that someone cares. They spoke of doctors who showed great love and compassion for their patients, who took the time to explain, to listen to the fears of patients and parents. They described the hospital that allows 24 hour visitation in the intensive-care unit. They told stories about medical personnel, clergy, neighbors, friends, and churches who uplifted them in the time of crisis.

Someone has wisely written that learning to die is part of living, and as we share together both the reality of death and the celebration of life, we might all dwell on the words of a ten-year old boy. He had a brain tumor, he had gone through months of chemotherapy, he was beginning to go blind, he was physically disabled, he was confined to a wheelchair, and he remarked one day to his mother, "I'm glad that I was born." To this day his parents are not completely certain what that statement meant to him, but the words are carved on his gravestone, "Glad to Be Born," and with this same sense of the celebration of life, with that same sense of thanksgiving for life, with that same sense of the dignity of life, we are called to handle with compassion and love the gift of life.

LITERATURE FOR YOUNG PEOPLE: NONFICTION BOOKS ABOUT DEATH
Joanne E. Bernstein

The nonfiction book about death and suicide is a recent phenomenon in literature for young people, beginning quietly in 1965 with an information book in verse by Audrey Harris, *Why Did He Die?* The movement then lay dormant for five years, until Herbert Zim and Sonia Bleeker wrote *Life and Death*. Momentum built slowly at first, and then the pace quickened. The middle and late seventies saw a spate of books on the subject. To this date, interest on the part of publishers, authors, and the public has not abated. Perhaps this is because Gerald Koocher's research has tapped a deep and meaningful truth. His young subjects revealed intense curiosity about all matters pertaining to death (Koocher 1973). Their need to know is being addressed at last.

To my knowledge, approximately twenty nonfiction titles about death have been published for children. In contrast to the fiction in this area, the number is very small. Yet at first glance it might appear that the nonfiction would be even more limited. After all, in fiction, the same themes can be successfully batted around endlessly because each author brings to the material a unique world view. In nonfiction, isn't there just so much information to be given to youngsters and that's all? This has not been the case. Each book published has accomplished something new, explored a different point of view, come from another background.

Witness the varied approaches: There is a book from an anthropologist, Turner's *Houses for the Dead*. Within are spirited stories of how various cultures have coped over time, from the ancients to the recent Irish. An historical perspective is taken by Stanley Klein in *The Mystery of Death* and by Margaret Coffin in *Death in Early America*. The former is unique in its overview of death prevention through the generations, while the latter is a solid reference work that demonstrates ways in which artifacts such as tombstones, coffins, and mourning paraphernalia are reflections of their times.

The biology and ecology people must have their say, too, and indeed they have, in a book for older readers (*Death Is a Noun*, by Langone) and in books for younger readers, such as Pringle's *Death Is Natural* and Simon's *Life and Death in Nature*. Pringle brings to his book a thought found nowhere else in books for the seven-to-eleven age group: The forceful idea that the human race may be in for self-imposed extinction and that, in addition, this would be acceptable and natural. "In the long view of the earth's history . . . the death of a species is no more remarkable than the death of one rabbit. . . . Other living things survive and change. . . . There is beauty, variety, and change, and death helps make it all possible" (Pringle 1977). Although Simon's title resembles Pringle's, Simon gives readers a dimension he has brought to his many other science books: experiments. Death experiments? you ask. Yes, in which earthworms are grown and their survival compared in crowded and uncrowded environments.

Some of the books are multidisciplinary in approach: Langone is more than biology. So is Segerberg's masterful title, *Living with Death*. Both approach the subject from anthropological, theological, historical, and thanatological vantage points. Both ask teenagers to philosophize and think more deeply.

Then there are the very specialized books—Klagsbrun's *Too Young to Die* and Madison's *Suicide and Young People* deal only with suicide, and the suicide of youth at that. Eda LeShan's *Learning to Say Goodbye* concentrates on the death of a parent. Like the three books above and *Living with Death*, my *Loss: And How to Cope with It* would be considered in the self-help category.

It is said that it takes ten years or so for adult trends in literature to reach books for young people. For much longer than ten years self-help books have been big sellers on the adult lists; their day is dawning only now in children's books.

Nonfiction books about death have been in the vanguard in the creation and promotion of new forms of writing for young people. Asinof's *Craig and Joan*, the story of two teenagers who committed suicide in order to speak out against the Vietnam War, is an example. Utilizing the finest journalism techniques, the author interviewed friends and relatives of the pair. Readers are compelled to ask, is altruistic suicide an appropriate choice? Are there better alternatives?

The use of case histories is another technique from adult literature that has been a part of books about death for younger readers. In *Death: Everyone's Heritage*, Landau reviews the lives of some who have had abortions, some who have tried suicide, and others who have tasted of death. Returning to Pringle, his case histories of animals are as interesting as those of human beings and as instructive. Klagsbrun, Madison, and LeShan also use this technique, in comprehensive, warm ways, and with ability to use studies in order to guide readers toward success in living with the survivors of death's ravages. Klagsbrun speaks of breaking the suicide cycle formed by guilt and poor self-esteem. Madison shatters common myths about suicide and successfully speaks to younger teens and some preteens. LeShan lovingly helps youngsters adjust to the possibility of a parent's second marriage. I, too, used case studies in *Loss*, and I hope I managed compassionate communication.

Compassion is a hallmark of another unique form developed in the nonfiction about death for young people—that form being the dialogue between parent and child. Earl Grollman uses this in *Talking About*

Death. In few pages and few words, a youngster and parent simply but eloquently discuss the death of the child's grandparent. Readers extrapolate to the person they both love and miss.

Dialogue is also encouraged in Stein's book *About Dying*. A dual narrative is introduced—one for the child to read or have read, the second for the parent to read beforehand. The adult narrative explains the psychodynamics of loss reactions.

Exploration of grief and mourning has been a part of the "death book" scene for children from the very beginning. *Why Did He Die?*, way back in 1965, even preceded the explosion of such books on the market for adults. Kubler-Ross says it well for *her* readership; Harris says it well for *hers*: "To lose what we love, and can never get back/ /Leaves us with a painful sore,/ /It's hard to think his Granddad's gone–/ /Jim won't see him anymore" (Harris 1965).

Perhaps the newest in adult forms to reach the young people's market is the psychohistory. Lifton and Olson's *Living and Dying* is of this genre. In an intellectually demanding book appropriate for late teens and adults, the authors investigate the relationship between music, poetry, and other arts to death imagery during the perilous nuclear age.

One of the most positive aspects of all the books about death and suicide cited is the fact that no matter what angle the author has taken, the level of scholarship has been extremely high. This, too, reflects a growing trend in nonfiction in general—only the highest levels of accuracy and honesty will do. In books about death, this means telling kindergarten students that, yes, children do occasionally die. This was part of *When People Die*, the picture book I did with Stephen Gullo. It's also part of Corley's *Tell Me About Death; Tell Me About Funerals* and Harris's *Why Did He Die?*

For the authors of most of the books discussed in this article, maintenance of high levels of scholarship meant in-depth probing of losses beyond one's own. Stein did this in consultation with the Center for Preventive Psychiatry in White Plains, New York, and other clinics specializing in crisis intervention. With her research giving her confidence, she could comfortably describe, both for the four-year-old and her mother, children's curiosity about corpses and their reactions to rigor mortis. Extensive research is what enabled Klagsbrun to take a deep breath and shock some parents and adolescents with self-recognition. She noted that some mothers and fathers want their children to be inactive so that things will be easier. Many youngsters strive to please by becoming passive and emotionless—dead for most purposes.

Careful research implies balanced examination of issues and dilemmas in today's society: the reversibility of death, euthanasia, cryonics, afterlife, and so on. Careful research is also called for in the presentation of religious beliefs and prescriptions for living. In contrast to some of the fiction about death, almost all the religious views of death in the nonfiction are handled cross-culturally, from a historical vantage point. One opinion and only one is rarely espoused. An exception is the Harris book, in which God is reported to be with the grandfather in the cemetery. Some authors are especially strong in their exploration of controversy, both religious and nonreligious. These include Langone, Lifton and Olson, Segerberg, and Landau.

Even though certain authors have given readers more than one side to think about, they are also unafraid to take a stance. Lifton and Olson expound upon transcendent experiences of many kinds as ways to counter overwhelming death imagery in a world gone crazy. In my own books and books such as Klagsbrun's and LeShan's, we espouse expression and communication as ways to exorcize death's pain and get on with the risk taking of life. Segerberg speaks to young people of this, also introducing life-affirming decisions versus death-seeking decisions. His plea is that youngsters stay away from drugs and cigarettes. Somehow, for me at least, none of these nonfiction books moralize. When Segerberg says that putting on a seatbelt is a decision favoring life over death, I'm impressed, and I remember his words every time I get into a car.

Meticulous research and point of view stretch beyond the main texts of these books. Many sport first-rate bibliographies—not just books but also listings of films and social agencies. As an example, Madison's book about suicide provides a state-by-state directory of treatment centers.

With all these virtues, it's not surprising to find that many of the books for young people have also reached and touched adults. Older readers are often unaware that they are reading material originally published for children. Within this category are *Death Is a Noun, Death in Early America, Houses for the Dead, Living and Dying, Loss, Living with Death, Learning to Say Good-bye,* and *Too Young to Die.* The last two books were afforded promotion on the *Today* show, and neither was introduced as a juvenile title.

You may wonder who these people are and how they came to write about such a topic. Almost all the books cited are by professional writers who've done other things. Some are science writers—Langone, Pringle, and Zim. A number specialize in writing about feelings—LeShan, Grollman, and Stein. Corley, the author of *Tell Me About Death* . . . is a funeral director. Some consider themselves to be thanatologists—Klagsbrun and her husband are leaders in the study of grief and mourning, as is Grollman, who is a rabbi. Lifton and Olson have devoted themselves to psychohistory, particularly as related to war.

Several authors speak in their books of how they wrote in order to help themselves cope with the loss of relatives. Besides me, also in this camp are LeShan and Turner. There are probably more. It's interesting to note that while Turner's book is a cross-cultural study undertaken primarily in the cool world of the research library, writing it warmed the heart of this author, whose mother had recently died.

In order to cope with the seriousness of the material, many of these books, for younger children especially, utilize a fictional device to get across information. *Why Did He Die?*, *Talking About Death*, *About Dying*, *Tell Me About Death* . . ., and *When People Die* all incorporate the death of a grandparent or elderly person into the manuscript, hinging the nonfiction material onto a concrete individual. When Steve Gullo and I did *When People Die*, the first draft had no main character. Was it ever depressing! We questioned, and others did, too, if readers would stay around to turn the pages. It seemed nearly impossible to grab interest at all without a focus. That focus became, for us, a fictional elementary school principal named Mrs. Michaelson.

When I read the book to classes, as I sometimes do, the youngsters have opportunities not normally available to library readers. Inevitably they ask me if Mrs. Michaelson is really dead. I then say, "No, she's alive and well and living in Connecticut." Some children are horrified that a book "lies." They are interested, however, when I then go into several aspects of the making of the book. I wonder if they realize how brave a woman in her eighties must be to pose in photographs as someone who has died. Surely they don't know that, in spite of the lifting of the death taboo, the photographer couldn't get anyone at all to pose in a cemetery. Finally my own family, the photographer and her husband, and two of my students formed the group. Coincidentally, the session took place on Halloween.

All the nonfiction in which a main character is developed has an older person do the dying. You may ask if this is a reflection of the author's discomfort or a reflection of statistical reality. Younger folks, even children, die in fiction for youngsters. I don't truly know the answer to this question.

Books about death are now available for all age groups—from kindergarten through high school. *About Dying*, for example, is written on a first-grade reading level, a typical page reading: "Be quiet. Grandpa is sick" (Stein 1974). On the opposite pole is *Living and Dying*, which demands of readers vast background in both history and psychology. Interestingly, though, adults have commented that they've been satisfied and reassured by books written for all the age groups. Some of the books for younger readers provide technical information that some adults are grateful to learn. *Tell Me About Death* . . . does this in distinguishing a mausoleum from a columbarium. Adults have also been comforted by emphasis in many of the books on the universality of human concerns.

The climate of the past decade has allowed these nonfiction books to surface. While each book offers a different thrust, all have stressed or implied the value in expressing one's feelings about the issues of the day. All have seen as an underpinning the idea that in aging and dying there is a natural end to the cycle of life, and that though one's life is finite, one has the capacity to continue in the minds and hearts of survivors in the form of memories.

Finally, all the books stress the point that the quality of one's life is more important than the length of its span. The celebration of well-lived years is expressed by Osborn Segerberg, Jr. (1976): "Death's sting is to die unfulfilled. A vaccine against this mortal sting is to live a full life, a rewarding life, and if possible, a long life."

REFERENCES

Asinof, Eliot. 1971. *Craig and Joan: Two Lives for Peace.* New York: Viking, Age 12+.

Bernstein, Joanne E. 1977. *Loss: And How to Cope with It.* New York: Seabury, Age 11+.

Bernstein, Joanne E., and Gullo, Stephen V. 1977. *When People Die.* New York: Dutton, Ages 6-10.

Coffin, Margaret. 1976. *Death in Early America.* New York: Nelson, Age 12+.

Corley, Elizabeth. 1973. *Tell Me About Death; Tell Me About Funerals.* Santa Clara, Cal.: Grammatical Sciences, Ages 6-10.

Grollman, Earl. 1970. *Talking About Death.* Boston: Beacon, Age 5+.

Harris, Audrey. 1965. *Why Did He Die?* Minneapolis: Lerner, Ages 5-9.

Klagsbrun, Francine. 1976. *Too Young to Die: Youth and Suicide.* Boston: Houghton Mifflin, Age 12+.

Klein, Stanley. 1975. *The Final Mystery.* Garden City, N.Y.: Doubleday, Ages 8-13.

Koocher, Gerald. 1973. *Childhood, Death, and Cognitive Development. Developmental Psychology* 9:369 1/N 75.

Landau, Elaine. 1976. *Death: Everyone's Heritage.* New York: Messner, Age 11.

Langone, John. 1972. *Death Is a Noun.* Boston: Little, Brown, Age 12+.

LeShan, Eda. 1976. *Learning to Say Good-bye: When a Parent Dies.* New York: Macmillan, Age 8+.

Lifton, Robert Jay, and Olson, Eric. 1974. *Living and Dying.* New York: Praeger, Age 14+.

Madison, Arnold. 1978. *Suicide and Young People.* New York: Seabury, Age 10+.

THE TOPIC OF DEATH IN CHILDREN'S LITERATURE
Phyllis L. Schneider

Until fairly recently, death, as depicted or referred to in literature for children, was something that happened to witches, pirates, dragons, and, occasionally, to beautiful princesses. In the case of the princesses, it was even a reversible condition once the handsome prince arrived on the scene. There was little in the portrayal of death in children's literature that had any relevance for them in real life or could help them to understand or cope with death and grief when they encountered it.

And yet great numbers of children encounter death, in one aspect or another, during their formative years. Death may enter the child's life when a loved pet, a relative, or even a plant or tree dies. Characteristically, parents and others working with children have little difficulty dealing with the death of inanimate objects such as plants and trees. It seems easy to acknowledge the finality of the life process when we are speaking of plants and trees, or even of animals. However, when the death of people arises, the situation changes.

It is inevitable that many of us, as educators and/or health professionals, will encounter children who are facing either their own death or that of someone dear to them, or who have just suffered the loss of a parent, brother or sister, or friend. What should we do, what should we say, how can we help when our own child, our student, or our young patient meets death in his or her life? We are told by many practitioners that we should help children understand and accept the loss and their feelings toward it; that we should treat the subject honestly and openly; that we should avoid euphemisms such as "She passed away" or "He has gone to sleep." Most of the advice we receive on helping children cope with death and grief comes in the form of "do's" and "do not's." There has been precious little guidance in the area of "how" to help.

Today, some "how to" assistance is becoming available through literature. In addition to the compassion and guidance that we can offer children, we now have available scores of children's books that we can employ in a bibliotherapeutic way to help children understand and cope with their feelings of grief and loss. Not only are many of these books sensitive to the topic, but they are good literature.

It is not within the scope of this paper to engage in a detailed discussion of the theory and practice of bibliotherapy or to suggest it as a universal panacea. It is, rather, my intent to provide information on specific children's books dealing with death, in the hope that people working with children will be able to render well-informed judgments on the use of books in helping children cope with the guilt, loss, grief, self-pity, and other feelings that often arise on occasions of death.

In addition to books designed for children, the last few years have also seen the emergence of several books, written for adults, that are concerned with helping children understand and cope with death. One of the best of these is Eda LeShan's *Learning To Say Good-bye*, a straightforward book concerning the death of a parent. LeShan tells the reader that her purpose in writing the book is to help people face the fact of death and to avoid situations such as the one LeShan's mother endured when, as a four-year-old, her mother died and the family attempted to shield the child from the truth. LeShan's mother went on for many months feeling deserted, lonely, and guilty, and without being able to discuss her feelings with those close to her. *Learning To Say Good-bye* is written so that children from about grade three upward can read it, but LeShan suggests that parents and other adults should read the book too. And despite the easy reading level of the book, the presentation is not too infantile for the adult reader. It seems to this writer that LeShan's book should first be read by an adult and then either a child might be directed toward it, or the adult could employ it in dealing with the child.

Earl Grollman has written a short, very good, book, *Talking About Death* for adults. In it, the ambivalent feelings of children are acknowledged, and the adult reader is supplied with specific reassuring, positive responses that may be made to children's commonly occurring questions.

Almost without exception, books for adults suggest that the first step toward being able to discuss death reasonably with children and to help them arrive at an understanding of their feelings is for adults to bring themselves to a realization of their own feelings and attitudes about death and dying. It is well known that many adults hold almost infantile attitudes on the subject. Masha Rudman, in a book for teachers, *Children's Literature: An Issues Approach*, provides a short questionnaire designed to assist adults in discovering their own feelings. Of course, one cannot help but suggest to the adult reader Kubler-Ross's classic *On Death and Dying*.

For many years, educators have been suggesting the use of children's books in a bibliotherapeutic manner. Underlying this suggestion is a belief that children can identify with literary characters and that such identification would be helpful in assisting children who are encountering death in their lives.

The concept of identification through literature has been explored by numerous researchers, one of the most prominent of whom was David H. Russell. Russell and Shrodes (1950) defined identification as the real or imagined affiliation of oneself (or sometimes a parent or friend) with a character or group in the story read (p. 336).

Huck and Kuhn (1968) note, "Although little is known about the process of identification, it seems likely that the reader who is able to experience problems, feelings, and attitudes of book characters will be more ready to identify with people he meets in life" (p. 651).

Based on his analysis of evidence existing in 1949, Russell (1949) developed several hypotheses concerning the concept of a child's identification with literary characters. He said that identification "is an active process. . . may help in the socialization of the child, and may have mental health values for the child" (p. 400-401).

These hypotheses become of especial importance in view of present trends in children's literature. Beginning in the late 1960's, there was a considerable movement toward much more realism, sometimes stark realism, in books for children and young adults. An integral part of this movement was the emergence, primarily in the 1970's, of stories in which a character dies, and the reader confronts the issues of loss and grief. The confrontation is usually handled in a natural, factual manner.

The treatment of death in many of these books has been sensitive and accurate, whether the death is that of a pet, an aged person (often a grandparent), a parent, or a peer. Feelings of grief are acknowledged and explored. Children's pangs of guilt at the death of a loved one are faced directly and often explained or resolved. Much of the mystery and secretiveness that frequently surround death are eliminated by the forthright treatment that many of the best books in this area offer.

While most of the books treating the subject of death are in the realm of fiction, there are several nonfiction books that help children explore their feelings and those of the people around them at the time of a death.

Life and Death, by Herbert S. Zim and Sonia Bleeker, is intended for children in the nine-to-twelve age range. It presents a factual, natural, scientific approach to maturation and dying. In addition to discussing life processes, it details customs surrounding death and burial in many cultures and even informs the reader of the clinical definition of death.

Older students find a reasoned, calm discussion of feeling about death as well as a great deal of information in John Langone's book *Death Is A Noun.* The author even considers contemporary controversial issues such as suicide, abortion, and euthanasia. Various viewpoints are presented and the young readers are left to make their own conclusions and judgments.

"Death is a natural part of life. Sooner or later, every living thing dies. We know this, but we usually don't think about death very much." With these words, Laurence Pringle opens a fascinating, informative book, *Death Is Natural.* Pringle is a former science teacher who is presently a free-lance writer and photographer, and the book presents death in both the plant and animal kingdom. His is a basically ecological presentation that focuses on change, maturation, and death as a part of natural law. The reader sees that as one animal or plant matures and dies, it aids in the inexorable progress of nature's cycle by providing food for other organisms. From time to time, Pringle gently introduces his reader to aspects of human death and some of peoples' feelings about death. Bountifully illustrated with black-and-white photographs, this is a superb book from both an informative and bibliotherapeutic standpoint. It introduces technical material in an understandable manner and evidences a genuine knowledge of and concern for the understandings and feelings of its young reader.

In the realistic fiction genre, there are now scores of books that treat death. Most of these, as indicated earlier, originated within the last ten years — a product of the virtual explosion in children's fiction of a realistic nature. Some of the more exceptional of such books will be mentioned in the present paper. However, the books included herein by no means constituted even most of what is available. To aid the health professional, educator, or parent in the search for additional children's books encompassing death, several reference sources that contain fairly extensive lists of books will be identified in the reference notes.

A book that was ahead of its time is *The Dead Bird*, by Marcia Brown, first published in 1958. It is a simple story of some children who find a dead bird and arrange a funeral for it. Perhaps the greatest virtue of Brown's book is the manner in which it shows the fact of the bird's death, the children's dealing with it, and, finally, their ability to matter-of-factly resume their daily activities, giving less and less attention to the death of the bird. Even though the children mourn the bird, there is evidenced a persistent feeling on their part of being glad to be alive.

Alvin Tresselt's *The Dead Tree* tells the story of a mighty oak tree and its part in the natural cycle of life in the forest. Tresselt paints a picture of a living, growing organism, which, at the same time as it grows, is harboring some of the elements of its eventual demise — carpenter ants and termites, fungus spores and rot. Without saying it in so many words, the author shows his reader that death is a natural part of the life and maturation process. After the oak has died and fallen to the forest floor, it is shown as the provider of a home for deer mice, rabbits, and other animals, a source of food for grubs, ants, and termites, and ultimately a provider of rich loam to sustain future growth of plants and trees.

In *Growing Time,* Sandol Warburg provides a well-written, sympathetic story of a boy's loss of his dog. Jamie at first rejects the consolation of his family when he learns that King is dead. Those around him tell Jamie, in a matter-of-fact manner, what death is and lead him to eventual acceptance of the pet's death. In addition to discussing the physical aspects of King's death, Warburg very skillfully presents a dialogue between Jamie and his grandmother in which the old lady introduces the boy to the concept of King's spirit. She tells him that what is buried up on the hill is only King's body; there is more to the dog than merely his bones and fur — there is his spirit. And Granny exhorts Jamie by saying:

> So remember this, child: the spirit of something you really love can never die. It lives in your heart. It belongs to you always, it is your treasure (p. 24).

Warburg deftly handles Jamie's sadness and anger at the loss of his pet and presents a realisic and supportive environment in which the boy can achieve understanding of the loss, cope with the grief it engenders, and go on to accept a new pet and allow it the "growing time" it needs.

"My cat Barney died last Friday." So begins Judy Viorst's book *The Tenth Good Thing About Barney*. The narrator informs the reader that a funeral was planned for Barney, and Mother suggests listing ten good things about Barney so they can be recited at the funeral. Alas! Only nine can be found! It isn't until after the child and his father have planted some seeds and talked about how Barney will change and become part of the ground that the tenth good thing is discovered: Barney is helping grow flowers. The book is very simple and straightforward. One small caution about Viorst's book is perhaps in order. Two children have an argument concerning where Barney is — in heaven or in the ground. Father attempts to settle the argument by stating, "We don't know too much about heaven . . . We can't be absolutely sure that it's there." (p. 14). Adults with religious beliefs encompassing the concept of heaven might want to prepare their child for the father's statements before exposing the child to this book.

At this point, the reader of this paper must be thinking that all the fiction for younger children relates to the death of trees or animals. Happily, such is not the case.

Charlotte Zolotow, one of our foremost authors of children's books, has written a poignant, sensitive treatment of death in *My Grandson Lew*. Six year old Lew awakens one night and tells his mother he misses his Grandpa, who died four years earlier. At his mother's urging, Lew recalls many experiences he had shared with Grandpa. The mother is amazed that Lew has so many accurate and fond memories of Grandpa, and they recall together various events in which Grandpa shared. Both acknowledge missing Grandpa, and, on the book's final page, agree to remember him together so "neither of us will be so lonely as we would be if we had to remember him alone" (p. 32).

Tomie dePaola presents a sensitive story of a boy's love for his grandmother and great-grandmother, *Nana Upstairs and Nana Downstairs*. First the great-grandmother and later the grandmother die. Tommy exhibits disbelief and hurt but is consoled by his mother's telling him that dead people can come back in your memory whenever you think about them. This is a very simple, warm book and could be read to children too young to read it themselves.

Annie and The Old One, by Miska Miles, is without a doubt one of the best, most sensitive, and most thought-provoking of all the children's books treating death. Annie is a Navajo girl whose most enjoyable moments are those times she sits at the feet of her grandmother — the Old One — and hears stories of long ago. A picture of joyful companionship and love between the two evolves. One evening the Old One, sensing the inevitable, tells the family that she will die ("go to Mother Earth") when the rug on the loom is finished. Annie's mother, who is dong the weaving, tries to help the child understand. But Annie decides the rug must not be finished. She misbehaves in school, hoping her parents will be called and thus her mother will miss a day's weaving. She releases the sheep so that finding them will use up a day's weaving time. When neither of these strategies works, Annie goes to the loom each night and pulls out that day's weaving. The Old One discovers Annie at the loom one night, and the next day the two of them walk out to the mesa and the Old One gently leads Annie to a genuine understanding that one cannot hold back time, that all things live and die. And then Annie takes up the weaving stick and begins to weave, just as her mother had done, just as her grandmother had done.

Students from about age eleven upward have available a plethora of recent fiction that includes the death of a main character. Many of these books are characterized by an honest, factual approach to the topic, and attitudes and emotions are frankly discussed.

Jenny Pennoyer loves her grandfather deeply, and a special relationship exists between the two, neither of whom relates well to the rest of the Pennoyer family. Author Norma Mazer develops, in *A Figure Of Speech,* a situation in which the reader shares Jenny's feelings of outrage when the family plans to move the grandfather to a nursing home. The old man, learning of the plans from Jenny, decides to "escape" to the old, long-abandoned family farm to live out his life. Mazer shows the doomed-from-the-beginning struggle of the old man and Jenny to survive on the farm, and, ultimately, the old man's surrender. A story well told, *A Figure Of Speech* is honest, realistic, and thought provoking.

Vera and Bill Cleaver, an accomplished husband-wife team, have many juvenile novels to their credit. Two of them encompass the topic of death. *Grover* is the story of a boy named Grover who must endure his mother's suicide, which occurs when she can no longer face her approaching death from cancer. We see the boy being shielded from the extent of his mother's illness and share his frustrations at the well-meaning relatives whose "smooth answers cheated him" (p. 25). Grover's father is completely unable to cope with his grief and becomes withdrawn and filled with what Grover discovers is self-pity. There is much to recommend this book in its treatment of the mother's death and the ways in which Grover and his father handle their grief.

Where The Lilies Bloom is also written by the Cleavers. The Luthers, an Appalachian mountain family, are motherless. When Roy Luther senses that he is dying, he makes Mary Call, his determined, strong-willed fourteen-year-old daughter, promise to keep his death a secret and keep the family together. Mary Call's struggles during the time of the father's dying and the intrafamily emotional turmoil engendered by their situation provide a realistic setting to foster discussion and understanding. Even though some readers may find the prospect of a teenaged girl being able to keep a family together rather far-fetched, the story is so well-written that this seeming incongruity is overcome by the novel itself. There is much in *Where The Lilies Bloom* to stimulate the reader's consideration of feelings and emotions when a parent dies. The narrative deftly handles the conflicts, guilt, denial, and ambivalence of feelings that often accompany such a loss.

A Taste of Blackberries has a different focus. In this first-person narrative, an eleven-year-old relates the story of the sudden death of his best friend, Jamie, from bee stings. Since he had felt that Jamie was pretending when he collapsed and therefore didn't help him immediately, the narrator experiences a special kind of guilt because he thinks he might have been able to prevent Jamie's death. This is a powerful, direct novel, and it realistically presents many questions, some of which do not have answers.

Paul Mather is an exceptionally good baseball player. But *Hang Tough, Paul Mather* is really a story of courage and ability in an arena far greater than just the baseball diamond. The twelve-year-old's dreams and hopes are shattered by the knowledge that he has leukemia. Alfred Slote performs a masterful feat in telling this story, as Paul relates it from his hospital bed. Paul emerges a strong, courageous youth who, with the help of a very understanding physician, faces death with a special kind of dignity and spirit. Slote minces no words, gives no candy coating to this tale. Details of Paul's treatment are candid, and his fear of approaching death is presented openly and compassionately.

Meg Chalmers has an older sister, Molly. Molly is charming, witty, attractive, and popular, always seems to do things well, and is understandably the object of Meg's jealousy. Lois Lowry, in *A Summer to Die,* tells the poignant story of Molly's terminal illness and of Meg's attempts to cope, to understand, to handle the guilt, to reconcile herself to the fact of Molly's impending death. The reader sees the telltale signs of Molly's illness, but Meg as narrator, doesn't acknowledge the problem until far into the book. Meg accuses her parents of being unfair by not telling her that Molly has leukemia. Lowry, just as Slote did in his book, refuses to gloss over some of the unpleasant facts associated with the illness and its treatment. We see in *A Summer to Die* the harshness, the unfairness, if you will, of Molly's death. At the same time, though, we view the beginning of a new life as Molly and Meg's friends have their baby. "Time goes on, and your life is still there, and you have to live it. After a while you remember the good things more often than the bad. Then gradually, the empty silent parts of you fill up with sounds of talking and laughter again, and the jagged edges of sadness are softened by memories" (p. 140).

Space just does not permit the inclusion in this paper of many superior children's books dealing with the topic of death. The reader should be assured that books mentioned herein represent only a sampling of those available. Additional reference sources may be found at the end of this article.

It is to be hoped that this brief exposure to some exemplary books on the topic and the rationale presented for their use with children will be useful to educators and health professionals as they try to help children adjust to death, accept its inevitability, and realize that death is a natural, inescapable component of life itself.

REFERENCES

Brown, Margaret Wise. 1958. *The Dead Bird.* New York: Scott.

Cleaver, Vera and Bill. 1969. *Where the Lilies Bloom.* Philadelphia: Lippincott.

Grover. 1970. Philadelphia: Lippincott.

dePaola, Tomie. 1973. *Nana Upstairs and Nana Downstairs.* New York: Putnam.

Dreyer, Sharon S. 1977. *The Bookfinder: A Guide to Children's Literature About the Needs and Problems of Youth Aged 2 - 15.* Circle Pines, Minn.: American Guidance Service. An annotated bibliography of 1031 children's books, indexed by subject, author, and title.

Kubler-Ross, Elisabeth. 1969. *On Death and Dying.* New York: Macmillan.

Langone, John. 1972. *Death Is a Noun: A View of the End of Life.* Boston: Little, Brown.

LeShan, Eda. 1978. *Learning to Say Good-Bye.* New York: Avon. Contains booklist for adults and children.

Lowry, Lois. 1977. *A Summer to Die.* Boston: Houghton Mifflin.

Mazer, Norma Fox. 1973. *A Figure of Speech.* New York: Delacorte.

Pringle, Laurence. 1977. *Death Is Natural.* New York: Four Winds. Contains a short booklist.

Rudman, Masha K. 1976. *Children's Literature: An Issues Approach.* Lexington, Mass.: Heath. One chapter is entitled "Death and Old Age." Rudman includes a fairly extensive bibliography, which includes books published up to 1975.

Russell, David H. 1949. *"Identification Through Literature."* Childhood Education 25: 397-401.

Russell, David H., and Shrodes, Caroline. 1950. *"Contributions of Research in Bibliotherapy to the Language Arts Program, I and II."* School Review 58: 335-342.

Slote, Alfred. 1973. *Hang Tough, Paul Mather.* Philadelphia: Lippincott.

Smith, Doris Buchanan. 1973. *A Taste of Blackberries.* New York: Crowell.

Stein, Sara B. 1974. *About Dying.* New York: Walker.

Tresselt, Alvin. 1972. *The Dead Tree.* New York: Parents' Magazine Press.

Viorst, Judith. 1971. *The Tenth Good Thing About Barney.* New York: Atheneum.

Warburg, Sandol. 1969. *Growing Time.* Boston: Houghton Mifflin.

Zolotow, Charlotte. 1974. *My Grandson Lew.* New York: Harper & Row.

THE IMPACT OF THE DEATH OF A PSYCHOTHERAPIST ON EMOTIONALLY DISTURBED CHILDREN
Boris M. Levinson

In our constant quest to understand the meaning of death and to help others deal with its impact, we sometimes overlook a source available to us as psychotherapists. Emotionally disturbed children in our care, whose defensive structures have crumbled, can often reveal what death actually means to them more openly than well-defended children or adults. Through them we can develop further insights into the dynamics of the human reaction to death.

The fear of death is expressed in different ways and takes different forms with each child, whether emotionally disturbed or not. The dynamics of how this fear is handled also differ as was clearly evident in a situation in which I was an active participant.

Two years ago, a beloved colleague and co-member of the psychotherapeutic staff of the Blueberry Treatment Center (Brooklyn, New York) died unexpectedly. Neither the staff nor the children had been prepared for this sad event. We had avoided telling the children that Richard (the name by which the children knew this psychotherapist) was undergoing an operation that entailed the risk of death, because we feared that this knowledge might sensitize them unnecessarily to the fact that they, too, would one day die.

It is not unusual for even sophisticated professionals in the mental health field to be culture-bound, as we were. Some vestigial belief in the power of the spoken word as a "hex" made us feel that to prepare the children by telling them about the possibility of Richard dying might invite the very disaster all of us found difficulty in facing. We acted as if Richard would not die if we did not tell the children. Obviously, we on the staff needed to master our own thoughts and emotions about the threat facing Richard. In retrospect, I know this was true for me.

Almost everyone past the prime of life has come close to death. Death came close to me at an early age—as close as a next-door neighbor. It followed me to school. Indeed, because of my condition, it was my daily companion. The way I handled this constant threat was largely determined by my Hebrew background. Our Hebrew daily prayers mention death frequently, although they talk of a God of love who loves life. Now, as I see it, I became alienated from death and learned to look at it as a fortuitous event, as something I didn't have to worry about or be concerned about. In general, death lost its terror for me. As a result, however, I had also become alienated from a part of myself, for death is only the other face of the coin we call life. In a sense, by escaping from thinking about death, I was escaping from myself. In a word, when coming face to face with death, I was able to relate only to the rituals of its public aspect and disregarded its more intimate, emotional aspects. Ignoring death had become part of my self-concept, instinctively I felt that if I talked about death, I would expose my alienated, naked self.

Many of these insights came to me as a result of my own reactions to the death of my beloved colleague and my observations of the children.

Richard had had open-heart surgery and was on the road to recovery. As a matter of fact he communicated with "his" children that he was returning to work. Then the blow fell, and we were told that Richard had died from internal bleeding. The news was like a thunderbolt on a sunny day. There had been no anticipatory grief. In addition, there was no participation by the children in the funeral and burial services. The reactions of the children in the Treatment Center varied, and the course of psychotherapy with some of them over the next few months was greatly colored by this event.

While Richard had been a well-known and loved member of the staff, he had never treated any of the children in my case load. Therefore, I am reporting the reactions of children who were not obliged to face the loss of their own therapist.

To "my" children, Richard's death was a symbolic loss. The children did not react so much to Richard's death as to what they were unconsciously reminded of by this loss. Obviously, these children had never completed their bereavement period. The vast majority of our child patients had been hurt before they came to us, by the loss of a vital love object. Richard's death seemed to precipitate bitter memories of this loss. Most of these children had lost one or both of their parents through separation or desertion. Usually the loss reinforced preceding traumas that had been caused by family quarrels and physical abuses. Death to these children meant separation and abandonment. Richard's death triggered memories of the terror, anguish, and despair these children had experienced before. They did not want to be abandoned again. Most of them were also severely alienated because of a lack of emotional closeness to their parents. They were afraid to become attached to their therapists for fear of suffering another loss. Many had made the transition and were developing faith in a relationship with another human being. With Richard's death, they had lost out again, and consequently they were somewhat bewildered and terrified.

While it is true that the subject of death always comes up directly or indirectly when one works with emotionally disturbed children, this time it was an unanticipated event and brought the children face to face with the issue. We decided to use the psychodynamics of the occasion therapeutically.

This, then, is a report both of the emotional contagion suffered by my child patients, who were only indirectly involved in the death, and of how I dealt with their reactions. Since not too much is known about the way in which emotionally disturbed children see themselves and their world after the death of someone closely associated with them, such as their therapist, my experience may increase our knowledge of the child's psychodynamics in these circumstances and aid in handling the therapeutic hours that follow such an event.

We sometimes feel that because children are emotionally disturbed, they long to die; we feel that death is welcomed by them. It became clear in these circumstances that this belief is not valid for most of our children. It also became apparent that when a death occurs in an agency, whether it be an attendant, teacher, therapist, or child who has died, the children who hear about it are deeply affected even though they may be only remotely involved.

Death to many of the children signifies a punishment for misdeeds. It was difficult for them, therefore, to understand Richard's death. Richard was admired and respected. He did not deserve to die. If Richard, who was good, could be struck down by death, how about themselves? They know they are bad. They had been told that a million times before they arrived at our Treatment Center. Are they also going to die? They became scared and anxious. The anxiety began to express itself in bedwetting, crying, clinging, thumbsucking, temper tantrums, and so on.

We must also remember that the children we see, whatever their age, have some ideas about death, inexact though they may be. Psychotherapy must start with this premise. To repeat, when Richard died they felt lonely and abandoned by yet another important protective figure. It became increasingly clear to the staff that we should have taken the children into our confidence before the death and allowed them to participate in the funeral ceremony. By not doing this, we permitted them to develop some peculiar ideas about Richard's death and burial. We strengthened the children's self-distrust by seemingly confirming to them that they could not be trusted with important information. How, then, could they trust themselves?

After Richard's death I tried to be repeatedly visible in the corridors and classrooms to reassure my children that I was still there. They ran to me, obviously very much distressed, anxious, and fearful. Was it true that Richard had died? they asked. Apparently they wanted me to deny this frightful rumor, which meant that one of their emotional supports and connections with the outside world had disappeared. Depending on the child's psychodynamics, various feelings, attitudes, and beliefs about death were expressed.

When I told them that the news was true, my voice reflected some of my sadness and grief. (Richard had been my college classmate, and with his death I felt that part of my own vitality, of my own life, had slipped away.) I indicated as simply as I could that Richard's death had hurt me deeply as well but that unfortunately there was nothing I or anyone else could do about it. Dead people remain dead.

The children thought I knew the reasons for Richard's death but would not disclose them. I told them I also wondered why he had to die at this time and that in many ways I was as ignorant as they were. (On many occasions the only difference between the children and me is the fact that they think I know all the answers and I know that I don't.)

It was hard for these children to comprehend how we could go on working as usual after Richard died. They were angry at us because they felt bereft of their idealized view of us as caring, loving, and concerned.

These deeply disturbed children—who supposedly had a "shallow affect" and were capable of little anger or emotion—began to cry on seeing my distraught face. Apparently they saw me as a model of how grief should be expressed. We cried together. Lollipops and chocolate were available as comforters.

One child curled up on my lap in a fetal position. Another, trying to comfort me and himself, kept touching my face and beard and kissing me. And so it went. We did not say much to each other. "Suppose," Steve asked, "I were to die. Would you cry this much for me?" He thus revealed his fear that he might suddenly die too.

Some days later I tried to explain to those of my children who cared to listen that Richard's death had been unanticipated, that such an event usually occurs in old age, and that he had not wanted to die and leave them because he loved them all, just as I did.

Harry, a schizophrenic, moderately retarded boy whose alcoholic mother preferred her lover to him, was angry and verbally abusive. He was going to kill the "sons of bitches of doctors" for letting Richard die or for killing him. This child tried to avoid the implication that death was inevitable and that he too would die some day. He reasoned, if Richard's death came from doctors' mishandling, don't go to doctors and you will be safe.

He was angry with me (whom on another occasion he had called his best friend) for permitting this to occur. I indicated that I understood Harry's anger and his disappointment that I was not powerful enough to protect Richard. I was very sympathetic and appreciative of the fact that he did not want to lose another friend. I said that I also understood that he was angry at me because he did not want to lose me and felt that his anger would hold me in check so that I would not die.

Freddie, who is subject to psychophysiological symptoms and is always ailing, became depressed. He did not want to speak and, according to his teachers, lost interest in school activities. Freddie felt that he was next on the death list, so why make an effort? I said that I understood how Freddie felt and that very often I, too, felt that way. It is only natural for people to feel that way. "Yes, Freddie," I told him, "you too will die someday. However, it will be at least another eighty

Christmases away." (Freddie longed for Christmas and its toys and joys, and he always complained that it took terribly long for Christmas to come around again.) Meanwhile, I assured him, he could look to the future and the fulfillment of his hopes of becoming a successful artist and having a good life. (Most of these children had been sick since early childhood. Most of their lives had been spent in the protected sanctuary of the Treatment Center. Since most of the grownups who worked with them were professionals, it was easy for some of these children to think that being grownup also meant becoming a professional).

Ellen, whose father had abandoned her family (a fact that she wished to deny), went about as if nothing had happened. Ellen apparently felt that Richard had abandoned his clinical children. By making believe that nothing had happened, she was confirming the fact that her father had not abandoned her family and Richard had not died.

Peggy, who was wearing her anger on her sleeve (apparently because she felt excluded), was irritable. She said that it was my fault that Richard had died. "Why didn't you die?" she asked. I said that I understood how angry she felt and that she preferred Richard to me. Most of us feel that way when we lose someone dear who appears irreplaceable. She then asked why we hadn't taken her to the funeral. I acknowledged Peggy's feelings that she could have done something for Richard and his family by being at the funeral. I explained the difficulties of making such arrangements and said I had been uncertain about how she would have reacted if asked to go. "Then why didn't you ask me about it?" she challenged.

Barry, who had previously expressed a fear of death, appeared indifferent, as if denying the reality of Richard's death. It was therefore necessary to work on the feelings we inferred he was having rather than on what he said or did. This child had unconscious death wishes toward me. This attitude of unconcerned denial of Richard's death was due to a need to deny ever having such ideas toward me who, after all, was always a protective and supportive figure. Actually (as he later rationalized), he was afraid to open his mouth for fear of bursting into uncontrollable tears and thus confirming in his own and everyone else's eyes that he was still a baby. (Sometimes the other children teased him unmercifully with such accusations.)

What are the implications for me as a professional?

The experience indicated that professionals often lose contact with the people we serve because our own attitudes toward death have not been thoroughly worked out. We have been alienated in certain areas from our child patients. Even with everything we have learned from psychiatry, neurology, and so on, we often show little ability in applying our knowledge to the children with whom we work. We find ourselves in a moral morass because we give lip service to what we have learned and cannot bring our ideals to life. Consequently, we cannot help our children.

I ask myself why this has happened to us? How come we have (temporarily, I hope) lost the basics, the fundamentals? Perhaps we have become alienated from ourselves and from our work. Perhaps we are dissatisfied with what we do, with our insignificant accomplishments, and wish we were elsewhere in a different occupation, doing something entirely different. Obviously, such a dissatisfaction would reflect itself in our work and in our attitude toward our children. Seymour B. Sarason, in his book *Work, Aging, and Social Change: Professionals and the One Life—One Career Imperative,* mentions the great disappointment professionals have in their chosen work. Apparently denial and withdrawal are how some professionals face the problem of their alienation from their life's work. How many, given the chance to live life over again, would choose their present occupation?

What are the implications for me as a psychotherapist?

From now on I have to reorient my therapeutic approach. What we usually overlook in therapy is the imperative of discussing the inevitable—object loss, separation, death. We should have used Richard's illness and then death as a focal point around which we could have discussed the feelings a child has about being absent, being temporarily away, and being away forever. Children have lost and will lose. We must emphasize the fact that loss is inevitable. Particularly, in connection with Richard's death, we overlooked the fact that his demise might have been used as a powerful searchlight to illuminate the children's hidden thoughts regarding death and separation. We need to educate our children for loss and separation, since it is everpresent and inevitable.

To illustrate, the children call me Grandpa Boris. Why Grandpa? Grandpa is older and thus nearer to death. Therefore I prepare them gradually and almost imperceptibly for the inevitable. The older you are, I tell them, the nearer you are to death. In a sense, then, my children are prepared for my death.

As a result of these experiences, and taking into consideration the developmental level of the children involved, I have considerably modified my therapeutic approach when potential separations are imminent. Whenever therapeutically feasible, I now try to anticipate events and tell children that death and separation are inevitable and try to help them to express their feelings. I also try to anticipate and share with my children any changes in their school, home, or placement that may affect them. If an occasion like this should ever arise again, I will fight for the right of my children to participate in the common grief by attending the funeral ceremony, seeing the body, and following the coffin to the cemetery. This would be done only after I had prepared them and explained what they might expect to see and hear. I shall in the future endeavor to give my children actual experiences, not the ersatz one of talking about and describing events and happenings that by their very nature are not real or comprehensible to them. I shall try to treat my children as far as possible as normal children, providing them with emotional experiences that may help them to fit more easily into the mainstream of American life and to get along better with their more "normal" peers.

May I close with a quotation from a book of great wisdom, the Bible – from one of its most fascinating books, *Ecclesiastes*.

>To every thing there is a season,
>and a time to every purpose under
>the heaven:
>A time to be born, and a time to die ...
>A time to get, and a time to lose.
>
>3:1 – 2,6

A CHILD'S DELAYED REACTION TO THE DEATH OF A PARENT: A CASE STUDY OF A THIRTEEN YEAR OLD GIRL
Phyllis Cohen

The following is a case study of a girl whose mother died of pancreatic cancer when the girl was 8 years 11 months old. During her mother's hospitalization, Stephanie was not permitted in the room with her, and her fantasies became far more frightening than any reality. Her father, relatives, teachers, and priest attempted to spare Stephanie pain by not discussing her mother's illness and death and dismissing her questions.

Almost three years after the death, Stephanie developed many symptoms and fears. Her major concerns were of dying of cancer, internal bleeding, poisoning, or other causes unusual for a girl of her age. As the case unfolded, it became apparent that Stephanie believed, as do many children, that her thoughts could make things happen. She began to feel guilty for her mother's death and believed that she deserved to be punished. When presented with an interpretation in therapy as to why Stephanie suffered from these symptoms, she readily integrated the information into her conceptual framework. Soon after, her symptoms began to disappear, and she started to verbalize long-suppressed feelings about her role in her mother's illness and death.

Description of Stephanie

Stephanie is an attractive, casually dressed, and well-developed 13-year-old girl. When she speaks she becomes easily excited, and she dramatically embellishes her stories by standing up, using her hands and body, and talking louder and louder. She is both verbal and articulate and she relates well in a one-to-one relationship.

In the first session and for several months following, Stephanie made many jerking movements and scratched and twitched various parts of her body. These movements were not always directly related to what material was being presented in the session, although at times they quite dramatically reflected Stephanie's reaction to what was going on inside her.

Family History

Stephanie's father appears much older than his forty-eight years, speaks English with a very heavy European accent, and has been working for the City of New York for 18 years. Since his wife died four years ago, he has not altered his lifestyle — he just took on the added responsibilities of raising his two daughters alone and of running his home.

Stephanie's mother was very much of a homebody, devoted to her children. To make extra money she did dressmaking in her home. She died when she was forty-seven years old, leaving two girls — Janice, age 12, and Stephanie, age 8 years 11 months. She was in apparently good health until she developed cancer, stayed home for several months with much of that time spent in bed, and then died three months after entering the hospital. During the time of her hospitalization, Stephanie was not permittted to visit her in her room, and her mother would stand at the window and wave to Stephanie, who was standing by herself in the waiting room. Stephanie's father said, "They were very close— Stephanie was her mother's baby." Stephanie's emotional reactions following her mother's death seemed to threaten her father's coping mechanism. He attempts to avoid and deny his feelings about his wife's death, and he becomes impatient when Stephanie is unable to do the same.

Mr. P. recalled that Stephanie had a normal early childhood and separated easily when she entered kindergarten. By the first grade she presented herself as a verbal, vivacious, and mischievous little girl who was disciplined often by her mother. Stephanie did very poorly in school after the death of her mother, yet she completed third and fourth grades without seeming to be too disturbed. In the fifth grade at a parochial school, she did not do passing work, and was held over. Mr. P. decided to transfer Stephanie to a public school. She entered a new school in the beginning of the fifth grade, being a full two years older than the other children in her class. During that time she began seeing the school social worker because of behavior problems and poor school performance. In March of that year she was referred to the New Hope Guild for individual therapy, and in October of the following year (when Stephanie was in sixth grade) I began seeing her once a week in psychoanalytic psychotherapy.

Onset of Symptoms

Stephanie says, "It all started when I went to see the movie *Jaws.*" She had gone with her sister and cousins, and she had had a little cut on her wrist. She had been picking on it. She had had started feeling that it was bleeding inside and that she was going to die; she had begun shivering and shaking and hiding under the seat, wishing for the movie to end. From that night on she started having nightmares.

This incident brought to her mind the day that her mother was called to the hospital and she had gotten yelled at for answering the phone. She had seen the movie *Poseidon Adventure* that day, and she felt it was the "bloodiest movie" she had ever seen — "people were dying all over the place."

Stephanie's symptoms began more than two years after her mother's death, when these two movies became linked in her memory to her mother's illness and death. The *Jaws* movie incident triggered off a long list of symptoms, phobias, and obsessions about death and bodily illness and injury. Stephanie became preoccupied with death and bodily injury, and she began to fear that she was going to get cancer. She asked the doctor about it constantly, because she recalled that her mother had cancer and didn't know that she had it. She asked her father, her cousins, her aunt, and her teachers in school. No one answered in a way that helped her feel better; their answers led her to raise more questions. None of their explanations satisfied her, and she became more anxious and preoccupied. Stephanie would say, "I'm going to die" or "Am I going to die?"

Father: Everyone has to die (or) You're not going to die.

Doctor: You're healthy. I just examined you.

Stephanie: But look at this lump.

D.: That's just your gland.

S.: But it's sticking out.

D.: There's nothing abnormally sticking out.

S.: But you don't see it the way I do.

Aunt: Stephanie, I have my own kids to worry about. Stop making a big deal over nothing.

Teachers: They tried to reassure her that she's OK, but she insisted that they don't know the extent of her condition.

Cousins and sister and boys on block: (Mockingly) Oh, my God, she's going to die. Quick, call an ambulance.

Priest: It's in God's hands. . . . If you're good . . . (etc.) . . .

Stephanie felt: If I'm bad, then God will punish me and make me sick and die. If I'm good, He'll take me as he took my mother, since she was good.

Therapy Sessions

She came into the first therapy session on October 3, 1977, with her father, and I was impressed by her verbal ability. She began to argue with Mr. P. in a manner that resembled a wife quarreling with her husband. The issue was whether Stephanie could have a moped; it was clear that her father decided it was "out of the question," while Stephanie had decided that she would use any tactic to get him to change his mind.

At the end of the session, I had the impression that Stephanie's father meant well but didn't know how to handle his daughter without becoming hysterical. While Stephanie called him names, he remained calm until he could't take it any more and he verbally exploded. Throughout the next session, when Stephanie and I were alone, she was picking on a scab on her arm until it started to bleed.

> Stephanie: It's bleeding, look at it.
>
> Therapist: Yes it is. You picked on it until you made it bleed.
>
> Stephanie: What do you think it is?
>
> Therapist: I don't know.
>
> Stephanie: Do you think it's dangerous?
>
> Therapist: I don't know — do you?
>
> Stephanie: [pause] I don't think so. [pause] I guess it's nothing.

(Very often these questions would be, "Do you think I'm going to die?" I would answer, "What do you think?" and she would answer, "No . . . I think I'll be OK." I once made the mistake of saying that I thought she was not in danger of dying, and she argued with me that I didn't really know how bad her condition was. I had inadvertently repeated the pattern established by other adults in Stephanie's life.)

Stephanie ended this session telling a story illustrating how "everything happens to me." She had once held a needle in her mouth and "all of a sudden it broke." She thought she had swallowed half of the needle, and she became so upset that her father finally took her to the hospital for x-rays to find the other half of the needle. They found nothing on the x-rays.

> "Would you believe?" she said. "When we got home from the hospital, I ran my hand on the floor where I was standing and, believe it or not, I found the half of the needle that I had lost before!"

In the fourth session she came in wearing a turtleneck sweater. She talked about how it was choking her as she pulled it away from her neck. Her face was red and she was getting tense. She asked, "Do you think it could make me choke to death?" I answered, "What do you think?" and she said, "I guess not." She seemed relieved. She went on to say that she thought her father was trying to poison her. When he is preparing dinner,

> Ajax is next to the sink and he leaves the food lying around while he washes dishes or cleans the stove with Ajax. Ajax has a bleach in it, doesn't it? Isn't bleach poison? When my father puts the can of bleach down, he bangs it, and the Ajax goes flying into the food.

At this point Stephanie began scratching her head, arms, and legs, while talking about how her sister made fun of her. Janice purposely put her toast on a battery and started screaming, "I'm going to die from the battery acid" as she ate her toast.

Stephanie's free associations then led to:

> Whenever I think things, if they are bad thoughts, they always happen. When I played on a skateboard, I thought I'd fall and I did, and when my friend was riding her new bike she had an accident when I thought that it was going to happen. Whenever I play out a bad thing, it always happens to that person.

These thoughts then led Stephanie to reveal an important link into how she developed her symptoms. Throughout this part of the session, she was still itching.

> It all started when I went to see *Jaws* with my cousins and my sister. It was scary and I had a little sore on my hand. I couldn't stop looking at it and thinking about it, and it started getting bigger and bigger right in front of my eyes. I kept shaking and crying. I asked my cousin how much longer the movie was, and she told me it had just started and and to shut up. I started to hide under the seat. I couldn't stop thinking I was going to die. I couldn't watch the movie because it was too scary. Everyone kept turning around and telling me to shut up.

> I remembered that the day my mother went into the hospital I saw the movie *Poseidon Adventure* and it was bloodier and scarier than anything but that didn't give me bad dreams. Even though when I got home my wrist was OK, still I couldn't stop worrying and having bad dreams that I was going to die.

As Stephanie was talking, she was going through contortions, scratching all over her body. When she finished, she seemed to be calm and relieved. When I told her that the session was over she replied, "Time flies so fast. It doesn't wait for no one. My mother told me that." This was her first reference to her mother directly.

In this session, Stephanie's guilt in relation to her mother's death became apparent. She truly believed that her bad thoughts had caused her mother to die. Her fears of dying or of bodily injury seemed to be a result of her fear of retaliation for what she had done.

After I had met Stephanie five times, I met with her father alone. He confirmed the fact that for over a year after her mother died, Stephanie had been fine and that she had changed after she saw *Jaws*. I asked Mr. P. about the circumstances of her mother's death.

> We had told Stephanie that her mother was coming home from the hospital. Stephanie was too young to visit her and she was too young to understand. She was very close with her Her mother had spoiled her because she was the baby. Her mother was a homebody and she never left Stephanie alone. When we told Stephanie that her mother died she felt like killing herself. She said, "You mean I'm never going to see her again?" She picked up a knife — a kitchen knife. Her sister and I took it away from her and so she ran into the living room and and opened the window as if she was going to jump out. She said she wanted to be with her mother.

In the seventh session, for the first time, Stephanie did not bite nails, crack knuckles, scratch, pull on her clothes, or display any other physical symptoms. She began talking about *Poseidon Adventure* again.

> It was on TV and I got the nerve to watch it. I was so excited to watch it again and then, would you believe, all of a sudden I started to feel guilty that I was enjoying watching other people die. It looked so real I forgot they were actors. I thought they all died. I should have known better than to watch it. Now I can't stop remembering the tidal wave. It's ruling my mind. I can't concentrate on my school work.

Then, for the first time since she had started treatment, Stephanie burst into tears and as she sobbed she said:

Stephanie: I feel guilty for what I did.

Therapist: What did you do?

Stephanie: I was only pretending. I pretended I was the captain on the ship when I played, and then all of a sudden, all the people were getting killed.

Therapist: It's very scary to you when you think that your thoughts are so powerful and could make things happen.

Stephanie: [continuing to sob and cry] It wasn't my fault.

She continued to cry for a few minutes and then talked some more about her bad dreams and bad thoughts. "Everything I play that's bad really happens." It semed that with all her anger she was asking to be physically controlled and punished so that she would be sure that they all cared for her.

By the nineteenth session, in February, Stephanie said that she knew she was getting better.

> I banged my knee in school today and I started to worry that I was going to bleed internally, but I watched it and I went to sleep and I realized I didn't die ... Also, I tried to open a Magic Marker cover and I had to use my mouth. Then I got some of the ink on my tongue. Once again I thought I was poisoned, but I lived.

In the beginning of March, Stephanie began to develop a negative transference toward the therapist. One time she said:

> No one can help me; not this place or any place. Not even you. There are four reasons why I can't be helped. The first is because I'm a hopeless case; the second is because of the stupid movie *Jaws* 2; number 3 is because of my stupid brain and body; and number 4 is, oh, I forgot.

The next two sessions showed more anger from Stephanie than previously; on the surface it seemed that she was getting worse.

> Why do I worry so much? — especially at night when I'm watching TV. It's all my teacher's fault — she had to teach us about veins in the neck. First my neck starts to click and then when I look in the mirror, I see red and then I start to taste blood in my mouth — I know it sounds funny and I know it's not true — but I can't stop worrying. Then I start sweating and I start to cry and choke . ... My sister said I'm the only one who can't stop worrying, but she doesn't understand. Tonight I'm not going to let myself worry — but I know my stupid brain will start worrying anyway. I wish I was a genie and could "blink" myself a new brain and a new ear [she has been scratching her ear and it is now very red]. My ear is so sore and I can't stop itching — do you see anything there? Is it bleeding? Do you think I could have cancer?

> Therapist: What do you think?

> Stephanie: I don't think so.

By the twenty-fourth session, Stephanie came in more frantic than ever. She had been up the entire night before, and she had run out in the street. She said:

> What a night. I can't stop worrying. I'm really getting worse. My sister and my father cursed me for keeping them up. They're all mad and I can't stop worrying.

She was wringing her hands and pacing back and forth. She continued:

> And I'm wasting his money here — you're supposed to make me better and I'm getting worse — I'm wasting his money. Even my doctor tried to tell me I didn't have cancer but I don't believe him. And my father told me I want to die and that's why I'm worried.

In the twenty-fifth session, Stephanie came in looking better than she had in weeks before.

> I had a good week this week — it wasn't as bad as before. I decided I wasn't going to break a vein in my neck because I asked God and He said, "No."

I asked her how she communicates with God and she said through her conscience. She also said that she had asked God if He loved her and if she was a nice girl and He had answered, "Yes." She then asked me, "Why does everything bad always happen to me?"

I then made an interpretation for Stephanie. I had planned it several weeks before and I had been waiting for an opportune moment. I said:

> Stephanie, I get the feeling that you feel so worried because you feel inside that you've done something terribly wrong. So you feel guilty about it and you begin to worry more. And then you feel frightened that you're going to be punished. You think your father is going to poison you [she interjected, "Yeah, I won't eat his food anymore"] and you feel that your teacher is always picking on you ["Yeah, she took me out of the good reading group and put me in the crummy one"] and that the boys are always picking on you ["Yeah, there were two boys in school who were bothering me and I almost killed them"].

The effect of this "interpretation" was to give Stephanie renewed energy. It was as if she felt she had finally been heard and understood. She began in a highly excited manner to talk about her body and her symptoms. She showed me the scratches she had given herself on her throat and neck.

> I know about the seven layers of skin that people have and how the skin protects the veins and so it's really impossible to break open your own vein and bleed to death — besides, veins bend because I looked at my knee and elbow and figured out that they must.

She then described a rash on her stomach (which she stood up to show me) and how she thought it was skin cancer, but she knew if she left it alone, it would get better. She showed me a cut on her wrist and a red spot on her neck in a similar manner.

> Stephanie: Oh, no, I'm getting itchy again. It's starting again [as she scratches her legs and arms].
>
> Therapist: It may be that these "symptoms or feelings" are inside you and they are causing this behavior that you feel you can't control. It may be that they start because you feel so guilty that you've done something wrong and now you're being punished.
>
> Stephanie: Yes, I feel so guilty that I went to church to confession to talk to God and He told me I'm not crazy.

The last words she said in this session were, "I guess it is helping me coming here. I'll see you next week."

In the next session (the twenty-sixth) Stephanie came in feeling excited, because she had gone on a class trip to Shea Stadium to see a Mets game and she had fallen "in love" with a ball player, Lee Mazzilli. Fantasies about him in relation to sex would occupy most of the time in the sessions to follow until the end of the summer.

When Stephanie returned to talking about "the bad things that happen to me," I again said the entire interpretation with all three parts: her feeling that she did something bad, her feeling guilty, and her fear of being punished. Her response was:

> If my mother weren't dead, I wouldn't even know what that word would mean. I can't even spell it [she was referring to the words "guilty" and "worried"]. I want to live 120 years and my father doesn't understand; there he is, worried about some water on his stupid knee, and he went to the doctor about it today so my sister had to come with me today. I don't know why he's so worried — he lived his life already — I didn't even have a chance yet. I haven't even reached my fourteenth birthday yet.

The next session, after describing having a good time in school, Stephanie said:

> Yeah, but then in school I started to worry. Why did I ever see that stupid movie *Jaws?* Ever since my mother died I can't stop worrying. If she were here, I never would have seen it in the first place. Then I would never have these problems.

For the first time since therapy had started, I asked Stephanie about her mother and what had happened when she died. She answered:

> My mother got cancer and died. When she went to the hospital, I said that she won't come out and that I would

never see her again. My sister blames me for saying that. But I know that whenever anyone is sick and they go to the hospital, they could die.

Once again I took this opportune moment to repeat:

Stephanie, it seems to me that you are feeling guilty because you think you had something to do with your mother dying. Sometimes people think that their thoughts could make things happen.

Stephanie was welling up with tears and she was becoming more and more upset. She blurted out, *"I DIDN'T KILL MY MOTHER. I KNOW I DIDN'T."* Stephanie began to sob. I continued talking:

Stephanie, you know sometimes people get angry at someone else and they say that they wish they would drop dead; if it really happens, that person feels guilty that he or she made it happen and . . .

Stephanie: [*interrupting*] Yeah, Janice used to fight with my mother and she used to scream at her, "drop dead." So how come Janice doesn't feel guilty and get these worries? How come these things have to happen to me? [*She went on without giving me a chance to answer.*] You know my cousin really has a reason to worry—she was hit by a car and she really did bleed internally. Imagine, she really could have died.

Stephanie then continued her session in her usual manner, and at the end of the session said, "I'm not coming back here any more if I get worried one more time."

In the twenty-eighth session, Stephanie was in the midst of her worst agony and suffering. She had gained some insight into her problems, and she couldn't close her eyes to them any more. As we walked to the therapy room, there was the smell of paint in the air. "Oh my God, there's no air in here – we're going to die." I replied very dramatically, "Yes, quick, open the window! There's no air." This kind of interchange continued until Stephanie began to laugh. "I'm not ready to die. I want to live a hundred years. My doctor said I'm healthy and I should."

Toward the end of the session, Stephanie began to cry.

Stephanie: I wish I knew who poisoned her food.

Therapist: Whose food?

Stephanie: My mother's. I didn't kill her and she didn't smoke or do bad things. People who smoke get cancer. If

I knew who poisoned her food, I'd kill them. [*She continued, sobbing*] Why doesn't my sister feel guilty? I always get blamed for everything . . . . They all make fun of me. No one gives me answers.

Therapist: No one understands you?

Stephanie: No one, especially my family. I hate everyone. [*looking at me*] Do you understand me?

Therapist: What do you think?

Stephanie: I don't know.

I went on to say that these feelings were very scary to her, and she was looking very depressed. She was obviously terrified of her thoughts being so powerful that she could make things happen. She had almost come to believe that she didn't kill her mother, but then she was bothered by having to find out who did kill her. I asked Stephanie, "What other things do you feel guilty about?" She answered that she felt guilty when people got cancer. She also said she felt guilty about her father not knowing that she was suffering, because he thought she was getting better. I repeated the basic interpretation, that it was scary to feel so guilty — as if she had done something wrong — and now to feel that something terrible would happen to her as a punishment. She then said, "I wish this day could go on forever." She continued, "So I would know I'd be alive forever."

The beginning of May brought nice weather and a new optimism for Stephanie. For the following three months Stephanie never became as upset or depressed as she had while she was trying so hard to understand what was going on inside her. She was able to joke with me about her symptoms, saying, "There I go again." I could even say, jokingly, "Stephanie, you have so much power that you could move this whole building — you just have to think it!" and she would laugh.

At one point she reverted to her symptoms — she began scratching her stomach and showed me a rash that she had provoked. I offered her a tissue, and she placed it between her skin and her sweater and said, "Now it's better." Previous to this, she probably would have said that a tissue couldn't help her or she would have continued scratching.

Stephanie then brought up a difficult problem that occurs very often in therapy. She was now feeling better and thinking of terminating treatment. In working with children, frequently if they "get better" the parent encourages terminating — and if they "don't get better," the parent also encourages termination. Stephanie was saying:

If I stop worrying then I'll be better and I won't have to come here any more. Then my father could put more money in the bank and we could go to more Met games.

At the same time there was ambivalence about ending our relationship without a "replacement" to talk to. I felt that although Stephanie had gotten to the reasons for her symptoms, she was not ready to end treatment. She was still afraid of her "bad power" and being a "jinx" — she discussed this in relation to the Mets losing a game while she rooted for them, but I knew it came out in other situations as well. Stephanie had continued to question who killed her mother and still had very sadistic fantasies related to expressing and receiving love. She was first learning how to deal with her anger and her upsets without "going crazy" and needed more time to practice her new behavior.

When Stephanie talked about getting better, she'd say she didn't know why but she wasn't worried any more. At those times I would say, "Maybe you don't feel guilty any more." One time she answered:

> Yeah, that's right. You want to see the place I used to worry about? *[She pointed at her elbow joint.]* I used to have veins sticking out here and now, you see, they bend. So it's OK.

She also said:

> This morning I almost worried. I was putting Proper PH on my face and some went into my mouth. I started to worry, but then I changed my mind.

In the next session (the thirty-first) Stephanie again referred to getting better. But anxiety in relation to terminating began to surface, and I was aware that her father had now talked to her about staying in treatment. In this session, first she started holding her neck. At first I imitated her, saying she might be feeling guilty again, and instead of responding in her usual manner, she said that her veins were different from mine and she was sure that something was wrong. She continued to hold her neck until the end of the session, when I brought up the issue of terminating and her "getting better." A little while later she said:

> I don't want to miss my appointment because I might start worrying again. You know sometimes I still worry. Sometimes I think my heart is bleeding to death and today my neck has something wrong with it. [*She was still holding her neck.*]

At this point I said:

> You know, Stephanie, you don't have to be worried in order to come to see me. We can still see each other

anyway. We have appointments at least until August.

During the month of June, Stephanie was involved in graduation rehearsals (from the sixth grade to go to junior high) and she was generally feeling very happy and excited. Once again, though, Stephanie's ambivalence about getting better came through. She said:

> You know, I don't worry any more. *NO MORE WORRY!* I only get pains in my neck sometimes. I say — "the hell with it" to the pain. I had some blood in my mouth the other day, but I wasn't worried about it.

> Therapist: Maybe you don't feel guilty any more.

> Stephanie: I never felt guilty anyway. I was always really feeling those pains. I won't watch *Poseidon Adventure,* though — even though it's going to be on TV again. I don't know if I'm strong enough to take it. Really, a grownup must make these kinds of decisions about whether or not to watch a scary movie.

Stephanie then began to rehash the story of the onset of her worrying about the movie *Jaws* — how it all started with a cut on her wrist and about the nightmare she used to get. She then wondered:

> Should I see *Jaws 2?* Am I strong enough? I don't worry anymore. How will I know if I am strong enough? Where will I go? With God or to the other place? If God would assure me of *when* I'm going to die, then I wouldn't worry "when" — I would know. My conscience doesn't tell me even though I keep asking. I want to live to a hundred. I have a lot of things going for me.

So many thoughts and reactions were going on within me as I listened to Stephanie during this session. She was expressing anger at her mother for dying by saying that she needed a grownup to tell her which movies to watch. It seemed almost as if Stephanie felt she needed to live to a hundred to spite her mother. She was also saying that she was afraid that she only seemed better and so stopping at this point might make her feel more anxious. She wasn't sure if she was really better or not.

The summer was now here and Stephanie was enjoying going to the beach for the first time in years. Before this summer, she had felt that the water was contaminated and that the sand carried germs and bugs and that these would harm her.

In the thirty-ninth session, Stephanie said:

> I saw a mummy on TV this weekend. It came to life. Are they real?
>
> Therapist: What do you think?
>
> Stephanie: I don't know. I got scared when I saw it. [*At this point she had started laughing.*] I guess if it were true, my mother could come back.
>
> Therapist: You are missing your mother and wishing there were some way for her to come back. It must have been very hard for you when she died.
>
> Stephanie: The day my mother went to the hospital, the phone rang. I answered the phone. It was the hospital. They wanted to speak to my mother, and my aunt grabbed the phone from me and was mad at me for answering it. She yelled at me that I shouldn't have answered the phone. But it was ringing, and I was only trying to be good. Then they told me that my mother was going to have to go to the hospital. I started crying and I said she wasn't going to come back. Janice said I shouldn't say that.

Stephanie then began referring to the fact that she has changed and gotten better.

> Therapist: You have grown up and changed a lot in this past year. I guess it is very painful for you to talk about old memories.
>
> Stephanie: I don't like to talk about it. They all knew before I did [*when she died*]. I used to visit the hospital, but I was only able to see my mother from the window. I was too young to go up and see her. I never saw her again. My cousins used to get dressed up and sneak up and my sister was old enough, but I had to wait downstairs in the waiting room. My mother was a good person. She used to wave to me from the window all the time. The day I came home from school, my family was there and I knew something had happened. They all knew before I did. When they told me that my mother was dead, I wanted to kill myself. I grabbed the knife and my sister and my father took it away from me. Then I ran over to the window. I wanted to jump out and be with my mother. But they stopped me. And when I saw the movie *Jaws* I started worrying.

There were more than two years in between her mother's death and the movie incident. No one had been able to sit down and talk to Stephanie about her feelings of guilt about her mother's death. It was very painful for the entire family of a forty-seven-year-old woman who had never been sick in her life to die of cancer five months after it was diagnosed. It was easier for everyone in the family to deny the feelings and act as if everything was normal and OK. All of this added to Stephanie's problems.

Shortly before summer vacation, Stephanie said:

> If I'm still living, I'll come to see you in September. I wish I would live a hundred years. Next week is our last week. Oh well, I guess I'll have to talk to Mr. Jaws in the ocean — that is, if he won't get too rough with me.

In the last session for the summer (the forty-second) Stephanie came in saying:

> I hate my father. My mother was an angel. She never cursed like he does. My sister thought I didn't remember the day it happened. But on August 3rd, I knew it was the day. And that was the same day this year that those six firemen were killed in that fire. Nobody said a word to me about the anniversary. Do they think I'm stupid?

Stephanie then went on to talk about how she hated her father:

> He's so cheap — he won't pay for tickets to the Met game, and he won't buy a new color TV. . . He won't buy me new clothes, and he won't fix the house. He'd spend all his money on his car and on his teeth, but not on me. I wish he wasn't my father — he's so stingy. When I get married, he won't come to my house. I hate him — he's such a jerk.

I tried to help Stephanie accept her ambivalent feeling by saying, "Stephanie, sometimes we hate parents and sometimes we love them." She answered, "No, I always hated him and I only loved my mother."

Stephanie not only survived during our five-week recess; she did quite well. When she came in for her forty-third session, on September 11, she was free of the old symptoms that she had had a year earlier. She talked about "here and now" realities of her life, and she referred to the fact that her sister was no longer a "goody-good," that she now cursed also. Maybe she was beginning to accept the realities of her mother's imperfections by observing her "perfect" sister being imperfect. She talked about her new school and about looking forward to Christmas this year. In this session there was a calm veil that had seemed to settle over the upheavals of Stephanie's past. I was optimistic that she had not reverted to her former nightmare and "bad thoughts" over the summer. Now we could look forward to dealing with new issues.

Summary

Although the case of Stephanie P. is unique in several respects, the primary one being that her symptoms did not appear until almost three years after her mother died, her situation has many implications for other children who face the death of a parent.

When Stephanie's mother became ill, she in essence lost both parents. During the time her mother was in the hospital, her father avoided discussing her illness or preparing Stephanie for her mother's impending death. Afterward, the father was involved in his own grieving process and once again withdrew from meeting his daughter's needs. Also, because Stephanie did not exhibit any obvious difficulties in adjustment until almost three years later, her father became angry rather than empathic when the symptoms first appeared.

At the time of Stephanie's mother's hospitalization, the little girl had said that she thought her mother would never come home again. Whether this was a verbalized Oedipal wish, subsequent events led Stephanie to believe that her words and thoughts made things happen – especially negative things. She began to feel guilty, as though she had in actuality caused her mother's death, and was convinced that she was deserving of punishment (Prugh and Eckhardt 1978; Nelson and Peterson 1975). As her father was not strict enough, her symptoms seemed to become self-inflicted punishment as well as a defense against the continuing aggressive thoughts and wishes (Anthony 1965).

After several months of psychotherapy, when Stephanie began to understand that her words and thoughts did not in fact cause her mother's death, she began to look elsewhere for a culprit. She had deified her mother as pure and perfect and started to see her father as a contrast, the evil parent. She began to blame him for everything, hinting that he might have poisoned her mother as she felt he was now trying to poison her.

When Stephanie was in therapy, she found an environment where her symptoms were taken seriously. She began to feel free enough to express her long-hidden fears about her role in her mother's illness and death. Although there is no way to predict how a particular child will respond to illness and death of a parent, indications are that Stephanie would not have suffered such a strong delayed reaction if the caring adults around her behaved differently.

When Stephanie had questioned her father, relatives, teachers, and priest about her mother's illness, they had all tried to shield her from pain by avoidance, euphemisms, or denial. This lack of direct communication had resulted in Stephanie's imagination working overtime, to a point where the fantasies were more grotesque than any reality could have been (Clay 1976). Her father had felt that Stephanie was too young to understand what was happening when her mother was taken to the hospital. Often, adults underestimate a child's capacity to comprehend and respond to a complex situation. Furman (1974) and others have presented evidence that even 3-year-olds can master the loss of a parent through a mourning process. If Stephanie had been able to face her mother's death through a period of mourning at the time, her suffering might not have stretched over a three-year period.

There are many lessons that adults can learn from Stephanie's case. If a caring adult had allowed Stephanie the opportunity to discuss and ask questions about her mother's illness and death directly, the child would have been encouraged to voice her fantasies and fears (Kubler-Ross 1978). The role adults can take on at this time is crucial, for they can act as facilitators or as guides (Keith & Ellis 1978). Thus can the child be helped to come to terms with the painful death in a manner appropriate to the child's developmental stage.

REFERENCES

Anthony, S. "The Child's Idea of Death," in T. Talbot, ed., *The World of the Child − Clinical and Cultural Studies from Birth to Adolescence.* New York: J. Aronson, 1967, 315-29.

Clay, V.S. "Children deal with death." *The School Counselor,* 1976, 23, 1975-83.

Furman, E. *A Child's Parent Dies: Studies in Childhood Bereavement.* New Haven: Yale University Press, 1974.

Keith, C.R., and Ellis, D. "Reactions of Pupils and Teachers to Death in the Classroom." *The School Counselor,* 1978, 25, 228-35.

Kubler-Ross, E. "Helping Parents Teach Their Children About Death and Life," L.E. Arnold, ed., *Helping Parents Help Their Children.* New York: Brunner/Mazel, Inc., 1978, 270-79.

Nelson, R.C., and Peterson, W.D. "Challenging the Last Great Taboo: Death." *The School Counselor,* 1975, 22, 253-62.

Prugh, D.G., and Eckhardt, L.O. "Guidance by Physicians and Nurses: A Developmental Approach," in L.E. Arnold, ed., *Helping Parents Help Their Children.* New York: Brunner/Mazel, Inc, 1978, 345-62.

A MULTIDISCIPLINARY APPROACH TO THE CARE OF THE TERMINALLY ILL PEDIATRIC PATIENT IN THE HOSPITAL
Joseph T. DiBianco and Irene Trowell

Increasing recognition is being given to the special problems related to the treatment of the terminally ill hospitalized child. The rapidly evolving medical technology has far outstripped the advances in dealing with the human and emotional needs of the patient, his family and his *caregivers*. The dying child evokes in all of us a degree of helplessness, pity, sorrow, guilt, anger, etc., that may be unparalleled in other areas of hospital practice.

Much has been written on the need for a "multidisciplinary approach" and for "coordinated care" in modern hospital practice. The actual day-to-day and situation-to-situation management of the dying child and his care is less well documented. In this brief article we will attempt to outline an approach to such care that has been followed by the Psychiatric Liaison-Consultation Service at Misericordia Hospital Medical Center. The coordination of the multitude of separate services such as pediatrics, nursing, dietary, social service, etc., in the treatment of the dying child and his family has been somewhat reluctantly assumed by the Psychiatric Liaison Service.

Shortly after the initial request for psychiatric evaluation of the dying child, the Liaison Team (psychiatrists, nurses, etc.) meet to discuss issues in the care of (1) the patient, (2) the needs of the family and (3) the problems faced by the pediatric staff.

I. Patient Care

We have been continually surprised at how many seemingly obvious and relatively simple maneuvers are often overlooked in making the arduous daily treatment more palatable, maneuvers such as eliminating excessive venipunctures and intramuscular injections, and the introduction of fun foods into the daily diet — such as milk shakes, hamburgers and french fries, etc., and bathing and grooming by someone who relates easily and well with the patient. The psychological effect of providing actual school work assignments when possible cannot be overestimated. It is a powerful stimulus of optimism and hope.

A prime issue is physical comfort of the patient with the expeditious use of analgesics. Psychological/emotional comfort can be assisted through explanation of procedures, listening to the child while respecting his/her feelings and opinions. Allowing the child to participate in the planning for care is most important. Spiritual needs may be met by support and religious services as desired by the patient. Diversional therapy must be appropriate for the patient's age and enjoyment.

II. Needs of the Family

Until recently the needs of the family of the terminally ill child had been, in large measure, benignly neglected. Many of their needs fall in the category of emotional, spiritual, and financial. Parental emotional support can be assisted through reasonable encouragement, open communication, explanation of all procedures, etc. Medical Social Service often provides assistance with social problems and financial matters. The involvement of pastoral counseling has been most fruitful for many of the families we have seen. The families accept their involvement enthusiastically.

III. Needs of the Staff

The needs of the Pediatric staff have only recently been acknowledged and addressed. Not unlike the staffs of dialysis units and intensive care units the pediatric staff from physician and nurse to aide and volunteer are drawn into the often high drama of the dying child. The caregivers are no less immune to the guilt, anger, depression, pity, etc. than the patient and his/her family. The knowledge of the impotence of their efforts to alter the final outcome often aggravates these feelings. Opportunities to openly discuss these feeling have been welcomed. The inclusion of times for such "ventilation" during planning conferences yields high dividends. There is less staff friction and we think less denial and increased ability to interact with patient and family.

Illustration: THE TERMINALLY ILL HOSPITALIZED ADOLESCENT AND MEDICAL STUDENT EDUCATION

We would like to present the management of a 15-year-old adolescent male who was in the terminal stages of a leukemic process when a medical student on a psychiatric clerkship assumed a crucial role in the final episode of the patient's life.

E.M. was a 15-year-old black adolescent male who had multiple hospitalizations for the treatment of a leukemic process that was discovered when the patient was 13-years-old.

The patient's mother stated that he learned that he had a fatal illness several months ago, and his response was one of withdrawal from family and friends with antagonism and resentment toward caregivers. He often spoke to his mother about his fatal illness and about death. He remarked to his mother that he was "born sick" and that he "had been sick all of his life." The patient has a seizure disorder which was diagnosed at age 7 and for which he required Dilantin daily.

The present and final admission was precipitated by uncontrollable bleeding from the mouth and rectum. He was sullen and withdrawn. Often he refused to speak or respond. He refused all medical procedures, medication, and even food. He felt that since he could not be cured he might just as well "die now."

The pediatric staff was distraught and frustrated. They could not deal effectively with E.M.'s rejection — nor could they find any way to motivate him differently. A psychiatric consultation was requested in the hope that some strategy could be proposed that might alter this deadlocked situation.

The psychiatric consultant was accompanied by a medical student for the initial evaluation. The picture was, indeed, as grim as had been presented by the pediatric staff.

Initially, the patient refused to acknowledge the psychiatrist and medical student. However, after a while the patient became somewhat involved. Serendipitously both the patient and medical student were avid chess players. An agreement was reached that the medical student would return "only to play chess."

The medical student saw the patient daily. Initially, they would play chess and often the medical student brought ice cream, malted milk, hamburger, and so forth. Within a short time, a strong relationship developed between patient and medical student that was to continue until the patient's death. While this primary relationship developed, the house staff was involved in coordinating activities of the other caregivers, namely, the pediatricians and nurses as well as working with the patient's family.

Joint conferences were held wherein various aspects of the therapeutic plan were discussed. These meetings included the dietician who would arrange to have the patient's favorite foods served; the lab technicians in order that only those technicians who had the best relationship to the patient would be involved in drawing bloods, etc.; the social workers who assisted with financial planning and arranged for care of patient's younger siblings while the patient's mother worked. These meetings also included the patient's minister who was actively involved in counseling both patient and family. The liaison team prevailed upon the hospital administration to provide a TV free of charge to the patient for the entire hospitalization.

The medical student carefully explained all medical procedures to the patient and served as a general ombudsman.

While E.M.'s discussion with the medical student over issues of death and dying were infrequent, it was obvious that much of his time was spent in struggling with these issues. He advised that he did not want his life artificially maintained: "I don't want to go on the machine because it would be too hard on my mother."

The dying child evokes emotional responses in all of us. In this particular instance, compassionate care was made possible by the special devotion of a medical student in his first encounter with a dying child. The psychiatric liaison team was instrumental in coordinating the best efforts of a multitude of caregivers to provide support for the patient and his family. When the patient finally slipped into a coma and died 48 hours later, the general sadness was tempered by the feeling that all that could humanly be done had been done.

CHRONIC ILLNESS AND DEATH IN CHILDHOOD:
Recommendations for Improvement of Current Educational and Management Deficiencies
Antoine K. Fomufod

This position paper will address three areas: For decades, the death process and the events surrounding it have remained distasteful issues for discussion even among health-care professionals. The extent to which death has been avoided is evident from its almost total exclusion from leading medical textbooks and other forms of medical teachings. Recent trends, however, indicate that the time has finally arrived for death and dying to come out of the closet! (Kubler Ross 1969) Current biophysical technology, by providing sophisticated diagnostic and therapeutic capabilities, is producing a subclass of patients who are being kept alive, artificially so to speak, almost indefinitely. Such innovations are creating an urgent need for greater understanding and better management of the psychosocial aspects of chronic terminal illnesses.

Current Traditional Management of Terminally Ill Children

There can be no doubt that the prerequisite for optimal management of any medical condition is adequate understanding of its pathogenesis. With no structured formal teaching in the area of death and dying in medical and nursing schools, is it surprising that, in general, present management of terminally ill children is far from satisfactory?

Current medical management and attitudes toward the crying child and family seem to derive from the personal experiences of caregivers, literature data and, only to a small extent, feed-back from the children themselves and their families. Personal experiences are unquestionably important, but their applicability to other situations has to be determined not only by the quantity and quality of these exposures but also by the individual situations. Even for the older physicians, the experiences that are helpful are only those in which death-related issues have been prospectively tackled or confronted with patient and family participation (Schulman 1976; Bluebond-Langer 1978).

Available literature has placed tremendous weight on the age of the child as a determinant of his understanding and reaction to terminal illness and death (Spinetta 1974; Anthony and Koopernik 1973). The under-ten-years-old are said not to understand the full meaning and finality of death, whereas teenagers do, although they might not accept personal involvement. The above is probably generally true, although perhaps the influence of observed parental and staff behavior upon the child's own reaction to death should also be heavily weighted. Recommendations based on age-expected reactions tend to be too generalized and often are unsatisfactory because immediate family and caregiver behavior can refine the individual responses. Even when the family and staff play the game of "mutual pretense" (Gyuley 1978) towards the child, it does not take long for the latter to figure out what is going on and then join the play.

Statements in the literature about what, when, and who should tell the child about his or her impending death are often contradictory — and maybe understandably so — because of the way in which the data on which they are based were collected. Only when we have first recognized the unmet needs of the dying child and the family will we be making any headway in this area.

Unmet Needs of the Dying Child, His Family and the Professional Staff

Our technological advances often appear to have outstripped our social institutions in relation to the ways in which each can be deployed beneficially for patient care. When we give the child's age primary importance, we relegate personal contact with the child to the background. The *person* of the child should be an equal factor with the age. Few discussions are ever held with the dying child alone even if these were nothing more than just lending a presence to listen to his venting of his feelings. He could, of course, also be more actively questioned about his thoughts on what will occur.

Rigid individual patient restrictions are often based on expected consequences — for example, on such physical activities as games and going to camp in summer; and there are also restrictions to certain diets in some medical conditions. Who is being helped, and to what objective, when these restrictions are routinely imposed — the child or the medical caregivers? I venture to say, not the child who *wants* to and *can* partake of these activities. Should not terminally ill children be allowed to self-learn restrictions through their own experiences?

There exists a stereotyped and preconceived characterization of parental behavior during chronic illness of their child. Although parental reactions might go through such stages as nonbelief, anger, and depression and then final acceptance, what happens in practice most often is that we predict parental reaction and proceed to try to spare their feelings by painting an ambiguous picture or giving a false hope. With few exceptions, most parents and relatives have stated in retrospect that they would have preferred the truth about the situation together with what to expect as soon as the medical facts became known for certain. Those who are going to disbelieve and want other opinions will do so whether we tell them today or wait until next month.

The public and/or society does not understand and share parental concerns. Society expects them to be superhuman, to continue giving support and care at all times and against all odds; anything otherwise is being insensitive, neglectful, cruel, and even criminal. Sometimes, there is a clash of opinions and interests between the public on the one hand and the institution of medicine through the physician on the other. The family is torn between the two: They either go along with public viewpoints, in which case thay have to find themselves an agreeable doctor, or go along with the physician and face the disapproval of society or the community.

Topping the list of deficiencies in medical care of chronic and terminally ill children is the lack of professional teaching and training in talking with dying patients and their families. A review of 12 leading current textbooks in pediatrics, internal medicine, surgery, and nursing showed that none contained a chapter devoted to the issue of death and dying! Some did not even have as much as a paragraph on death and related issues.

Certainly there are published articles on the issue of death and dying, but these are in isolated specialty journals. Doctors and nurses have been trained to cure, and consequently can see the dying patient as a failure on their part. Pathology is a required course in colleges of medicine. Autopsies are done, demonstrated, or discussed. Histology is also taught and learned. But the chronic transitional state between acute clinical illness and pathology – the dying patient – has been left void. One might ask what is so distasteful about terminal illness that is worse than the very end – autopsy, gross pathology and histology? With such a void, is it any surprise that a generation of doctors has problems handling the dying patient, the family, and the professional staff?

Recommendations for Improvements in Care

The unmet needs identified above can be regarded as a few among many. Consequently, the recommendations that follow, which are based on such needs, cannot be considered to be comprehensive, although they could go a long way as a start.

A. Educational
1. There needs to be a concerted effort to offer required courses on the subject of death and dying to medical students, physician assistants, and nurses. This should not in any way compromise enthusiasm for cure as the primary objective of any patient-physician encounter. Quite early in the course of medical education, attention should be called to the fact that even in optimal circumstances, there are always patients who cannot be cured. For such patients, the teaching should be "When you cannot cure, care." The patient and family should never be abandoned or cleverly avoided when we have exhausted our clinical capabilities: they probably need us more than before.

2. Writers of standard and leading textbooks should not regard their books complete until they have included a chapter on terminal illness, death and dying. Rather than depending on

monographs and special journal articles, would it not be better to have a chapter in a major medical, surgical, or nursing textbook on "The Dying Child, Death and Dying, Chronic Terminal Illness – Patient, Family and Hospital Staff?" In this context it is very gratifying to note that one pediatrics textbook has done just that (Hoekelmar 1978). Such a bold departure from tradition is highly commendable and should be emulated by others.

3. The time seems ripe for the creation of a subspecialty of medicine devoted to death and dying. Even to suggest that such a creation could be viewed as defeatist and not in line with the goal of every doctor is to continue to deceive ourselves at the same time that we render suboptimal total health care to our terminal patients and their families. Why should it be so difficult to see the need for one or two such well-trained specialists in any institution? Not only would they teach other professionals, but also they would serve as management consultants for all parties concerned. What is surprising is not, in my opinion, the suggestion of a subspecialty but how long it has taken us or is going to take us to see the need for such specialization. We have clergy and professionals in psychosocial sciences, but how often have we asked them to give relevant structured courses and lectures to medical and nursing professionals? How often have we made them full-fledged members of the therapeutic team in cases of terminal illnesses?

B. Management Issues

Even if it is going to be a long time before sound and satisfactory management recommendations are laid down, it needs to be recognized that current methods are so deficient that there is need for change or modification.

1. Having accepted that patient responses and reactions to terminal illnesses, whether expressed or not, are determined and modified by the multiple factors of age, family and relatives' support, stage of the illness, society norms, and previous experiences, caregiver staff must now set aside preconceived notions and *listen* to what the children and parents are saying or asking; they can then take cues from them and answer their questions on the basis of the known facts of their particular illnesses. With honesty, respect, and good patient-family-professional relationships as the sine qua non of optimal care,

there should be no room for the "mutual pretense" game.

2. The desertion of the patient and family at the very end is totally unacceptable whatever the reasons. The cause usually lies within us, the professional staff; maybe we see in the patient our own vulnerability or the failure of our science. If we recognize that our technology and abilities have limits, then we should face up to that fact and help the patient and family as best we can. This is not to imply that this is an easy task, far from it. Staying away, however, is not the answer either.

3. After the child dies, what do we have for the family? There should be a comfortable place that is physically convenient for first absorption of the death event and any initial mourning. The facility will permit the family a leisurely, last-hospital-contact with their loved one. The family could remain a while longer, if they wish after the body has been removed to the morgue. A postdeath conference one to two months later should be part of the total health care. Some families may require encouragement to agree to come to this but should never be coerced. This is the best time for detailing the autopsy finding where one has been done.

The above cannot be regarded as the only therapeutic areas needing improvements and changes. The do appear, however, to be the ones where our actions are farthest away from the most desirable course.

REFERENCES

Anthony, E.J. and C. Koupernik, eds. 1973. *International Yearbook for Child Psychiatry and Allied Disciplines*. New York: Wiley.

Bluebond-Langner, M. 1978. *The Private Worlds of Dying Children*. Princeton, New Jersey: Princeton University Press.

Gyuley, J.E. 1978. *The Dying Child*. New York: McGraw-Hill.

Hoekelman, R.A. 1978. *Principles of Pediatrics: Health Care of the Young*. New York: McGraw-Hill.

Kubler-Ross, E. 1969. *On Death and Dying*. New York: Macmillan Company.

Schulman, J.L. 1976. *Coping with Tragedy: Successfully Facing the Problem of a Seriously Ill Child*. Chicago: Follett.

Spinetta, J.J. 1974. "The Dying Child's Awareness of Death." *Psychological Bulletin* 81: 256.

THE CHILD AS A HOSPITAL PATIENT
Anneliese Sitarz

During the pre-terminal and terminal phases of catastrophic illness, the two most important needs that any human being has are to obtain necessary medical care and not to be alone. If the patient is a child, the latter is especially important. The child who is very ill needs to be close to and feel the support of his or her family. The child who is too young to understand the meaning of death understands and fears separation from loved ones. I can recall a six-year-old girl whose parents explained that, if she were to die, she would become an angel. The child accepted the explanation quietly when it was given, but at bedtime, she became very frightened and agitated. When a nurse tried to comfort her, the child said that she would like to become an angel, but would her parents be angels too or would she be alone?

Separation from loved ones is, in my opinion, the basic cause of anxiety in the younger child and, perhaps, in most human beings. There is no question that the familar home setting can best supply the proximity of loved family members and cherished objects. Still there may be situations where, by necessity or choice, a child is hospitalized during the terminal days of illness. In many ways this can be a positive experience for the child and for the family. For the child who has developed close relationships with members of the hospital team, nurses and social workers as well as the doctors, during previous admissions, hospital staff becomes an extension of the natural family. Often the hospital has been associated with past experiences of medical support and of getting better. When feeling ill, a child can be more relaxed and less fearful in familiar hospital surroundings, even though he would like to be at home. (A sixteen-year-old girl had cried bitterly to leave the hospital. When she was finally allowed to go home on a pass, she requested that she be allowed to return to the hospital, for she felt more secure there.)

Because of the need for certain treatments or blood products, specifically platelet transfusions for hemorrhage, the child must return to the hospital. At these times, the warm support of the medical team can be helpful in making the child and the family comfortable. The presence of other children requiring similar treatments is reassuring to the child. Misery likes company, and even painful procedures are more tolerable if other children are undergoing them too. In addition, there are numerous opportunities for the child to ask questions of the medical team. By receiving truthful answers to these questions commensurate with his age and level of understanding at each stage of the illness, a child is helped to be more in control of his situation. The older child needs to retain as much of this control as possible.

The changing body image, as weakness, pain and, at times, disfigurement occur, is especially difficult for teenagers to accept. What one tells them must be individualized. In general, questions should be encouraged and should be answered directly and simply. The more candid one is from the start, the freer the child will feel about asking further questions. This greatly facilitates getting his cooperation for treatments or other procedures. The answers can often be limited to the condition of the moment, without extrapolation to the ultimate outcome. Whenever possible, it is important to interject an element of hope. for example: "Yes, your hair may fall out, but that shows that the medicine is working and it will get rid of the cells, the bad ones."

People wonder about what to answer if the child asks if he is going to die. The answer must be realisitic, and yet allow hope. "Yes, one can die from this disease, but everything possible will be done to make you better." Children quickly learn whether their questions create anxiety, or whether they can feel free to ask them. The hospital staff has an advantage over the family for its members can be more objective and allow the child greater freedom to question. It should be realized that the older child may already know, or at least suspect, what his disease is and his imagination may make the picture worse than it is. A frank discusssion may relieve rather than increase anxiety.

It can be difficult for parents to accept this concept. They feel that they are protecting the child from reality by not being truthful with him. This can lead to significant communication gaps between an older child and his parents, with each party "protecting" the other by not expressing thoughts they feel to be difficult or painful for the other party to hear. The staff and the hospital setting as go-betweens can relieve a burdon that would otherwise be borne in silence by parents and children.

Much depends on the relationship established during the early days of the illness. All members of the treatment team need to become involved with the child and the family at the time of diagnosis, and to remain involved throughout the illness. Sometimes the child actually enjoys being in the hospital, away from siblings where he can have his parents' undivided attention. In the hospital setting, parents can obtain answers to questions more quickly than they might at home, preventing a buildup of their anxiety.

At times, parents are puzzled by young children's reactions to them. A young child may appear to ignore his parents when they come to visit even though he was crying for them only moments before. This may mean that in the presence of the parents, the child feels comfortable enough to play or go to sleep. Or it may be a silent expression of anger. The presence of parents can alleviate a child's anxiety even if the child does not appear to respond in the hopeful way. At other times, a child may express frank anger at the mother, which is most difficult for her to understand. This may be the only way for the child to vent feelings of anger and frustration that accompany his predicament. The mother is the only safe person to vent it on, for the child knows that she will still love him. Staff explanation of such behavior can help parents perceive the problem aspects of the situation and mitigate the already strong feelings of guilt that these parents share. Also, when warm relationships are established, members of the staff can be an effective substitute for members of the extended family, who may not be available at home either. In these days of family mobility, as the child's condition worsens, a gradual detachment from life occurs and there may actually be jealousy and hostility directed toward well and active family members who are not present. The actual locale in which the patient finds himself may gradually assume less importance than who is with him. The children occasionally wish they were at home, yet acknowledge that they might not feel as secure or as comfortable there.

Parents should be with the sick child as much as possible, and siblings should visit when a wish for their presence is expressed. Familiar toys, a special blanket, or pictures of relatives or a pet can make the hospital room more homelike. On the other hand, it is extremely demanding and exhausitng for a parent to be at the bedside for extended periods of time. Not only is it emotionally draining to see a child so sick, but the constant companionship of a very young child can be wearing. The hospital setting makes it possible for a trained and loving person whom the child knows to allow parents to get away from the bedside or the hospital for a while. Obviously, the hospital setting is the place to provide types of treatment that would be difficult or impossible to receive at home. A child's death almost universally produces guilt. The fact that the child died in the hospital helps to relieve parents of the additional guilt and fear that more could have been done for the child. The staff is available to discuss the desirability of doing something more, or, very importantly, doing nothing more.

In summary, the hospital can be a warm and supportive place for the terminal care of the child with a catastrophic illness. This is especially true when there has been a team caring for him throughout his illness — a team whose members realize the child's needs, those of the family, and last, but by no means least, their own need to support each other.

PSYCHO-MEDICAL INCONSISTENCY IN PREADOLESCENT AND ADOLESCENT LEUKEMICS
William James Liccione

In her study of leukemic children, Bluebond-Langer (1978) theorizes that these children "come to know themselves and their world" through a socialization process which gradually increases their awareness of two related, albeit distinct, dimensions of their illness: 1) their self-concept and 2) their knowledge of their illness. In addition, the author argues that there is a necessary relationship between these dimensions such that the child cannot accept the full implications of his illness unless he first had a sufficiently morbid self-concept (Bluebond-Langer 1978: 170). For example, the child cannot accept the fact that he has a disease involving powerful drugs with side effects, painful procedures, and a series of relapses and remissions which may result in death, unless he first thinks of himself as "seriously ill" or "dying."

This paper maintains that there is no necessary relationship between these psychological and medical dimensions of illness. Indeed, some leukemic children display an impressive knowledge of their medical condition while continuing to think of themselves as quite normal, even during the advanced stages of their illness. These children are characterized here as having *PSYCHO-MEDICAL INCONSISTENCY*, since their self-concept does not follow from their knowledge of their condition.

The concept of psycho-medical inconsistency is discussed below, along with its implications for both the leukemic child and his parents.

PSYCHO-MEDICAL INCONSISTENCY

Although the relationship between a leukemic child's self-concept and his knowledge of his illness may be inconsistent in a number of ways, this paper is concerned, specifically, with cases of psycho-medical inconsistency in which the child 1) continues to think of himself as relatively normal and healthy 2) despite knowledge that he is in the advanced stages of leukemia. Following cognitive consistency theory (see, for example, Festinger 1957), it is reasonable to assume that such cases generate stress in the child, as well as a desire to eliminate that stress by changing either his self-concept or his medical knowledge so that one follows from the other. Since the latter is substantiated by medical fact, and more or less stable, he is likely to try improving his situation by changing the former. For example, if he knows his illness sometimes results in death, he may begin wondering how healthy he really is.

Whether or not psycho-medical inconsistency in these cases actually results in a morbid self-concept depends, among other things, on how much JUSTIFICATION the child receives from his parents for continuing to think of himself as relatively normal and healthy.[1] When the parents provide sufficient justification, the child is able to divorce the implications of his condition from him, personally.[2] For example, the leukemic child in uncontrolled relapse may convince himself, with sufficient prompting from his parents, that even though other children in his condition die, in his case a miracle is only a matter of time. Under these conditions, the stresss generated by his psycho-medical inconsistency is reduced, and he has less desire to change his self-concept. However, if his parents do not provide sufficient justification he is likely to find it difficult to ignore the implications of his condition, and begin thinking about how healthy he really is. Under these conditions, a morbid self-concept usually develops.

From this perspective, the parents' ability to provide their leukemic child with enough justification for maintaining a normal self-image is, perhaps, the single most important factor is determining whether or not he develops a morbid self-concept. In some cases, of course, parents choose to allow their child to begin thinking of himself as seriously ill or dying because they consider it best for any number of reasons. But in other cases they may make a deliberate effort to help him retain a relatively normal, healthy self-concept as long as he possibly can. In these cases, their success depends upon the age of their child, and creates a number or issues which must be resolved if they are going to be comfortable with their decision.[3]

PSYCHO-MEDICAL INCONSISTENCY IN PREADOLESCENCE

When the leukemic child is a preadolescent, his parents are often successful in providing him with sufficient justification for retaining a relatively normal, healthy self-concept, even when he is in the advanced stages of his illness. This seems to be the case for at least three reasons. First, preadolescents often consider their parents very credible sources of "self-knowledge."[4] In Rosenberg's (1979) study of the preadolescent and adolescent self-concept, between 67 percent and 78 percent of the respondents 8 to 11 years of age held that, in the event of disagreement with their parents over one of the components of their self-concept, their parents would be right (Rosenberg 1979: 243). In addition, 79 percent felt that their mothers knew what they thought and felt "deep down inside," while 63 percent were willing to say the same for their fathers (Rosenberg 1979: 245). The degree of consensus indicated by these and similar data is so striking that Rosenberg (1979) suggests that "in part it reflects a faith in adults (and parents, in particular) bordering on the religious" (p. 248). It also suggests that when parents choose to help their preadolescent child ignore the consequences of his medical condition, he will listen to them.

Second, preadolescents conceive of themselves largely in terms of what Rosenberg (1979) calls a "social exterior" (p. 195), consisting of overt, especially behavioral, characteristics and activities. Since this exterior is directly observable, parents usually have first-hand information on the things that count most to their child. Quite literally, they *KNOW* what they are talking about. Coupled with their credibility, this allows parents to effectively communicate with their child, pinpointing many of his fears and anxieties during the course of treatment.

Third, the parents of a preadolescent leukemic have the ability to strongly influence their child's activities. In many cases, their child is able to engage in routine school and play activities even during the advanced stages of his illness. Since he often defines himself in terms of these activities, parents who continue to encourage them actually encourage the maintenance of a social exterior necessary for their child's healthy self-concept.

The case report below illustrates a parent's ability to maintain her preadolescent child's healthy self-image, even during the advanced stages of his illness.

Case Report

Ken was 5-years-old when he was diagnosed as having leukemia in late December, 1978. During the following months he demonstrated a better understanding of his medical condition than patients twice his age. He understood the meaning of terms such as "remission," relapse," etc., as well as their relevance to him. He knew the names of the drugs used in his chemotherapy, and the side effects associated with each. He knew the names of the procedures he underwent, and details on how each was performed. And he knew that he had leukemia — a serious illness that sometimes resulted in death.

Ken responded well to initial induction therapy, and was in remission within a month. At this point, he thought of himself as hardly sick at all. He was an excellent student in school, and an indefatigable young man who delighted everyone he came in contact with with his irrepressible curiosity and wit.

Unexpectedly, his first remission lasted only 4 months. Although he again responded well to induction therapy, his second remission did not last either. Finally, after a series of relapses and remissions, Ken's mother was told that tests now indicated that he was in advanced stages of Acute Myelogenous Leukemia, and had virtually no chance of recovery.[5] Experimental chemotherapy was offered as the only hope of inducing yet another remission, although even that could not be expected to last. Faced with a choice between 1) allowing Ken to remain in relapse and enjoy his remaining days as long as his condition would allow, and 2) consenting to experimental chemotherapy which would probably produce extreme side effects, she decided to allow Ken to remain in relapse without further treatment (other than palliative care).

At this point, Ken's mother made a deliberate effort to maintain her son's still healthy self-image by providing justification for him to continue thinking of himself as a relatively normal child. She kept school officials fully informed, and encouraged him to remain in school even after he no longer could walk the quarter mile from his home.[6] She encouraged his play activities with neighborhood children even after he had difficulty negotiating the porch steps in front of his house. She encouraged talk about Halloween, Thanksgiving, Christmas, and other future events which he anticipated with relish. And she allowed him to attribute the increasing discomfort he experienced from being in uncontrolled relapse to causes unrelated to leukemia.[7]

As a result of his mother's efforts, Ken continued to regard himself as a relatively normal child. Even after tests indicated that he had a white cell count of approximately 200,000 and 80 percent of his bone marrow was blast cells, he spent hours each day playing with neighborhood children; and was preoccupied with issues such as whether or not to wear shorts or long pants to school on warm days; whether or not he would return from clinic visits in time for gym class; and whether or not he could handle all the math homework he recently had been assigned.[8] Neither his mother's, nor my, conversations with him indicated that Ken yet seriously considered alternatives to getting better.

Finally, when she learned that he had little more than a week to live, Ken's mother decided to allow him to spend his remaining days at his grandparents' house surrounded by his extended family.[9] During this period, there was a coordinated effort to help Ken justify his healthy self-image as long as he was comfortable with it. At the same time, everyone tried to create an environment which was conducive to questions he might have concerning his medical condition, death, etc. For example, discussion of future events were allowed when Ken initiated them, although they no longer were encouraged. Christian perspectives on death, and life after death, were openly discussed when there was an appropriate reason for doing so; and care now was taken to explain to Ken that his symptoms were attributable to the fact that the doctors had been unable to control his leukemia.

Ken remained at his grandparents' house for two weeks. During this time he expressed open irritation with his increasingly severe symptoms, and did have a discussion with his mother about what his death and life afterwards might be like. However, on balance, he devoted little time to such concerns. He remained future-oriented, and retained an interest in a number of routine activities (to the extent that he was now able to perform them).

Finally, Ken's mother decided to admit him to the hospital when she no longer could control his bone pain and evidence of internal bleeding developed. He remained there five days. During this time his mother and/or members of his extended family were with him continuously, and all were willing to openly discuss any fears he may have had. However, Ken never lost faith that he was going to recover. He remained future-oriented, repeatedly expressing the hope that he would be home for Halloween; and continued to attribute even his most severe symptoms to causes unrelated to leukemia. For example, when, after he was virtually blind from retinal hemorrhaging, I asked him if he was not concerned abut his trouble in seeing, he said "No. I think I'm tired and just need more sleep."

On Tuesday, October 30th, Ken died. His family took comfort in the belief that he truly would be "home" for Halloween.

Implications Of Psycho-Medical Inconsistency For The Parents Of Preadolescent Leukemics

The above case illustrates the success parents often have maintaining (or justifying) their preadolescent leukemic child's healthy self-image, even during the advanced stages of an illness. However, their ongoing attempts to do so generate a number of issues which they must resolve if they are to remain convinced that they are "doing the right thing." Perhaps most importantly, these parents must convince themselves that they are actually maintaining their chid's self-image. By their actions, they attempt to establish (at least for a time) a "closed awareness context" (Glaser and Strauss, 1965:29) in which their child remains unaware of the seriousness of his medical condition. However, if the child suspects that he is going to die, he may instead be unwilling to express his fears, thinking that his parents prefer not to talk about it. Hence, parents must be sure that their child's apparently healthy self-image is what it seems to be; and that they are not simply making it difficult for him to express his underlying fears and anxieties.

Even when the child is truly unaware of the implications of his medical condition, parents who decide to help him continue thinking of himself as relatively normal and healthy must be willing to structure their grief around the requirements of maintaining that self-image. Since they may care for him for months after knowing his poor prognosis, they are likely to begin grieving in anticipation of his death. However, they will not be free to express their "anticipatory grief" (Fulton and Fulton 1976) with their child as long as they are committed to maintaining his self-image.

In addition to the above, these parents must be prepared to cope with the unreality of their child's self-image. According to social psychologists (e.g., Sherif and Sherif 1969) people have a basic psychological need to "pattern" their experience (or awareness) so that things "fit together" in their mind, and there is a basic unity to them. When they cannot do this, they are likely to experience various degress of stress depending upon the importance of the situation they find themselves in. Parents who decide to maintain their leukemic child's healthy self-image find themselves not only in an extremely important situation, but also in a situation in which they have difficulty patterning their experience because things do not quite fit. It is as if their child's self-image is a constant reminder to them of the difference between appearance and reality: even though their child thinks of himself as basically healthy, and may be doing things that healthy children do, medically speaking he is not.[10]

PSYCHO-MEDICAL INCONSISTENCY IN ADOLESCENCE

When the leukemic child is an adolescent, his parents are often unsuccessful in providing him with sufficient justification for retaining a relatively normal, healthy self-concept when he is in the advanced stages of his illness. This seems to be the case for at least two reasons. First, adolescents often do not consider their parents very credible sources of self-knowledge. In Rosenberg's (1979) work, less than 50 percent of the respondents 15 and over were willing to take their parents' word over their own in a disagreement over one of the components of their self-concept (Rosenberg 1979: 243). In addition, only 53 percent of the respondents 12 to 14 years of age and 40 percent of the respondents 15 and over, felt that their mothers knew best what they were like "deep down inside"; while only 10 percent of the former and 9 percent of the latter were willing to say the same for their fathers (Rosenberg 1979: 247). Because parents often are not a credible source of self-knowledge, when they choose to help their adolescent child ignore the consequences of his medical condition the child often refuses to listen to them.

Second, adolescents conceive of themselves largely in terms of what Rosenberg (1979) calls a "psychological interior" (p. 195), consisting of reflections on their inner life of thoughts and feelings. Since this interior is not directly observable, parents often are unaware of many of their child's fears and anxieties when he chooses not to discuss them. This makes effective communication with him difficult; and often leads to a complete breakdown in communication during the course of treatment.

Even when the adolescent shares his concerns with his parents, they often are helpless to much about them. Because of the nature of his self-concept, he is likely to spend a considerable amount of time thinking about death, and its consequences for him personally. Kastenbaum (1967) underscores this point in the following:

> Intellectually, (the adolescent's) mind now has the power not merely to view life, but to review and preview. With an increased ability to think symbolically, to "think about thought," the adolescent can philosophize, daydream, plan criticize, imagine. Possibility is as important to him as reality. He begins to explore the alternatives, the options that lie before him.
>
> Sooner or later the adolescent is likely to turn his new intellectual resources to the subject of death. Previously he had been led to believe certain propositions about "life after death"

— now he may be inclined to examine these propositions critically. Furthermore, it is not enough to acknowledge the bare reality of death. Somehow, this reality must become integrated into his total view of life. As the adolescent begins to form his own purposes and make his own decisions he becomes aware that all his hopes, expectations, ambitions, require *TIME* for their actualization. The adolescent stands here at a certain point in time. Off in the distance, on the other side of time, stands death. This new self that he is developing and these new purposes that are emerging confront a natural enemy in death (pp. 104-105).

When the leukemic adolescent confronts his parents with fears that his dreams and ambitions will go unfulfilled if he dies, he confronts them with fears about which they can do relatively little.

Under these conditions, helping him maintain a healthy self-image becomes a difficult, if not impossible, task. In essence, their child has reason to think otherwise.

For all the above reasons, the adolescent leukemic usually cannot ignore the implications of his medical condition, and maintain a healthy self-image during the advanced stages of his illness. In the case report below, an early adolescent actually is willing to consider himself moribund when he realizes his prognosis is bleak.

Case Report

Mike was 12-years-old when he was diagnosed as having Acute Myelogenous Leukemia in January, 1979. He did not respond well to induction therapy, and his medical condition worsened. During the following months he began to tire easily, experience frequent pain, and run high fevers. However, for a time he retained a relatively healthy self-image. Although he knew he was ill, he did not consider alternatives to getting better. He remained in school, retained an interest in many activities, and looked forward to the time when he would be well enough to again swim and play basketball.

Several months after diagnosis, Mike began experimental chemotherapy, but his medical condition continued to decline. In addition to his other symptoms, he now experienced extreme side effects from the drugs he was taking, and was forced to drop out of school and spend much of his time in bed. By this time there were noticeable changes in his disposition: he often seemed depressed and was cantankerous with those around him. However, aside from general complaints about his physical condition and painful treatment procedures, he did not, indeed would not, talk with anyone about his illness. His mother expressed repeated frustration at her son's unwillingness to talk with her, and began to feel despondent because she felt she could do nothing to help relieve his anxiety. When she was asked to join a parents' support group at the hospital she declined, believing that nothing could relieve her feelings of helplessness.

Finally after several months of experimental chemotherapy, Mike told his physician that he refused to endure another procedure. The physician responded compassionately, explaining to him that his leukemia had progressed beyond the point where recovery was likely, but that without further treatment he would certainly not survive more than a short time. She suggested that he and his parents think about his decision in light of what they had been told and call her in a few days. Two days later Mike called to say he had not changed his mind – he would not accept any more treatment. His parents supported not only his right to make this decision, but also the decision made.

One month later Mike died. Home visits by the oncology nurse, private conversations with the mother, and reports by the mother and father during group therapy sessions they attended after their son's death all indicated that his last month was among the most peaceful of his 8½ month illness, for both him and his family. [11]

Implications Of Failing To Maintain Psycho-Medical Inconsistency For The Parents Of Adolescent Leukemics

When the parents of an adolescent leukemic are successful in maintaining their child's healthy self-image, they face all of the problems discussed above with respect to preadolescents. However, when they are not, as is characteristically the case, they often become frustrated by their sense of helplessness or loss of control in the situation (Kastenbaum 1978); at a time when they desperately want to "make a difference" in their child's condition, they are unable to do so.[12] Unfortunately, the stress generated under such conditions often adversely affects their relationship with their child, making him even less willing to allow them to help than he was earlier.

PARENT SUPPORT GROUPS

A parent support group consisting entirely of the parents of preadolescent leukemics, or entirely of the parents of adolescent leukemics, is a valuable resource for coping with the problems associated with psycho-medical inconsistency.[13] Parents of preadolescents, in particular, often express a strong desire to talk with others in their situation. These parents realize they will have a strong impact on how well their children cope with their illness, and are concerned about dealing with this responsibility. For them the group becomes a means of "reality testing": it allows them to find out what other parents think of psycho-medical inconsistency, and how they deal with the issues associated with it. Few people have more credibility for the parents of a leukemic child than another parent who has faced the same crisis. Hence, the support and advice offered by the group is often invaluable in helping them cope with their fears.

Parents of adolescents often express less interest in talking with others in their situation than parents of preadolescents do. More often than not these parents feel they have little control over their children, and are ready to discount the group as a way of improving the situation. However, those who decide to participate often find the group a valuable therapeutic aid: while their helplessness may be quite real, they now can talk about it in an understanding, supportive environment. In addition, the group can sometimes suggest ways for these parents to help their children cope with their illness when they have overreacted to their sense of helplessness.

The group therapist's effectiveness in these situations obviously depends on an understanding of the psychosocial dimensions of childhood leukemia. However, it is no less important that he have a sound medical knowledge of the various types of therapy offered, and the side effects associated with each, since these account for a substantial portion of parents' concerns.

---

1. Although this discussion focuses on the intact, two parent family, it also applies to situations in which one or both parents are absent, and parent surrogates assume responsibility for treatment.

2. It is important to distinguish between "divorcing" one's self from the implications of an illness and "denying" them. According to Weisman (1976), denial generally is regarded as a defensive *REACTION TO* a threatening situation. However, when the leukemic child divorces himself from the implications of his illness he, in essence, *RETAINS* his ignorance and prevents a threatening situation from developing in the first place.

3. The parents' decision to help maintain or not maintain their child's healthy self-concept is, itself, an important issue which unfortunately cannot be discussed within the confines of this paper.

4. By "self knowledge" is meant parent's knowledge concerning the preadolescent's self-concept.

5. Ken's mother and father were divorced, and his mother assumed almost total responsibility for his care during his entire illness.

6. After Ken's legs were so weak that he had difficulty walking the full distance from his home to school, his mother began pulling him in his cart on nice days — an event he (and she) came to love.

7. During his last month, Ken repeatedly attempted to explain his symptoms by attributing them to causes unrelated to leukemia. For example, he suggested that his increasingly intense bone pain was due to arthritis and that his increasingly frequent stomach pains were due to being constipated. Until his last days, his mother did not discourage such reasoning.

8. A normal white cell count in bone marrow which is not infiltrated by leukemic blast cells is between 4,000 and 11,000.

9. Ken remained a popular student at school until the day he left for his grandparents' house. When his mother called school officials to notify them of her decision, and why, they expressed utter amazement that a child with Ken's disposition could possibly be so near death.

10. Balanced against all of the problems discussed is the parents' belief that, by maintaining their child's healthy self-image, the quality of his remaining days will be far better than it would be otherwise. This, of course, is an extremely important belief; and often compensates for the problems they feel they may encounter. Hence, one cannot generalize and say that either maintaining or not maintaining the child's psycho-medical inconsistency is preferable in most cases.

11. From the above perspective, Mike's peacefulness after considering himself moribund is an indication not only of the stress which sometimes accompanies psycho-medical inconsistency, but also of the relief which follows from resolving it.

12. It is of course, true that parents of a preadolescent who fail in their efforts to maintain their child's health self-image are subject to the same sense of helplessmess.

13. Since the parents of preadolescent leukemics face a number of problems which are different in nature from the problems faced by the parents of adolescent leukemics, it is desirable to have separate support groups for each. In my experience, the parents themselves are the ones who are most supportive of this segregated approach to group counseling.

REFERENCES

Bluebond-Langer, M. 1978. *The Private World of Dying Children.* Princeton, N.J.: Princeton University Press.

Festinger, L. 1957. *The Theory of Cognitive Dissonance.* New York: Harper and Row.

Fulton, R. and J. Fulton, 1976. "A Psychosocial Aspect of Terminal Care: Anticipatory Grief." In R. Fulton, ed., *Death and Identity,* Bowie, MD: Charles Press.

Glaser, B. and A. Strauss. 1965. *Awareness of Dying.* Chicago: Aldine Publishing Co.

Kastenbaum, R. 1967. "The Child's Understanding of Death: How Does It Develop?" In E.A. Grollman, ed., *Explaining Death to Children,* Boston: Beacon Press.

Kastenbaum, R. 1978. "In Control." In C.A. Garfield, ed., *Psychosocial Care of the Dying Patient,* New York: McGraw-Hill

Rosenberg, M. 1979. *Conceiving the Self.* New York: Basic Books, Inc.

Sherif, M. and C. Sherif. 1969. *Social Psychology,* New York: Harper and Row.

Weisman, A.D. 1976. "Denial and Middle Knowledge." In E. S. Shneidman, ed., *Death: Current Perspectives,* Palo Alto, Ca: Mayfield Publishing Co.

ISSUES OF CONSENT IN THE TREATMENT OF THE CHILD WITH A DEADLY DISEASE
James L. Gibbons

The treatment situation has changed remarkably in recent years for those with potentially fatal illnesses. The number and potency of therapeutic agents and procedures, and the sophistication of life support techniques, have confronted patients and families, as well as physicians, with competitively alternative courses of treatment. The complexity of treatment planning, at various junctures of a disease process, has drawn patients, their families, and physicians into increased collaboration and has enriched the concept of "informed consent." Informed consent is certainly a more substantive issue when the amount of information to consider has multiplied and when there are genuine choices to be made between competing treatment approaches.

The treatment situation today places heavier responsibilities on the patient to participate in treatment decisions. This is a proper role for patients even if it is one for which we are rather unschooled. Such participation allows increased influence in treatment decisions by those most affected by them.

Children with deadly diseases present many additional complications to the already difficult decision-making situation just described. A child's intellectual ability to collaborate in the treatment situation is obviously a crucial variable, but so are factors related to psycho-social development and family dynamics. Three situations will be presented that will provide an opportunity to sketch some of these added complications to the issues of consent in the treatment of the child with a deadly disease. These complications place additional burdens on the family and on the treatment team.

THE ABSENCE OF PATIENT COLLABORATION

Children are often unable to provide the kind of collaboration that assists the doctor with the adult patient. Making the best treatment decisions for children often requires information that the child is not able to provide. Newborn infants present the extreme example of being unable to assist in clarifying the consumer interest aspect of the decision regarding their treatment. Parents, or guardians, must then act for the child, giving or withholding consent for treatment. The painful process confronting staff and parents in such a situation can be seen in the following example:

> Based on the experience of aggressive treatment for 1,000 spina bifida babies in England, Dr. John Lorber asserts that it is possible to say with confidence "on the first day of life whether that baby would have an existence compatible with health, dignity, and all other factors which contribute to a

reasonable quality of life."

If a baby is born with any one or more of the following characteristics, the medical staff would recommend parents that treatment not be begun:

1) A site for the spina bifida in the lower half of the back (leading to severe paralysis, incontinence, and probably severe hydrocephalus).

2) Paralysis (the loss of muscle power will be non-recoverable).

3) Gross distortion of the spine (coorelated with severe handicaps and the tendency toward deterioration).

4) Gross hydrocephalus.

5) Other gross congenital malformations (such as congenital heart disease and/or mongolism).

In a 21 month survey period, thirty-seven new spina bifida patients were seen and firm recommendations were made to the parents. Only one couple rejected the recommendation. Of the thirty-seven children, twenty-five were not treated due to the severity of their condition. The hoped-for outcome of the failure to treat was an early, painless death. The untreated infants were given nursing care and appropriate food. Parents could take their children home if they wished. "If they became infected by a disease of any kind, they were not treated with antibiotics." The outcome of this approach was that three children died "within a few days, eighteen within three months, and twenty-five within nine months" (Lorber 1974).

There are a host of ethical questions that surround the treatment experience described above, not the least of which is the validity of all "quality-of-life" arguments. However, the situation described here involves "quality of life " issues that are being argued, necessarily so, by people other than the patients whose well being is most directly affected by the treatment decisions. As Dr. Lorber has defined the situation, there is no neutral ground to stand on for either the staff or the parents. The staff are in the position of being advocates for a certain treatment course based on predetermined medical criteria. The parents are cast in the role of making the final decision regarding their infant's care pursuant to the medical assessment and recommendation of the physicians.

One can see aspects of a role shift that has occurred for physicians through the model of this situation. In addition to the traditional roles of diagnosis and treatment, we here see the physicians establishing criteria for determining " a reasonable quality of life." They assume the further role of advocating a specific treatment direction based on their understanding a reasonable quality of life. From an ethical point of view, it is entirely appropriate to ask if such advocacy is moral, and equally appropriate to ask if the failure to take such a position of advocacy is moral. My point, however, is not the ethical correctness of their position, but the added complexity of their role given their increased range of therapeutic agents and procedures.

The role that was assigned to the parents of these 37 children was also one of increased intricacy. The parents were not merely being asked to give consent for the therapeutic course of treatment with the best promise of success for their child. That was a more traditional role for parents. In this case, parents were also being asked to subscribe to a "quality of life" concept and to master, to their own satisfaction, a complex set of medical information to inform their final decision.

In the above situation, it is interesting to observe how the whole concept of consent gets a rather new meaning. Ordinarily, the medical team advocates a course of therapy to which the patient or their guardian consent or refuse consent. In a majority of cases, the physicians were recommending against therapy, so that to consent to the recommendation was to consent to non-treatment. To seek treatment really required the parents to refuse the recommendation and to demand that therapy be begun. Still, the parents have a very critical decision to make on behalf of their newborn infant, and it is reasonable to assume that the parents are as likely to represent the interests of their infant as might any other unrelated person. The genuineness of the parents' decision was reinforced by Dr. Lorber and his associates by the assurance that maximal therapy would be available for those infants of parents who opted for that course of treatment even against medical recommendations. Again, the central issue raised regarding the spina bifida patients was one of probable quality of life, and the parents were given the assignment of representing the child's best interests.

THE COMPETING INTERESTS OF PATIENT AND PARENTS

A somewhat more murky and equivocal situation can be found in the following case study. This example raises questions about the wisdom of parents being allowed such a unilateral authority to represent the interests of their child. Also, it subtly points toward the issue of the competency of consenting adults:

> Roger is an 11-year old boy who was first referred about two years ago to a university hospital because of a conspicuous abdominal mass. Consulting physicians were agreed that the first stage of treatment would be surgery which would provide tissue for diagnosis and would also de-bulk the tumor if it was not totally resectable. The tumor was found to be

quite widespread. One kidney had to be removed along with extensive tumor tissue. Some liver tissue was removed before it became clear that the tumor was too extensive to be resected. As the surgery progressed, serious bleeding began from some of the excision sites. Hypotention was noted, blood was given, surgical oversuturing done, the abdomen closed and the patient was sent to pediatric surgical ICU.

Within the hour, Roger suffered a cardiac arrest, was resuscitated, returned to surgery for more attempts to stop internal bleeding. Subsequently, note was taken that Roger had sustained severe brain damage, the extent of which could not be immediately determined. Several hours later, Roger again "arrested," was again resuscitated and his condition stabilized.

About one and one half weeks later, chemotherapy was begun at the insistence of the parents even though very minimal brain function was detectable. The treatment was "successful" and the patient now flourishes, although he cannot walk, sit, talk, see, feed himself, control bowel or bladder functions, or give any indication of intelligent cognition. Family life has been adversely affected by Roger's condition with the mother emotionally abandoning the husband to devote herself to round-the-clock care of Roger.

The pediatric oncology team, which followed the family before and after the surgery, included non-medical personnel who were trained in psychosocial aspects of pediatric oncology. It was the observation of the oncology team that Roger's situation had provoked strong feelings of guilt and responsibility in both parents, but especially the mother, even before the surgery. In an attempt to better the family economically, the mother had been working for several years, leaving Roger and his sister in the care of her mother except on weekends. This arrangement was contrary to her own upbringing and contrary to the teachings of her family's church. When Roger became ill, both parents, but especially the mother, were inclined to see Roger's condition as a punishment that had been visited upon them. When the surgery resulted in the disastrous consequences, this seemed to intensify their feeling of guilt and responsibility. The influence of these feelings was easy to trace in their insistence upon maximal care for Roger even after most of his brain function was lost. No amount of counseling from the oncology team was able to ease the feelings of self-blame that were especially pronounced in the mother. It was, in fact, only many months of almost total devotion to Roger's care, after release from the hospital, that began to restore for the mother her sense of worth as a parent.

This situation in some respects appears to this observer to be quite typical in its portrayal of the issues of consent in the care of potentially dying children. Roger had a fatal illness. Roger was unable to give consent for treatment because of his age and then because of his medical condition. The oncology team would probably have preferred not to treat Roger with chemotherapy, since there was no clear benefit that the patient could derive from therapy and since it was painful to Roger. The parents were severely impaired in their ability to perceive and act on behalf of the patient's best interests because of the compelling quality of their emotional needs in the situation. The parents are technically competent to serve as proxy decision-makers for Roger, since they are neither mentally ill nor morally deficient.

The search for the "good" and moral resolution to this type of situation is difficult indeed. If one were to approach the question strictly from the point of view of what is the patient's best interest, the issue might not be too difficult to resolve. That is to say, with the patient's minimal ability to realize any benefits from therapy and his clear ability to appreciate the pain that accompanies therapy, it would appear that the patient's best interest would be served by not commencing chemotherapy. The consequence of such a decision would be that the nonresected tumor would quickly resume its growth, leading to probable death within a few months.

On the other hand, if the pediatric oncology team interprets itself as serving the interest of the family unit, rather than just the interest of the patient, the situation would read quite differently. Roger's parents very much needed him to survive or at least needed heroic attempts to be made in that direction. They needed an approach to treatment that would not excerbate their feeling of guilt and one that would perhaps provide them with time to resolve some of their conflicted feelings about their parental responsibilities. In support of the treatment approach that developed, it could be argued that the patient actually had minimal interests needing protection and that the conspicuous need of the parents appropriately prevailed. On the other hand, if the therapy should prove to be completely successful, the parents have created for themselves a lifelong burden from which there would be little promise of release.

The pediatric oncology team determined that regarding the treatment alternatives, no compelling case could be made for what would best serve the patient's interest. Furthermore, they determined that, at least from a legal point of view, the parents could not be disqualified from the role of deciding on the course of treatment to be pursued with their son. The combined efforts with the oncology team to assist the parents to obtain some relief from their feeling of guilt toward Roger were unsuccessful in the short term. Consequently, it was decided that

that there was no alternative to beginning therapy and assisting the parents to live with the consequences of that decision.

PSYCHOSOCIAL DEVELOPMENT AND FAMILY DYNAMICS

One other situation not infrequently presents itself as a complication to the issue of consent in the treatment of potentially dying children. This situation is that of a child resisting treatment that has good promise of saving his or her life. Not infrequently, the patient may adopt such a position against the stated wishes of the parents and of the treatment team. A complex of factors again can serve to make the issues of consent anguishingly difficult to resolve. Consider the following case example:

> Ryan is a 14-year-old boy who was diagnosed with Hodgkins disease. The diagnosis workup revealed that the disease was at a stage which has a very favorable prognosis for cure if therapy is undertaken. Ryan was a difficult but compliant patient through the diagnostic phase of his care, especially during hospitalization. However, radiation therapy had hardly begun before Ryan refused to come to the hospital for treatment.
>
> The family situation is that Ryan is in the care of his mother as is his only other sibling. His mother and father are divorced although the father is frequently in the mother's home for visitation purposes, especially so since Ryan's illness. The father had a history of serious drinking resulting in employment difficulties and marital discord. Subsequent to the dissolution of the marriage, Ryan has become "his own man" and cannot be depended upon to "obey" either parent. Ryan has enjoyed the extra attention from both parents which the "sick role" has provoked. He also suggested to his mother that she and his father should get back together again.
>
> Ryan was referred for psychiatric consultation in view of his difficulties in cooperating in treatment, but he refused to go.

Here we have a situation with a number of difficult problems from the point of view of obtaining consent for treatment. Ryan has a favorable prognosis, and his interests are clearly best served by proceeding with therapy. Ryan's guardians are very clear that they would like him to proceed with therapy and have given consent as well as endorsement to that course of action. Ryan considers himself something of an "emancipated minor" and frequently, though not constantly, refuses therapy. The treatment team does not feel that it could or even would wish to proceed with therapy that had to be literally forced on the patient.

This is a case in which the issue of consent is clouded by the age and emotional immaturity of the patient. It is further complicated by the status of the family and the relationship of the divorced parents. Ryan may well have been using the situation of his illness and his intermittent willingness to cooperate in therapy as a tool with which to manipulate his parents toward some end of his own design. Regardless, the situation is that of an adolescent of questionable judgment and motivation who is able to resist therapy successfully, to exercise a refusal, because of his status in a somewhat disorganized family.

In a sense, the issue of consent in this situation must be temporarily set aside until the difficulties that surround the patient and his family can be managed, if not fully resolved. In my view, a heavy obligation exists on the part of the treatment team to assist the divorced parents to collaborate in resolving the problem with their son so that together they can get to the issue of consent for therapy. A similarly important responsibility rests with the oncology team to effect an alliance with Ryan that will at least provide the basis for a good working relationship once the family and personal conflicts have been resolved.

The issues of consent in regard to treatment of children with potentially fatal illness are more complex than the issues of consent for the treatment of adults. As the cases here have illustrated, additional complications can and frequently do exist: (1) the absence of data from patients on the basis of which informed proxy consents can be based, (2) the issues of the interest of the patient in competition with the interests of the family as a whole, (3) the issues related to the competency of the parents as proxy decision-makers when their judgment is clouded by factors related to the child-parent relationship, (4) the problem of the emergent autonomy of the early adolescent whose cooperation in therapy must, to a large extent, be voluntary, and (5) the complications of intra-family dynamics, which intervene to prevent approaching the treatment decision as a decision about treatment.

The complexity of issues of consent in the treatment of children with deadly diseases argues for great care in addressing the ethical dimensions of treatment planning. This complexity argues equally strongly for a multidisciplinary team able to respond to the psychosocial dynamics within the child and the family.

Lorber J. 1974 "Selective Treatment of Myelomeningocele: To Treat or Not to Treat?" *Pediatrics* 53:307-8.

ON THE SIDE OF LIFE: LIVING WITH A LIFE-THREATENING ILLNESS
Iris Cutler

Cystic fibrosis (CF) is a genetic, chronic, progressive, incurable, and ultimately fatal illness.

As the counselor/social worker for the Cystic Fibrosis Center at Hahnemann Hospital, I have witnessed and been intimately involved with the deaths of many children ranging in ages from infancy to adulthood. I use the word *child* advisedly, because to bereaved parents "it does not appear to make a difference whether one's child is three, thirteen, or thirty." It just doesn't seem in the natural order of things for a parent to outlive a child.

However, instead of addressing myself to the many issues involved in helping dying children and their families cope with what is frequently called the "ultimate tragedy," about which much has been written, I have chosen to write about life and living. The purpose of this paper is to share some insights and understanding about how young people with CF have learned to *live* life in a meaningful way, knowing that they have a life-threatening illness, and how a group experience can prove to be mutually beneficial and supporting, while it provides us with new knowledge that can be used to help others.

Twenty years ago very little was known about CF, and most children died from this disease before they reached school age. Ten years ago they possibly lived to become adolescents. Today, because of continuous research, better understanding of CF, and more effective methods of treatment (which involve a great investment of effort and time on the part of the parents and the patients), many children are living into adulthood. The Cystic Fibrosis Foundation reports that 16 per cent of patients with CF are eighteen or older, and out of the 30,000 people known to have the disease in this country, 121 are over the age of thirty, as compared with only five in 1966. As of the time of writing this paper, one-third of the patients in our CF clinic are over the age of seventeen. This means that for the first time in the history of this disease, we have a new generation of patients with CF who can serve as the models for others, and in a true sense be our teachers. As we have learned from Elisabeth Kubler-Ross, "the best possible way we could study death and dying was to ask terminally ill patients to be our teachers." We also believe that the best way we can learn about how to help younger children with CF to grow up to become happy, well-adjusted adults is to find out from our older patients what helped them.

I was particularly impressed with a number of young adults who appeared to be living very normal lives: going to college, getting married, carving out careers for themselves, and in some instances having children, and still taking good care of themselves. I wondered how they were coping with all the physical, emotional, social, and financial stresses that are inherent in a chronic and ultimately fatal disease.

Although they seemed to be doing well from an achievement point of view, I questioned how many of these young people were feeling isolated and alone with their problems and wondered if perhaps there was a need for me to create an opportunity and an atmosphere whereby they could come together and begin to share feelings and discuss mutual concerns.

I knew I was right in my assumption that forming a young adult group was a good idea when seven young adults ranging in age from eighteen to twenty-three agreed to attend our first meeting. Three and a half years later, we are still meeting on a monthly basis, with an average attendance of ten to twenty patients ranging in age from sixteen to fifty-one, who are sometimes accompanied by their spouses, boyfriends, or girlfriends. What started out as a pilot project proved to be not only very nurturing to its group members and a learning experience for me but also the source of inspiration to 150 parents, siblings, friends, and health care professionals who attended a Family Forum that was organized and presented by the young adult group in the hope that their life experiences and new insights would benefit others. The focus of this forum was on the quality of life, no matter how long. Ten of the group members shared with the audience what it has been like for them to grow up with CF and what the ingredients were that helped them have such a positive outlook on life, despite their problems. In other words, it was a way of looking not just at pathology or what went wrong but also at what was done right to help these children grow into such beautiful young adults.

To give some idea of what each of the participants shared with the audience, and to illustrate the diversity of their backgrounds and the similarity of their attitudes, the following is a brief summary of each presentation.

The first young lady to speak was Betsy, a beautiful twenty-two-year-old college graduate. She is one of four children. She has one sister and two brothers, one of whom is sixteen and also has CF. Although they both had symptoms most of their lives, Betsy was not diagnosed until age thirteen. Her brother was seven at the time of his diagnosis. Although the family was relieved to have a name for their disease at last, having two children diagnosed as having CF at the same time precipitated a real crisis. However, as a result of this, her parents reached for more spiritual help, which she believes brought the family closer than ever. She is presently working in the patient relations department of a university hospital and attends that university at night in order to achieve her ultimate ambition of becoming a physician, because she is depending on medical science to discover a cure for CF. Betsy has a great outlook, she sees life as a pocket; the more she can stuff into each day, the better!

Jim spoke next. He's twenty-three and an only child. He was diagnosed at nine months of age and has lived with the knowledge of CF all his life. However, because of the encouragement that he received from his parents, his close friends, and his doctors, Jim is living a very active and meaningful life. Among his many accomplishments are receiving a BS degree in mechanical engineering, being the news editor and advertising manager of the school newspaper, and working as an auto mechanic during the summer, as well as building miniature furniture and playing the piano and guitar in his spare time. He is working on two master's degrees, one in engineering and one in business administration. The way he sees things, CF isn't the end of the world. The only limits on your life and what you accomplish are those you set yourself. He believes that your own personal attitude toward life is 90 per cent of the battle, that you sink or swim on your own motivation, but you must "remember to let go of the side of the pool."

Chip, who is now twenty-seven years old, was also an only child. He was diagnosed at birth. He had a very normal active childhood, not ever really understanding that he had anything really wrong with him until he was about seventeen years old. Except for his original diagnosis, he had not been in the hospital until he was twenty-two, when he had a collapsed lung. Up until that time he had graduated from junior college and had worked full-time as an expediter and part-time as a newspaper reporter; he was also a football manager. He married a nurse whom he met while in the hospital, and was married for about three years. He has since been divorced and has become much more limited because of his impaired health. However, in spite of all these obstacles, he has carved out a new career for himself as a successful artist. He has had a one-man show, has been on TV, and has had articles written about him. He also has a waiting list of people wanting to buy his paintings. He too believes that good friendships and the understanding he gets from the group members have helped him to get through the bad times.

Marcia, twenty-eight years old, is another example of determination and courage. She has a master's degree in elementary education and psychology. She taught emotionally disturbed children for four years and has been married to a veterinarian for three and a half years. She was not diagnosed until she was fourteen years old, which compounded all the other problems that any adolescent faces. She has an older brother who does not have CF. She has also had several setbacks physically during the past few years and has had to work hard to keep up her spirits. Although she is not employed, she does meaningful volunteer work. She has learned the importance of being flexible so that she is able to bend with changing circumstances and readjust her goals. Her philosophy is that one's worth doesn't come from what one does or how one earns one's living but from what kind of person one is. Everyone has something to offer!

Mark, age fifteen, is the youngest "young adult" in the group. He was diagnosed as having CF at age two, and his parents have encouraged him to take part in sports. He has played soccer, baseball, and basketball. He also bowls, golfs, and lifts weights and has played in a marching band in spite of several hospital admissions over the past five years. He has three Siberian huskies that are his pride and joy. He plans to go to college, get a job, and get married (in that order). His parting message was that living with CF, like any other challenge, takes persistence, courage, and self-motivation in order to live a more healthful and more prosperous life.

Kay is twenty-four years old and has four handsome brothers, none of whom have CF. She was diagnosed at two years of age and accepted taking her pills as a way of life, since she had the impression that the difference between little girls and little boys was that all little girls took pills! She believes that what really helped her to grow up and mature was that she was not overprotected by her parents. She was expected to do her share of the family chores and was disciplined just as her brothers. She had a very normal, active childhood, and although she took her pills and had physical therapy, she pretty much ignored the fact that she had CF. It wasn't until she graduated from college and had a full-time job as a medical secretary that her illness started to catch up with her. This, of course, curtailed her goal at the time of getting her own apartment and establishing her independence. This was a severe blow to her. Since then, Kay has had to adjust to becoming gradually more and more limited and changing her lifestyle. She is a beautiful example of what one can do when one has to. She has not only met all her new challenges but has surpassed them with courage, good humor, and a positive attitude. She has a strong faith and personal relationship with God, and has been able to reach out to others in both accepting and giving love. She looks at each day as a precious gift and quotes Jack London in saying, "The proper function of man is to live, not to exist. I shall not waste my days trying to prolong them."

Al is twenty-five years old, has been married for three years, and works full-time as a design draftsman. He also has a seventeen-year-old brother who has CF. Both of them were diagnosed later in life, which did not make things easier by any means. Al has always been interested in physical fitness, but ever since he was diagnosed at sixteen and a half years this has become an obsession with him. He spends a great deal of his time working out, running, and developing his skills in the martial arts. He also enjoys doing magic, and he is very good at this. Bruce Lee has been an inspiration to Al, and he lives by Lee's philosophy: "A man is born to achieve great things if he first has the potential to conquer himself." Al has invested much time and effort in developing himself both physically and mentally, and there is hardly a challenge that he does not try to overcome, usually with great success. He believes "when you stop trying to be better, you stop being good."

Georgette is atypical of most young adults with CF, not only because she is now thirty-three years old but also because she is the mother of a healthy twelve-year-old daughter. When Georgette was diagnosed at six months of age, very little was known about CF and how to manage it, so she spent much of her childhood in and out of hospitals. She is the third child in a family of four, with none of the siblings having CF. As a result, she received all the secondary gains of being sick, such as a lot of love and attention. The love and faith her mother had in her seems to have been most instrumental in helping her meet all of life's many challenges. In college she studied business management. While working her way through school, she married. She went to Bible college in Florida. She was in and out of several businesses with her husband and has moved around quite a bit. She does her volunteer work, loves music, and has a very positive attitude toward life. Her greatest compliment was received when, in talking to her preadolescent daughter about marriage and children, her daughter said, "You know, Mom, it really wouldn't be so bad having a child with CF. Look how well you have done."

Craig, now twenty-seven years old, was diagnosed at birth but was never overprotected by his parents. He had two siblings who have already died from CF, a brother at five weeks and a sister who was twenty-six years old. As his mother shared with us, "We decided early in raising CF children that we wanted them to live normal lives and not wrap them in cotton. They never thought of themselves as being handicapped." Craig is living proof of this philosophy. He leads a very active and productive life, partaking in sports and going away to college, where he earned a BS degree in business. As editor of the school newspaper he was nominated to *Who's Who in American Colleges and Universities*, and as a member of the rifle team was named to *Outstanding College Athletes in America* for two years. He held a full-time job until about a year ago. He hardly knew he had CF most of his life, since all he ever had to do was take enzymes. He didn't know what physical therapy was until his health started to go downhill and he resigned himself to his fate. After all, he was then twenty-six years old, and that is the age his sister was when she died, so he believed that this was the beginning of the end for him. It was at this time that he was hospitalized, but his doctors saw things quite differently. Not only did Craig's health improve, but he met and married the head nurse on the floor, and has since started a business that designs, manufactures, and sells trophy and award plaques.

Craig learned a lot of valuable lessons during the past year—mainly that life is not a matter of enjoying material things, it's a matter of enjoying human things. Friends came to see him in the hospital not because he was productive or measuring up to some kind of mark, but because he was Craig, and in some way or form they loved him. He said that he wasn't up there to paint a pretty picture, because it is not a pretty picture, but everyone in the world has a problem. He said that what we really need and really want is help, patience, and, in the end, love.

Jody at age fifty, calls herself the "senior citizen" of the young adult group. Although she was born with CF, she was not diagnosed until age forty-eight. She had been sick most of her life, in and out of hospitals, and was actually relieved when the proper diagnosis was finally made. She has been married for twenty-five years, and since she was never able to become pregnant, she and her husband adopted a son, who is now nineteen years old. Although her health was never too good, she managed to live a busy married life, raising her son, taking trips with her husband, and going to the theater and to sporting events. Her family has always been very supportive of her. Most of her friends and acquaintances know of her disease. She says she is not shy about it. The way she figures it, there are worse afflictions, and she is glad she doesn't have them. Since Jody is one of the oldest known persons with CF, she offers inspiration to all of us.

Although the one thing these people have in common is the fact that they all have CF, and they have all been hospitalized at one time or another, their life experiences have been different in many ways (see Table 1).

What this experience has taught me is that regardless of how old these patients were when they were diagnosed; how may siblings they had or did not have, with or without CF, living or dead; what their education was; whether or not they were single, married, or divorced; whether they did or did not have children; and whether their family was intact or not, these people have managed to develop appropriate defenses that have enabled them to cope with their anxieties about their illness and uncertain futures in such a way that, despite their disease and limitations, they are living meaningful lives. This doesn't mean to say that all patients who attend our clinic enjoy the same quality of life. I learned that there is no blueprint or script that can be given to any parent, and there is no one answer to any question. It also became evident that while the group experience had proved meaningful and growth-producing for those who have chosen to attend the meetings, a group is not for everyone. We have many patients who attend our clinic who do not participate for various reasons. It is a very individual matter, depending on the child, the family in which the child lives, attitudes and philosophies about life and death, belief systems, support systems, and many other things.

However, the presentations of those who shared their experiences in the group and in this Family Forum, had several common themes which could be used as guidelines to help others, such as the importance of:

1. Maintaining hope and daring to plan for the future.
2. Receiving love, support, and encouragement from the family and friends and also developing the ability to give the same to others.
3. Not being overprotected by parents.
4. Living as normal a life as possible and being encouraged to be independent but knowing that it is often necessary to ask for help.
5. Spending time and effort to develop oneself physically and mentally.
6. Having high self-expectations, interspersed with flexibility and realistic goals.
7. Developing determination and courage by accepting and overcoming challenges successfully.
8. Living each day at a time and making every day count.
9. Having a positive mental attitude, and never thinking of oneself as handicapped.
10. Realizing that life is an ever-evolving process with constant changes and developing the ability to accommodate to new situations.
11. Developing a philosophy about life and death.
12. Having a strong faith in God.
13. Maintaining a sense of humor.

To substantiate that these guidelines had some very valuable effect on their lives, all we have to do is look at some of their accomplishments. Just this past year, five of our young adults graduated from leading universitites. One young lady was accepted at medical school and is now attending; one young man is working on two master's degrees in engineering and business; one young man is in a master's program for languages. Others are putting their education to work in job-related areas. One of our group became a proud mother last year, and another member, who is now thirty-three years old, has a twelve year-old daughter. In addition, many of them have been very active in sports, such as baseball, rifle shooting, basketball, bowling, martial arts, and hunting, as well as developing hobbies and talents, such as playing the piano and guitar, building miniature furniture, being editor of the school newspaper, and learning to be a magician. While people with CF are thought of as having a handicap, these young people have clearly demonstrated from their accomplishments so far that they are in no way disabled!

What did the group exeprience mean to them? For one thing, they learned that they were not the only ones who had lived past childhood, and they were happy to meet others "who had made it." By sharing their concerns about taking pills in front of others, coughing, going away to school, getting financial aid, interpersonal relationships with peers and family, indecisions about whom to tell and when to tell others that they have CF, their need for independence, the possibility of marriage, children, career choices, and the probability of an early death, they realized that they were not alone. The group experience further helped these young people to develop new skills and self-confidence and to understand themselves and others better. They were able to talk about feelings, perhaps for the first time, because they were sharing with people who had the true empathy that can only come from having CF oneself. A cohesiveness developed within the group, and new friendships were made that have subsequently provided an important support system in times of need. They learned that "it is not the length of one's life, rather it is the breadth of his sympathies for others; it is the depth of his understanding of life's meaning; it is the height of his aspirations that are important." Most crucial of all, they learned the importance of attitude. They were helped to understand that although they could not always change the realities that they were handed in life, they could change their attitude and how they allowed their circumstances or situations to affect the quality of their lives. In other words, instead of dwelling on the negative aspects of their disease, which might immobilize them, they could choose to direct and channel their energies in a constructive way that would motivate them to get as much out of life as possible.

They also began to realize that there is a big difference between who they are and what they have. In other words, they and their disease are not synonymous. Cystic fibrosis is a noun, not an adjective. We seem to have a habit of labeling people with their illnesses, and they begin to identify with them. We call a person with heart trouble a cardiac, a person with diabetes a diabetic, and people with cystic fibrosis cystics. Kids thus grow up believing that they are their disease. This really hurts in terms of developing a good self-image. They were helped to realize that each person has all the worth in the world by virtue of the fact that he or she is a human being. They just happen to have an illness that is called CF, and their challenge is to figure out the best way to live and cope with it. I believe that those who are challenged in this way have to dig down inside of themselves a little deeper than most of us and find the courage, strength, and the philosophy they need to continue on in life in spite of their problems. Their presentations reaffirmed my belief. They seem more concerned with how they live their lives rather than how long they live, and their motto seemed to be "courage is not the absence of fear but the affirmation of life despite fear."

By adopting Orville Kelly's philosophy of "make today count," they do not look at each day as another day closer to death but as another day of life to be appreciated and enjoyed. They truly are our teachers and an inspiration to all who know them.

TABLE 1

	NAME	AGE	EDUCATION	AGE AT DIAGNOSIS	SIBLINGS	MARITAL STATUS	PARENTS
1.	Betsy	22	BA degree	13	3 – 1 with CF living	Single	Together
2.	Jim	23	BA (working on masters degrees)	9 months	None	Single	Together
3.	Chip	27	Associate degree (jr. college)	Birth	None	Divorced	Father dead
4.	Marcia	28	BA and masters	14	1 brother, no CF	Married	Father dead
5.	Mark	15	High school	2	None	Single	Divorced
6.	Kay	24	Associate degree (jr. college)	2	4 brothers, no CF	Single	Together
7.	Al	25	Associate degree (jr. college)	16½	1 brother with CF	Married	Together
8.	Georgette	33	Bible School and Business College	6 months	3 – no CR	Married with daughter 12 years old	Divorced
9.	Craig	27	BS degree	Birth	3 – 2 with CF died	Married	Together
10.	Jody	51	High school	48	1 brother	Married with 19 year old son, adopted	Father dead